The Musician's Way

The Musician's Way

A Guide to Practice, Performance, and Wellness

Gerald Klickstein

OXFORD

UNIVERSITY PRESS

2009

OXFORD
UNIVERSITY PRESS

Oxford University Press, Inc., publishes works that further
Oxford University's objective of excellence
in research, scholarship, and education.

Oxford   New York
Auckland   Cape Town   Dar es Salaam   Hong Kong   Karachi
Kuala Lumpur   Madrid   Melbourne   Mexico City   Nairobi
New Delhi   Shanghai   Taipei   Toronto

With offices in
Argentina   Austria   Brazil   Chile   Czech Republic   France   Greece
Guatemala   Hungary   Italy   Japan   Poland   Portugal   Singapore
South Korea   Switzerland   Thailand   Turkey   Ukraine   Vietnam

Copyright © 2009 by Gerald Klickstein

Published by Oxford University Press, Inc.
198 Madison Avenue, New York, New York 10016

www.oup.com

Oxford is a registered trademark of Oxford University Press.

Library of Congress Cataloging-in-Publication Data
Klickstein, Gerald.
The musician's way : a guide to practice, performance, and wellness / Gerald Klickstein.
p.   cm.
Includes bibliographical references and index.
ISBN 978-0-19-534312-0; 978-0-19-534313-7 (pbk.)
1. Practicing (Music) 2. Music—Performance. 3. Musicians—Health and hygiene. I. Title.
MT75.K74 2009
781.44—dc22   2008043840

7   9   8

Printed in the United States of America
on acid-free paper

Preface

I'll never forget the day that my parents brought home my first guitar—the awe I felt as I reached for the strings and was enveloped in the silken tone. My command of those strings has come a long way since then, yet I still feel that same sense of wonder whenever I unlatch a case and take a guitar in my hands. If you're a musician, too, you know exactly what I mean.

What is it about music that grabs the heart and fires the imagination? Victor Hugo wrote, "Music expresses that which cannot be put into words and that which cannot remain silent."[1] Words are destined to fall short when it comes to capturing the essence of music, but the skills involved in making music *can* be pinned down. And for aspiring performers, those skills are priceless.

The Musician's Way articulates fundamental skills that bring about musical excellence. It merges concepts drawn from current research with the insights that I've gathered across three decades in the performing and teaching professions. Part I, *Artful Practice,* describes strategies for practicing creatively and efficiently. Part II, *Fearless Performance,* maps out a route to conquer nervousness and connect with audiences. Part III, *Lifelong Creativity,* equips readers to look after their most important resource: themselves. It shows how musicians can prevent occupational injuries, boost creativity, and thrive amid the demands of their field.

The chapters and sections are best read in order, but they're also designed to function independently so that a musician interested in a particular topic can singly read the relevant portion. To achieve such independence, some points are reiterated, albeit sparingly.

Many sections incorporate case examples. Such narratives are composite sketches of students with whom I've worked, although identifying characteristics have been modified so that none depict specific persons. The book also employs a companion website, *musiciansway.com.* The site compiles useful links, instrument-specific tips, and more—it provides readers with easy access to web-based information and allows the book to address issues concisely.

The Musician's Way can aid all vocalists and instrumentalists who are seeking to improve their abilities. Nonetheless, it's framed around the learning environment of first-year, university-level music students performing in the Western music traditions. It's intended as a companion text to music lessons and classes and also as a guidebook that music lovers can explore on their own. Whether you're enrolled in school or not, if you have a passion for music, I hope that these pages will be a beacon on your journey toward limitless artistic growth.

Acknowledgments

The Musician's Way arrived at its present form owing to the support of diverse people and institutions. I'm grateful to the University of North Carolina School of the Arts Foundation for funding the sabbatical that enabled me to concentrate on writing. At Oxford University Press, I'd like to acknowledge Suzanne Ryan, Senior Editor for music books, as well as Associate Editor Norman Hirschy, Production Editor Liz Smith, and Editorial Assistants Katharine Boone and Lora Dunn. And to the individuals, listed alphabetically below, who gave sage advice, read various drafts, or otherwise made helpful contributions: Thank you.

Angela Myles Beeching	Court Huber	Joseph Pecoraro
Guy Blynn	Sarah Johnson	Steven Pologe
Alice Brandfonbrener	Adele Klickstein	Marion Pratnicki
Sheila Browne	Steven Lankenau	Ellen Rosenberg
Kris Chesky	Eric Larsen	Judith Saxton
F. Joseph Docksey	Barbara Lister-Sink	Glenn Siebert
John Ferri	Kathryn Lucktenberg	Mary Siebert
Arlene Gostin	Eric Maisel	Jeffrey Solow
Paige Greason	Linda Moore	Taimur Sullivan
Ann Grimaldi	Thomas L. Murray Jr.	Ransom Wilson

The photographs were produced thanks to Rick Lee Photography and these models:

John Beck, marimba	Laura Gutierrez
Sheila Browne, viola	Ryan Layton, guitar
Ronnal Ford, oboe	Genevieve Leitner, guitar

Daphne Nichols, piano   Judith Saxton, trumpet
Taya Ricker, violin   Paul Sharpe, bass

Notice

This book includes research-derived information regarding how musicians can flourish or become harmed in their occupations. However, the ideas presented here are not offered as substitutes for expert medical or psychological advice. Before you make decisions concerning your health and prior to beginning any exercise, diet, or wellness regimen, consult a healthcare professional.

Contents

Part II   Fearless Performance

Part I

Artful Practice

Getting Organized

In this chapter:

- Defining practice
- Equipping a practice space
- Planning and scheduling practice sessions
- Choosing new material
- Self-recording

Artful Practice

It isn't where you came from, it's where you're going that counts.
—Ella Fitzgerald, singer

Wherever you hope to travel on your musical journey, practice is the only route to getting there. You may wonder whether you possess the talent to reach your goals, but musical progress depends more on practice than on talent. Talent symbolizes your underlying potential; practice enables you to realize that potential. But not just any sort of practice will do.

Part I of *The Musician's Way* combs the fundamentals of *artful* practice, the kind of practice that results in comprehensive musical excellence. This chapter looks at organizational concepts that furnish a stable footing for your work. Chapters 2–5 describe strategies to mature your practice skills and bring pieces to concert readiness. Chapter 6 explores collaborative music making. In total, the information here is meant to empower you to steer your creativity in whatever direction you choose.

Defining Practice

Practicing is not forced labor; it is a refined art that partakes of intuition, of inspiration, patience, elegance, clarity, balance, and, above all, the search for ever greater joy in movement and expression.

—Yehudi Menuhin, violinist

Practice holds a place of honor in the life of a musician. How then does it sometimes earn a reputation as "forced labor"? Author Edith Hamilton supplies us with the answer: "It is not hard work which is dreary," she said; "it is superficial work."[1] For your practice to vibrate with excitement, it has to be both skillful and meaningful. So, to get to the core of how to deepen your practice habits, let's begin by boiling down what practice is.

When you engage in serious practice—as opposed to when you casually play or sing for fun—you're basically striving to learn repertoire or to enhance your functional abilities by working on things like technical exercises. And through that process of absorbing repertoire and polishing skills, you become a better artist. You build "patience, elegance, clarity, balance." You ascend toward endless artistic growth.

But beyond personal fulfillment, the decisive aim of practice is to prepare performances because, as an art form, music centers on the interaction between performer and listener. In a few words, then, practice is the deliberate, creative process of improving musical ability and of mastering music for performance.

Looking through the prism of that definition, you can see that to become a capable practicer, you require expertise in both artistic and practical realms. You need to gather insight into the expressive language of music while you also amass technical skills. Plus, you have to be socially adept to rehearse effectively with other musicians. Topping that off, there are the issues surrounding how to prepare secure, spellbinding performances.

Practice, therefore, isn't a simple act; it includes a constellation of factors. We'll be teasing out those factors throughout part I. Before doing so, however, let's turn to the matter of *where* you practice.

Creating a Practice Environment

The studio, a room to which the artist consigns himself for life, is naturally important, not only as workplace, but as a source of inspiration.

—Grace Glueck, journalist

I'd like to put forward two ideas here. First, you should arrange your practice space to optimize your productivity. Your studio or practice room doesn't have to be fancy for you to make impeccable music, but there are some things without which musicians flounder. Second, whether your practice setting is stylish or ordinary, you can transform it into a creative temple, a place where inspiration flows.

How can ill-equipped practice rooms leave musicians floundering? Poorly sized chairs contribute to backache; dim lighting provokes eye strain; missing metronomes can give rise to a distorted rhythmic sense. You see what I mean. Table 1.1 presents an inventory of essentials, aside from an instrument, for setting up a practice space. Bear in mind that some musicians won't need all the items listed. Few pianists, for example, require electronic tuners.

Table 1.1 **Practice Room Essentials**

1. Suitable chair
2. Music stand
3. Notebook and pencils
4. Electronic metronome and tuner
5. Clock
6. Mirror (for monitoring movement habits)
7. Audio recorder (p. 16)
8. Instrument stand/holder
9. A bottle of water (drink plenty of water)
10. Adequate lighting and climate control
11. Relative quiet and privacy
12. Hearing protection (p. 277)

To transform your practice space into a creative temple, designate it as such every time you work. When you prepare to practice—whether at home, at school, or on the road—make sure that your equipment needs are met and that your materials are in order. At the same time, remove distractions: Switch off the phone; shut down your computer.

Next, take a minute to acknowledge the extraordinary opportunity before you to make music. Just as religious devotees may perform rituals when entering houses of worship, adopt prepractice customs. Prior to your musical warm-up, breathe, release tension, and affirm the value of your artistic work (see *warming up*, p. 37). Then, leaving your troubles behind, enter the exquisite realm of music making.

The Five Practice Zones

> *The secret of getting ahead is getting started. The secret of getting started is breaking your complex, overwhelming tasks into small manageable tasks, and then starting on the first one.*
>
> —Mark Twain, author

To put your practice sessions together, you have to coordinate not only your environment but also your goals and yourself. Goals and people, however, don't remain static. Each day you're faced with a new you and with fresh hurdles. For instance, there are usually pressing obligations to meet, such as cleaning up a part for an impending performance. All the while, long-term objectives call for your attention—chiefly, you need to acquire musical and technical skills and accrue a repertoire. There can be so much to cover in a practice session that it can seem overwhelming.

To work on a large quantity of material efficiently, I recommend sorting it into five zones. Three of those zones encompass the repertoire that you practice; the other two organize the work you do to improve your functional abilities.

The Five Practice Zones

- New material
- Developing material
- Performance material
- Technique
- Musicianship

For starters, when you pick up an untried piece, you consign it to the *new material* zone. In that zone, you get an overview of a composition, split it into sections, and then, as detailed in chapter 3, you absorb the artistic and technical content through precise practice. A slow to moderate tempo is the norm. When you can easily play or sing a piece at a preliminary tempo, it graduates to *developing* status. With *develop-

ing material, your aims include refining interpretation, increasing tempo, and, when applicable, memorizing—those topics are investigated in chapter 4. Once the music reaches a final tempo and is artistically whole, it's ripe for the *performance material* zone. Then you renew the interpretive and technical particulars, maintain your memory, and, most of all, practice performing as chronicled in part II of this book.

Apart from repertoire, for the items you practice to upgrade your skills, I suggest sorting them into two zones: *technique* and *musicianship.* In the *technique* zone, you hone your scales, arpeggios, etudes, and so on to assemble the building blocks of high-level execution. The *musicianship* zone incorporates activities such as sight-reading and improvisation practice. Chapter 5 scrutinizes tactics for working in both the *technique* and *musicianship* zones.

To make significant progress, music students need consistent practice in all five zones. In contrast, scattershot work leaves musicians wanting. For example, if you're eager to learn an intricate new piece of music, but you seldom go over material in the *technique* and *musicianship* areas, then you probably won't have the component skills that complex music demands. By the same token, if you primarily practice technique, then, when you plunge into a lengthy composition, you'll lack the facility to mold an interpretation and perform securely.

Seasoned musicians, therefore, balance out their practice across the five zones. In reality, the coordinating of materials and time involves a knack of its own. And it all begins with planning.

Planning Your Practice

> *To achieve great things, two things are needed: a plan, and not quite enough time.*
>
> —Leonard Bernstein, composer and conductor

A well-crafted practice plan divides your materials and time into viable units. Here I offer strategies for managing material. The ensuing section examines ways to carve up time.

To keep abreast of material in the five practice zones, I advise student musicians to document it on paper or computer files. Documenting guarantees that you won't lose track of any goals. For musicians in ensembles, writing down rehearsal objectives also averts misunderstandings about who is supposed to prepare what.

Two low-tech formats that I've found worthwhile for documenting practice aims are a one-page sheet and a notebook. Two model practice sheets are

---

Model Practice Sheet

New material
> Divide into sections
>
> Establish interpretive/technical plan
>
> Slow tempo

Developing material
> Refine interpretation
>
> Increase tempo
>
> Memorize

Performance material
> Practice performing
>
> Maintain memory
>
> Renew and innovate

Technique
> Scales
>
> Arpeggios
>
> Diction
>
> Instrument-specific work

Musicianship
> Sight-reading
>
> Theory/ear training
>
> Composition/improvisation
>
> Listening/study

Figure 1.1. Model practice sheet no. 1.

included in this section. The first is a starter sheet that shows the five practice zones (figure 1.1). To use it, a student would note material under the relevant headings and then review the sheet daily to formulate a practice plan. A musician working on a modest amount of material might be able to list it all on one side of a sheet; a person with more music to practice would use both sides or employ several pages. You can download practice sheets and other helpful documents from *musiciansway.com*.

The second practice sheet comes courtesy of a freshman guitar student

---

Keith's Practice Sheet

New material

	Divide into sections	*Solo: Caprice*
60	Establish interpretive/technical plan	*Duo: Fandango*
	Slow tempo	

Developing material

	Refine interpretation	*Solo: Vals español*
40	Increase tempo	*Duo: Madrigal*
	Memorize	

Performance material

	Practice performing	*Estudio*	*Allegro*	*Nocturne*
20	Maintain memory	*Chanson*	*Spanish Study*	*Andante*
	Renew and innovate	*Ballade*	*Pavane*	*Duo: Minuet*

Technique

	Scales	*Open-position chromatic; three-8ve chromatic; chromatic octaves; closed-position major & minor; long scales in C, Amin, G, Emin, D, Bmin, A, E*
30	Arpeggios	*Method book, pp. 90–92, 99–109, 162, 170; Carcassi Etude #2*
	Slurs	*Exercise in 5th–9th positions; Etude by Sagreras*
	Velocity	*Right-hand sweeps; scale bursts in 5th–9th positions; Etude by Pujol*

Musicianship

	Sight-reading	*Reading book, pp. 24–40 (w/metronome)*
	Theory/ear training	*Workbook, pp. 38–41(spell, sing, and play seventh chords)*
30+	Composition/improv.	*Invent melody over I-ii-V-I progression; improvise variations*
	Listening	*Attend classical concerts Tues. & Sat.; listen to Wes Montgomery recording*
	Study	*Read online bio of Wes Montgomery*

Figure 1.2. Model practice sheet no. 2.

named Keith, who had studied with me for two months after taking lessons from other teachers for eight years. Although Keith's sheet catalogs both solo repertoire and also music for his newly formed guitar duo, it applies to his solitary practice agenda for only a single week (figure 1.2).

Keith intended to practice three hours daily, excluding time spent on warm-ups, breaks, and any reading or listening assignments. The numbers to the left of the sheet roughly indicate how much time he would spend practicing in each zone per day. Although his main interest was classical guitar performance, I was encouraging him to compose, improvise, and learn about jazz. His small assignments in those realms appear in the *musicianship* zone.

Keith didn't practice everything on his sheet on any one day. He worked on his new and developing pieces daily, but many items he practiced on alternate days. To prevent his routine from becoming predictable, I counseled him to tackle material in varied order. After warming up, he could start with and then move on to material from any zone.

The advantages of using the practice-sheet format are that you can view material at a glance and quickly devise a practice plan. Then, as you work, eyeballing the sheet helps you track your progress through different zones. It's a handy efficiency booster. The downside of such a format is that it doesn't leave room for registering lots of material or for specifying objectives. A practice notebook (or the digital equivalent) does the trick there.

With a notebook, you can apportion ample space to a zone, piece, or exercise. Let's say that, in preparation for an audition or a solo concert, you want to buff up a composition in your *performance material* zone: Write the title at the top of a page, and make a checklist of practice goals beneath. Similarly, for scale practice, you might allot a page to your artistic and technical aims: Artistic goals could involve producing full tone, relaxed vibrato, and a bevy of rhythm variations; technique-wise, a string player might seek to play scales with seamless position shifts and a variety of bowings. If you need reminding of such multipart objectives—and many students do, especially when studying with unfamiliar teachers—then a notebook is the way to go.

Keith, at the beginning of the school year, used a notebook in conjunction with his practice sheet, bringing it to every lesson. In it, I'd write comments and tips. He preserved more extensive remarks on his audio recorder, from which he later transcribed notes. Keith also used his notebook during practice sessions to jot down questions he wanted to ask in his lessons. Partway through the school year, he abandoned the one-sheet layout and employed a notebook exclusively, assigning a page or more to each zone.

Together with his notebook, Keith employed four folders to manage his scores. He had one folder for his ensemble pieces, one for his solo *performance material,* one for his *new* and *developing material,* and one for the music in his *technique* and *musicianship* zones. All of those folders he kept in a vinyl case that he carried in a backpack.

Given how beneficial it has proven for students like Keith to use notebooks, folders, and practice sheets, I urge all students to do the same at least for a while, until they arrive at personalized methods of organization. I also encourage you to experiment with alternate strategies. Whatever organizational system allows you to maximize the efficiency of your practice, that's the system you should use.

Scheduling Practice Sessions

A schedule defends from chaos and whim. It is a net for catching days. It is scaffolding on which a worker can stand and labor with both hands at sections of time. . . . It is a lifeboat on which you find yourself, decades later, still living.

—Annie Dillard, author

How you shape your practice schedule will in many ways determine the course of your creative life. An effective schedule enables you to achieve your musical goals without becoming exhausted. However, putting together an art-nourishing agenda is far from simple. Misguided scheduling leads numerous musicians down paths to either erratic, fruitless practice or overpracticing and to injury and despair. Therefore, this section proposes five scheduling guidelines and untangles related issues of practice management.

Scheduling Practice Sessions
1. Practice regularly
2. Arrange multiple, shorter stints
3. Take breaks
4. Increase gradually
5. Live a balanced life

1. Practice regularly

Your artistic evolution is best served by steady, judicious practice. Aim to do a similar amount of playing or singing each day, being mindful not to exceed your physical limits. Also, consider reserving one day a week for rest or low-intensity practice only.

If you're renovating your practice habits, you may find it useful to log when, what, and how you practice. Come up with an original logging format, or use the model available from *musiciansway.com*. Few musicians use logs on an ongoing basis, but when making changes to your practice patterns, logging for a week or more will shed light on your habits and could help lift your productivity.

2. Arrange multiple, shorter stints

To stave off weariness and promote deeper learning, arrange several practice sessions each day, preferably at comparable hours throughout the week. Myriad performers have given corresponding advice, among them, violinist David Oistrakh: "Start off in the morning; put the violin away; practice in the afternoon; put it away; practice at night; put it away; practice before bedtime."[2]

If prolonged rehearsals are ever necessary, such as when you work with a group that can't meet often, rest beforehand, take breathers, and listen to your body. If you feel fatigue or discomfort, stop for the day. Ideally, halt playing or singing before tiredness sets in. Spent muscles and voices are more prone to injury, and once your mind dulls, practice becomes useless. Chapter 12 sifts through the injuries caused by excessive practice.

3. Take breaks

As a general rule, rest 10 minutes of each hour that you spend in the practice room. Rest more if you're working vigorously or adopting new techniques. A sensible practice-to-rest ratio, widely recommended by teachers and medical authorities, is to practice no more than 25–30 minutes before pausing for a 5-minute respite. Many musicians opt for more frequent breathers and rest 2–3 minutes every 15 minutes or so. With large-group rehearsals, however, an entire ensemble might pause for 10 minutes after practicing for 50, provided that the material and rehearsal pace aren't strenuous.

How you rest merits special attention. Instrumentalists should pass up hand-intensive tasks during breaks; singers should sip water and curb vocal use. Breaks are covered in greater depth on page 75.

4. Increase gradually

College-level music students commonly devote two to three hours per day to solitary practice. Singers, on average, rehearse less to prevent overusing their voices. Some instrumentalists practice five hours or more, although four or five hours a day appears to be the upper limit for most players. Nevertheless, the musicians who can be productive for hours have built up their stamina in stages. So, when designing your schedule, balk at sudden increases in your total practice and performance time. Abrupt upswings in playing or singing time are prime causes of injury to musicians.

How much can you safely increase? Physician Ralph Manchester, editor of the journal *Medical Problems of Performing Artists,* counsels musicians to confine any rise in playing or singing to a maximum of 10–20% per week.[3] If you normally make music two hours per day, then your topmost increase would be anywhere from 12–24 minutes a day for one week. Even so, if you step up for three straight weeks, it might be prudent to practice less on the fourth week so that you don't get worn down.

On certain occasions, however, increasing isn't appropriate. If you make technical changes, rehearse arduous material, or obtain a new instrument, it's safest to reduce your practice time and then build it back up. In so doing, you give your body a chance to adjust to novel movements. But that restriction applies only to your physical practice. You can still do copious mental rehearsal and score study, thereby raising your productivity without depleting your physical resources. Techniques for mental practice are presented in the chapters to come.

5. Live a balanced life

Effective scheduling entails harmonizing all the aspects of your life—your health, relationships, school, and employment, as well as your music making. As you chisel out a practice regimen, strike a balance. Make room to exercise, eat nutritious foods, relax with friends, and do first-rate academic or other work. A balanced lifestyle is essential to your well-being and therefore to your long-term success as a musician.

As an example of how you might apply these guidelines, suppose that you intend to practice three hours each weekday and that you'll do so in three separate sessions. You participate in ensemble rehearsals, too, and you do some gigging on weekends. Given your workload, your solo practice needs to be highly productive and minimally fatiguing.

A reasonable arrangement would be to start a practice session with 10 minutes of warm-up and then work in three 20-minute practice segments with 5-minute breaks in between. You could then finish with a 5-minute cooldown, perhaps integrating gentle scales and stretching, after which you'd spell out the goals for your next practice installment.

The duration of your session would be 85 minutes, not counting any setup time. So, on your daily calendar, you'd reserve three 90-minute time slots. One could be in the morning; the others might fall in the afternoon and evening. On the weekends, you could abide by a matching schedule for one day; on the second day, you might practice lightly, play or sing for fun, or enjoy other activities.

To conclude this section about governing the quantity of your practice, I want to mention the other side of the artful practice equation: practice *quality*. To learn vast amounts of repertoire and develop professional-grade skills, students require substantial practice over a span of years. Still, no matter how clever you become at coordinating your time and materials, hours of sloppy run-throughs will produce nothing of value. Both quantity and quality of practice are critical to musical achievement.

As you settle into a practice schedule, make it your top priority to raise the quality of your practice and not merely control the quantity. Practice quality is contingent on what materials you select and how you practice them. Chapters 2–6 delve into the *how* of practice. For now, let's consider what music you choose for your *new material* zone.

Choosing New Material

The wise musicians are those who play what they can master.
—Duke Ellington, composer and bandleader

Whatever styles of music you perform, choosing new material involves three factors: You have to weigh your musical preferences, your creative capacity, and your short- and long-term plans. Teachers exploit those same criteria when selecting repertoire for students. If you study with a teacher who assigns material, the better your teacher understands your taste, capacity, and plans, the more optimal those repertoire choices will be. So, whether you choose your own material or you work with teacher-assigned music, here's how these factors operate.

1. Taste

First and foremost, you should enjoy the music that you learn. That's not to say that every composition you take on has to be a favorite, but the storehouse of repertoire you accumulate should reflect your artistic personality. Besides, excitement for a piece of music will motivate you to practice. Furthermore, try to be broadly literate about music so that you can enjoy an assortment of genres. As a student, you don't get to choose all of the titles that you play or sing. When you're assigned an unfamiliar composition, hold off passing judgment—tune in to the piece's expressive language by listening to recordings and reading about the music's origins. Then, whatever your personal style, bring the music to life. Doing so will make you a more versatile performer.

2. Capacity

Your creative capacity is determined by your musical and technical abilities, along with your available practice time. Your capacity will increase as your strength and skills grow. However, for you to make progress with basics such as on-stage confidence and ease of execution, your repertoire choices must be within your capacity. Musicians who pick unattainable pieces foster destructive habits, such as anxiety and tension, and they miss out on learning how to present secure, poetic performances.

3. Plans

As you search out music that lines up with your taste and capacity, you also have to keep an array of goals in mind. In the long term, a musician with professional aspirations needs to master numerous skills, stockpile an expansive repertoire, and become conversant in a range of styles. In the near term, a concert could be coming up in a few weeks.

Your best bet for meeting all of your goals is to find pieces that serve both your immediate and your ongoing objectives. Seek compositions that aren't just appealing and reachable but also contrast with other titles in your repertoire. You might select certain pieces because they introduce you to new genres or expressive techniques; other compositions might be apt because they complement your previously learned pieces and would fit with them in concert or audition programs. To widen your pool of repertoire possibilities, regularly attend performances and visit libraries, retailers, and websites where you can peruse scores and recordings. Also review your plans with your teacher. A veteran educator will possess encyclopedic knowledge of music that suits you.

In addition to these factors, if you're looking to conquer performance jitters or overcome technical problems, then, until your fundamental skills gel, all of your new repertoire should be highly accessible. You should choose pieces that you can master in a week or two because for you to gain expertise with practice and performance skills, you must repeatedly go through the process of preparing music for the stage.

Some of you may be wondering, "If I practice only music that's highly accessible, how will I advance? Shouldn't I stretch my limits?" Of course you should stretch your limits. For the most part, etudes and exercises in your *technique* and *musicianship* zones will target your functional weaknesses. In those zones, as chapter 5 explains, you'll often push the envelope to ramp up your facility. But if you haven't yet acquired the skills to execute pieces fluently and be poised under pressure, then the repertoire you practice must not exceed what you can readily handle.

Case in point, all of the new, developing, and performance material on Keith's practice sheet (p. 9) was of the accessible type. Even though he had eight years of lessons behind him, when he arrived at my studio, he needed to complete some groundwork to quell performance nerves, cultivate solid technical habits, and lock in memorization skills. Accessible material enabled him to attain proficiency quickly. In the process, he collected a sizable repertoire that he loved to play.

How did Keith locate pieces that met his educational needs? He didn't. That was his teacher's responsibility. Nobody expects students to be connoisseurs of pedagogical music. Accordingly, I searched out material on Keith's behalf by applying what I had discovered about his taste, capacity, and plans. For example, after asking him about his favorite composers, I singled out promising repertoire and asked him to rate the pieces on a 1–10 scale of appeal, with 10 as the highest rating. We agreed that he'd play only the ones that he rated at six and higher.

At first, Keith learned pieces selected from my music library, and all of the scores included technical and expressive indications. Preedited music gave him a model of how to prepare a score and interpret a composition. In time, once Keith had formed an interpretive-technical knowledge base, I ceased providing edited scores, and he independently devised interpretations and fingerings for his new pieces.

As Keith devoured accessible titles, he ratcheted up his foundational abilities with both simple and challenging material in the *technique* and *musicianship* zones. All told, he enlarged his practice and performance skills while assimilating the ingredients necessary to play tougher repertoire. In six months, with an arsenal of basics in place, he tackled more intricate music of his own choosing.

Self-Recording

> *There is nothing more fatal for our musical sense than to allow ourselves—by the hour—to hear musical sounds without really listening to them.*
>
> —Tobias Matthay, pianist

Keen self-listening is central to musical excellence. Without it, performers heedlessly sing off pitch, play out of rhythm, or otherwise mangle their music. They sound good to no one but themselves. With high-quality recording devices, however, accurate self-assessment comes within the reach of all musicians.

This section focuses on audio recording. Video recording is discussed in later chapters in the contexts of sprucing up technique and stage presence. I begin by surveying the five main benefits of self-recording and then describe types of equipment.

Benefits of Self-Recording

1. Sharpens musicianship

Recording a portion of your practice sharpens your musicianship in that you can gauge every facet of your sound with an impartial ear. Whether you record a single phrase or a full-length piece, you can stand back and listen to the music as if someone else had performed it. You can then refine your execution in line with your insights.

2. Prevents distorted perception

Self-recording prevents distorted perception because it gives you an opportunity to evaluate your performance without any interference from the actions of producing the music. For instance, if you unwittingly rushed your timing during a thorny phrase, you would hear the flaw on your recording and be able to make corrections promptly. You wouldn't be reliant on a teacher to reveal your gaffe. Also, for many musicians, especially vocalists, their self-perceived tone quality necessarily differs from what their audiences hear. A recorder enables you to perceive how you actually sound to your listeners.

3. Heightens practice efficiency

Self-recording heightens efficiency in practice by not only thwarting distorted perception but also boosting accuracy. If you've ever realized at a lesson or rehearsal that you had practiced a passage wrongly, then you know how wasteful inaccurate practice can be. Self-recording, combined with acute listening, helps you be precise from the start.

4. Enhances lessons

Recording your lessons will enhance your learning because, following a session, you can review and take notes. Given that music lessons encompass profuse subjects and that there's seldom time to write down every detail, self-recording will ensure that none of the advice you receive is forgotten.

5. Promotes objectivity

The last benefit I'll cite is that, when musicians rehearse in groups, self-recording allows them to appraise their work objectively and minimize conflict. Rather than arguing over whether someone was out of tune or played too loud, group members can record an excerpt to uncover faults.

Types of Self-Recording Gear

The prospect of buying recording equipment may seem daunting, but, to record for self-study purposes, you don't need elaborate gear. First, decide how compact your self-recording setup should be. Highly portable gear probably suits you best because you'll be recording yourself in varied locales, and you'll want to listen at your convenience, perhaps while riding public transportation.

Opt for pocket-sized digital devices that record in stereo using onboard mics and operate at several sampling rates, including MP3 and CD levels. Current models are a bit bigger than cell phones; they store data on removable memory cards that permit you to transfer audio files to and from computers (see *musiciansway.com*). Recording with a laptop computer is another option, but take into account the limited portability of computer-based recording setups. Nonetheless, using a moderately priced microphone and interface, along with free or low-cost software, you can record onto your hard drive and listen through headphones or speakers.

Regardless of how little money you can spend, having *some* means of self-recording will be vital to your musical development. Don't splurge on high-end products, though, unless you're going to record to industry standards and you can get guidance from an audio engineer. Superior recording gear will sound terrific, but it won't make you a more capable performer. Decent gear and artful practicing will.

2

Practicing Deeply, I

In this chapter:

- Habits of excellence
- Essentials of artistic interpretation
- Mental imaging
- Guidelines for warming up

Practicing Deeply

That inner voice has both gentleness and clarity. So to get to authenticity, you really keep going down to the bone, to the honesty and the inevitability of something.

—Meredith Monk, singer and composer

As chapter 1 points out, practice is both a many-sided task and a quest for boundless artistic growth. Despite the wonders and the intricacies, however, the inner workings of practice have much in common with other avenues to learning and self-improvement. Simply put, certain ways to practice music or study academic topics lead to profound understanding, whereas others cause material to be shaky and easily forgotten.

For instance, on the shaky side, if you do a cursory job of preparing an ensemble part, your performance will be uninspired, if not edgy, and you'll be unlikely to extract any musical benefit. Correspondingly, if you cram for a math test, you might be able to pass, but the formulas you studied will soon vanish from your mind if you don't use them again. Such shallow learning doesn't yield tangible changes in your knowledge or skills, whatever the subject.

Deep learning occurs when knowledge transforms you—when you don't just study a math problem for a test but also apply it, perhaps to designing a sculpture. Then a math principle comes alive and persists in your memory longer than any exam. Deep practice involves an even more comprehensive process. When you practice deeply, you explore multiple aspects of a piece or exercise, and every element draws your interest. You work until you reach the authentic place that Meredith Monk alludes to above. At that point, you can be secure and artistic on stage.

This chapter and the three that follow plumb the components of deep practice. Here you'll read about general concepts. The ensuing chapters then describe strategies tailored to the five practice zones that chapter 1 introduced. You'll see that deep practice entails achieving mastery, integration, and transcendence with everything that you play or sing. That is, you start from a mastery-oriented perspective and strive to attain the utmost clarity with your music: You divide a piece into sections, assimilate the ingredients, and then merge the parts. At the same time, deep practice integrates all that you are—your body, mind, and spirit. Third, deep practice is transcendent. No pitch is merely a pitch; each one has a living quality. The humble exercise and the glorious composition alike present opportunities for you to make music and assert your style.

> **The Foundations of Deep Practice**
>
> • Mastery
> • Integration
> • Transcendence

As you read the upcoming suggestions for deepening your practice, remember that there is no one "correct" way to absorb a piece or become a better artist. Capable musicians employ related principles of learning, but individual systems of practice necessarily include customization. What's more, profound learning isn't the sole attribute of deep practice; there's also the efficiency angle. It's not enough to know how to master repertoire and refine skills; you additionally need the know-how to accomplish your goals as swiftly as possible. To quote David Soyer, longtime cellist with the Guarneri String Quartet, "Practicing well is virtually an art in itself—the art of achieving economy of time and means."[1] With that in mind, the information here, beyond offering practice strategies, is intended to promote your artistic independence and equip you to shape your own creative yet efficient approach to musical development.

Habits of Excellence

> *We first make our habits and then our habits make us.*
>
> —John Dryden, poet

Your habits in the practice room make you the musician that you are. And given that the foremost goal of practice is to prepare performances, your work should instill the habits needed on stage. This section highlights seven indispensable habits that are elaborated on throughout this book—five deal with musical execution; two speak to states of mind. When you emphasize all seven in each moment that you practice, excellence becomes your "default setting" both in rehearsal and under the spotlights.

Habits of Excellence
1. Ease
2. Expressiveness
3. Accuracy
4. Rhythmic vitality
5. Beautiful tone
6. Focused attention
7. Positive attitude

1. Ease

Masterful performers exhibit ease in all that they do on stage. Their performances appear easy because they *are* easy for them, thanks to the fact that, in practice, such artists invariably execute with a minimum of effort. Student musicians might believe that they can struggle in practice and, over time, will garner similar fluency. But experts know otherwise. Ease is a habit that has to be fortified at every turn.

Although ease includes many physical features, such as supple movement, facility originates in the mind. It arises from building awareness of your material and of your playing or singing actions. Nonetheless, the amount of brainpower that you can expend to be aware is finite. The more attention you use up supervising technical elements, the less you have available for artistry and coperformer communication. The key to easeful performance is the ability to command your music making in an integrated manner without exhausting your capacity.

To foster easeful habits, choose manageable material, and practice with your effort meter far out of the struggle zone. Establish a standard for easefulness whereby you make the quality of your experience while playing or singing as significant as the quality of the music you produce. In the words of violinist Kato Havas, "Playing is never difficult; it is either easy, or it is impossible."[2]

2. Expressiveness

The only way that you can become an expressive performer is to be an expressive practicer. Still, transcendent musicianship isn't based on arbitrary emoting. Gripping interpretations result when musicians respond to the expressive grammar embedded in their music. If, instead, musicians perform contrived renditions—swelling the volume, for example, irrespective of a composition's energy—their expression sounds meaningless at best and bizarre at worst.

To permeate your practice with eloquence, as the next section shows, bring out the peaks of phrases and taper your sound as phrases repose. Also make strong beats strong and weak beats weak rather than thumping along with undifferentiated pulses. Crank up your imagination, too, even with the plainest of materials: Put some punch into scales and exercises such that you're always creating shapes. "Treat everything you play on your instrument as an important piece of music," urges trumpeter Wynton Marsalis, "even if you are just warming up."[3]

3. Accuracy

Many students begin working on new pieces by doing heaps of sketchy run-throughs and sloppy repetitions. Then, after forming error-ridden habits, they're obliged to spend countless hours trying to overwrite their flawed programming.

A more masterful strategy is to start with accuracy and continue being exact at each phase of ripening a piece. To instill accuracy, however, you have to not only select material that fits your level but also work in ways that make slip-ups rare. Some of those ways, explained later on, involve splitting pieces into digestible portions and learning them systematically. Of course, to discover interpretive ideas you might experiment freely. When you repeat material, though, you must uphold precision of thought and action. Then your performances will be likely to contain few mistakes because your practice didn't introduce muddled habits.

4. Rhythmic vitality

Music exists in time, so musicians must become connoisseurs of timing. But artistic timing isn't only about maintaining a steady pulse and precisely subdividing beats. Vitality in rhythm results when you also create forward motion that propels a phrase toward its summit and brings it firmly to a conclusion.

As discussed in the coming pages, one device for transmitting motion is to lock onto a baseline pulse and then drive from upbeats to downbeats—for example, when appropriate, to group four notes as 2 3 4 | 1 instead of | 1 2 3 4 |. Another constituent of rhythmic vitality, as with expressiveness, is to adjust the strength of beats to fashion a diverse ecosystem of accents. "Always try to find variety," said cellist Pablo Casals; "it is the secret of music."[4]

5. Beautiful tone

The quality of your tone will probably have a more immediate impact on listeners than any other feature of your execution. And each tonal shade that you create will cast an emotional spell either for better or for worse. If you emit a harsh tone, let's say, then even when you craft your timing with care, your phrases will leave listeners grimacing. To entice an audience, your tone has to beguile, and you should have on hand a palette of tonal hues to complement any composition.

Whenever you practice, ensure that your normative tone is full and rich. If you perform acoustically, develop a tone that will project to the back of a hall even at your quietest levels. Also search out ways to tint your sound so that every piece you perform comes with brushstrokes of color, as tenor Plácido Domingo has explained: "I then realized that I could never be satisfied again with the mere natural charm of my voice," Domingo recalled, "that I had to constantly paint when singing, melting all the colors, expressing reds and blacks that had to be less primary but bursting with subtly colored combinations."

6. Focused attention

Imagine being on stage, about to begin a performance. Are your thoughts typically focused, or does your mind race? If you feel jittery, do you know how to attain a centered presence? Disciplined mental habits in practice will lay the groundwork for you to direct your thoughts under pressure. In contrast, if you routinely let your attention drift as you practice, then it's questionable whether your mind will be steady when your stress level climbs.

To cultivate focused mental habits, set explicit practice goals, and then keep up a calm, alert disposition as you work. If your attention wanes, take a break. Permanently shun mindless repetition.

7. Positive attitude

In your quest to upgrade your proficiency, some artistic and technical problems will be easy for you to figure out; others will challenge you severely. You won't get far as a musician, though, unless you meet problems head-on.

Accrue reservoirs of optimism by regarding difficulties not as personal failures but as opportunities for learning. If a passage baffles you, use the problem-solving tactics in chapter 3, get help if you need it, and proceed confidently, knowing that the route you take to unravel an impasse, no matter how convoluted, will lift you to new heights of competence.

Essentials of Artistic Interpretation

There must always be a sense of progression or movement towards definite landmarks.

—Tobias Matthay, pianist

Many years ago I had lunch with two music teachers who advocated what I call the "notes first" practice method. In their estimation, students should practice new repertoire mechanically—that is, students should "get the notes"—and pursue interpretation afterward. I knew that numerous teachers shared that opinion, but I argued for the reverse approach. I still do.

Whatever music you play or sing, your aim is to express musical ideas, not spew out notes. Without interpretive notions at the forefront, what part of you will be in the lead as you practice? Not the artistic part. And what habits will you implant if you ignore the emotional soul of a composition? Not musical habits. Besides, "notes first" practice is woefully inefficient. At the outset of learning a piece, a performer's technical decisions have to be rooted in an interpretive blueprint. Otherwise, randomly chosen breath locations, fingerings, and so forth will largely conflict with a piece's phrase structure. "Notes first" practicers don't just ingrain mechanical habits; they're also burdened with reworking their habits later on—after they've deciphered what a composition is about.

In sum, when learning a new piece, your objectives are to master the music efficiently and then perform artistically, so artistic expression should be front and center at each stage of the mastering process. Therefore, before we dive into practice procedures, let's look at seven essentials of artistic interpretation to apply whenever you practice or perform. By integrating all seven, your every phrase will shimmer with life.

> **Essentials of**
> **Artistic Interpretation**
>
> 1. Capture the mood, style, and tempo
> 2. Shape the dynamics
> 3. Color the tone
> 4. Mold the articulation
> 5. Contour the meter
> 6. Drive the rhythm
> 7. Express the form

1. Capture the mood, style, and tempo

Suppose that you're an actor who has been hired to perform in a play. When you receive the script, what will you do first? Will you sound out your opening word, then the second? Hardly. You'll begin by getting an overview of both the story and your character. After you've studied the entire script, then you can infuse your lines with fitting emotions.

Interpreting a piece of music entails making similar connections. As chapter 3 portrays, when you pick up a new piece, rather than first being concerned with execution, it's best to capture the mood, style, and tempo by listening to recordings, studying the score, and researching background information. Cellist Yo-Yo Ma says, "Only after I have become familiar with the style and character of the work can I start shaping an interpretation."[5]

2. Shape the dynamics

On a primary level, musical interpretation conveys fluctuations in emotional intensity, and one of the principal means to communicate changes in intensity is to vary volume. More volume equals more emotional power, so you can set out to create an interpretation by increasing and decreasing volume to complement the gradations of intensity you perceive.

For instance, when melodies ascend, they often grow in vigor; upon descent, they might repose. As a rudimentary strategy, therefore, you could raise and lower the dynamic levels along with the melodic arc. In example 2.1, the dynamic markings were specified by the composer. Repeatedly play or sing the example and enjoy shaping the dynamics.

Example 2.1. From Mario Castelnuovo-Tedesco, Sonatina for Flute and Guitar, op. 205, second movement, measures 5–8.

Musical intensity, however, isn't generated from melodic layout alone. As chords depart from the tonic harmony, intensity rises dramatically, so you should adjust your volume in response to harmonic energy, too. Play example 2.2 on a keyboard or cello and sense how the harmonies call out for dynamic shading as they progress away from and then return to the tonic chord.

Example 2.2. From J. S. Bach, Suite BWV 1007 for unaccompanied cello, measures 1–4.

With vocal music, the text guides the shifts in melodic and harmonic power. In example 2.3, the melody, harmony, and text align such that, as the melody and text rise and fall in intensity, the harmony moves in step.

Example 2.3. From Franz Schubert, Erlkönig D. 328 for voice and piano, measures 93–96.

What if a melody descends and the harmony becomes more potent? Harmonic intensity usually trumps melodic outline. Even so, use your best judgment with any musical situation—make an interpretive choice that feels honest, and then expand and contract your sound accordingly. Also take into account that a piece may be structured with a single climactic peak that merits the loudest treatment. Hence, you'll often want to regulate your volume over the long haul so that you arrive at *fortissimo* only once.

3. Color the tone

Dynamic shapes will give your phrases surging dimensions, but when you also modify tone color, an expressive gesture gains even more clout. As an illustration, in example 2.4, the composer suggests abrupt dynamic changes. Leaving the tone color the same for both volume levels would make for a drab effect, but darkening the tone for the *forte* and brightening it for the *piano* dramatizes the contrast, drenching it with character.

Prelude

f [darker tone]   *p* [brighter tone]

f [darker tone]   *p* [brighter tone]

Example 2.4. From J. S. Bach, Suite BWV 1012 for unaccompanied cello, measures 1–4.

Vibrato is another component of tone coloration that's linked with dynamics. In example 2.5, the melody blooms in the third measure when the soloist intensifies and then relaxes vibrato in tandem with the dynamics.

Allegro moderato   *[vib. intensifies - vib. relaxes]*

p

Example 2.5. From Franz Schubert, Sonata D. 821 for arpeggione and piano, first movement, measures 10–13.

4. Mold the articulation

For many styles of music, the prevailing articulation for instrumental melodies is legato. But merely connecting one note to another doesn't make for a flowing line; multiple features combine to knead a legato phrase into a creamy texture. Take vibrato, for instance. If a soloist playing example 2.5 halts the vibrato before the end of the B (si) in the first measure, then the dulling of the B's conclusion will create a sag in the line, and the impression of legato will be lost. When vibrato comes into play, legato articulation often hinges on continuity of vibrato.

Many other aspects also contribute to producing a legato effect, among them tone color, accent, and, for vocalists, diction. Listen closely as you practice, and meld your legatos such that the seams between pitches disappear within the arc of a line.

The ability to deliver a liquid legato is crucial, but silence is the ingredient that punctuates musical ideas. In example 2.6, I've inserted apostrophes—or "breath marks"—to indicate where expressive silences fit in the melody. Such silences, though, don't add time to a measure. Instead, the duration of the pitch preceding the silence is reduced.

For instance, the quarter note that concludes the fourth measure of example 2.6 could be performed as an eighth note or a dotted eighth note, with silence occupying the remainder of the pitch's value. The dotted half note at the end of the second line might be held for approximately five eighth notes in duration followed by about an eighth note of silence. Play or sing the example a few times to gauge how much silence you feel the melody needs at each breath.

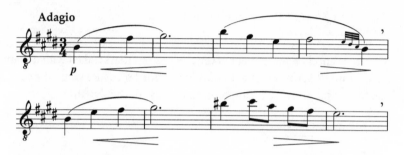

Example 2.6. From Franz Schubert, Sonata D. 821 for arpeggione and piano, second movement, measures 4–11.

Here's another application of the same articulation principle. Execute the breaths in example 2.7 by playing or singing the eighth note before each apostrophe as a sixteenth note followed by a sixteenth-note rest.

Example 2.7. From Domenico Scarlatti, Sonata K. 159 for harpsichord, measures 1–5.

Silences not only punctuate phrases but animate staccato pitches as well. And the amount that you detach your staccatos will alter the character of the music you create. Play or sing the melody in example 2.8, and toy with varying the staccato articulations: Fine-tune the duration of each silence; polish the way you attack and release every pitch.

Example 2.8. From Joaquín Rodrigo, En los trigales for guitar, measures 1–12.

Example 2.9 demonstrates a more modern use of articulation. Here the text implores the north and south winds to blow, and the composer uses articulation, rhythm, and melody to create a capricious, windlike effect in the line—an effect that a performer would want to put across. Also notice the serial composition technique: The first three measures form a phrase that contains twelve different pitches; the pitches in next phrase start off in the reverse order.

Example 2.9. From Igor Stravinsky, Canticum Sacrum for voices and instruments, measures 47–53.

5. Contour the meter

In the hands of an artistic performer, meter translates into a voluptuous topography of stronger and weaker beats. For you to create a stirring metric terrain, however, and not a mechanical-sounding one, you have to cunningly vary the weight of the beats, first, in keeping with the time signature and, second, in relation to the music itself.

To form a smooth metric contour, as would be apt with example 2.6, the onsets of beats must never be angular or hard hit. Conversely, to generate a punchier line, some downbeats need to be palpable, and other beats will call for assorted emphasis. For instance, play or sing the melody in example 2.10, and investigate how varied accentuation affects the music.

Example 2.10. From Fritz Kreisler, Liebesfreud for violin and piano, measures 1–9.

When deciding how much to accentuate pitches, in addition to assessing their metric positions and surveying any expressive notation in a score, consider where pitches lie in an arching phrase. If a phrase tapers into a downbeat, that downbeat will characteristically be softened, even though a downbeat is normally the strongest beat of a measure. In example 2.11, the four-measure phrases conclude with diminuendos: The final pitch of each phrase would probably be the quietest one, whereas the preceding downbeat would be the strongest.

Example 2.11. From Franz Schubert, Sonata D. 821 for arpeggione and piano, third movement, measures 17–24.

Long notes or dissonances that fall on weak beats are ordinarily stressed, thereby overriding their subordinate metric positions. Play or sing example 2.12, and experiment with adding emphasis to the pitches that I've marked *tenuto.*

Example 2.12. From Enrique Granados, Danza española no. 5 for piano, measures 48–55.

To produce accentuation, on top of sounding strong beats louder, you can enhance metric stress through subtly stretching the duration of weightier pitches. In example 2.13, the notes marked "long" could be sustained slightly beyond their notated values, and then the ensuing eighth notes would be tumbled forward in a sly *accelerando* to land, in time, on the subsequent downbeats.

Example 2.13. From Bernardo Gianoncelli, Bergamasca for lute, measures 1–8.

Overall, to bring your meter to life, flavor each beat in proportion to its rank in the musical hierarchy. Tweak your accentuation with both volume and duration such that, depending on the music's mood, you create sonic landscapes that undulate, flow, or spike in dramatic peaks.

6. Drive the rhythm

Rhythm comes alive when it propels a listener forward through a phrase. Aside from choosing a tempo that fits a piece's nature, two ways to create irresistible motion are to steer shorter notes into longer ones and to move from upbeats toward downbeats without halting at the bar lines. Cellist Diran Alexanian, in the preface to his edition of the Bach cello suites, termed this propulsion "rhythmic attraction,"[6] and numerous other musicians have put forward the same concept. In his book *Note Grouping,* for instance, hornist James Thurmond discusses how an upbeat initiates motion toward a downbeat just as an in-breath (upbeat) activates the need to release on an out-breath (downbeat).[7]

In example 2.14, the gravitational tug of rhythmic attraction pulls the melody notes in each of the bracketed groups forward. Play the example—or sing the melody—and drive the shorter notes toward the longer ones that conclude each group.

Example 2.14. From W. A. Mozart, Sonata K. 333 for piano, first movement, measures 1–4.

When the note values in a composition are more uniform than those in example 2.14, one tactic to express rhythmic attraction is to minutely extend the duration of prominent pitches and then push the subsequent pitches forward. Repeatedly play example 2.15 on a keyboard or cello and, as shown, propel the sixteenth notes following a strong beat toward the strong beat to come. Such note grouping, however, shouldn't distort the baseline pulse. As you play the example, ensure that the first and third beats in each measure coincide with the pulse of a metronome (the second and fourth beats might or might not line up with the metronome).

Example 2.15. From J. S. Bach, Suite BWV 1007 for unaccompanied cello, measures 1–2.

Although music needs forward motion, your rhythmic propulsion shouldn't be relentless. Example 2.16 presents a melody in which a performer could seductively manipulate the motion in each of the bracketed phrases. Play or sing the example, and try this: In the first two phrases, after lingering a tad on the upbeats, move forward through the middles of the phrases and then relax the motion as the phrases end. Next, press onward through the eight-measure phrase, putting a slight delay before the closing pitch.

Example 2.16. From Fritz Kreisler, Liebesleid for violin and piano, measures 49–64.

If these rhythmic inflections seem subtle, they are. Yet expressive timing forms the backbone of artistic music making. Mozart wrote, "The most necessary, most difficult, and principal thing in music, that is time."[8] Continually try out ways to imbue your rhythm with motion and personality, and then run your rhythmic experiments by your teacher.

7. Express the form

The word "form," as it's used in music, refers to a piece's structure. Many traditional dance forms, such as minuets and gigues, have binary designs: There are two halves, and each half might repeat; they're typically performed AABB. Folksong forms, by comparison, often comprise several verses with an intervening chorus. Rondo forms can incorporate any number of sections, but the main theme keeps coming back; some are structured ABACADA. Rondos tend to be entertaining because they mingle familiarity with freshness, so they customarily turn up as concluding movements of Classical-era sonatas.

But that's only the macroview of form. On a smaller level, form affects the way that groups of notes clump into phrases and phrases join to create sections. In microterms, form operates on the level where melodic, harmonic, and rhythmic forces cause handfuls of notes to coalesce into figures or motives. Form equates with the way letters adhere into words, words group into phrases, phrases assemble into sentences, sentences constitute paragraphs, and so on. Extending that analogy to literature, large-scale compositions resemble novels. When you set about learning them, it takes time to grasp their designs, their many characters, and their emotional sweep. Binary forms are like short essays that make a single point; there's one prevailing mood, the storyline is more evident, and just a few characters are involved.

To express the form of a piece, you employ the preceding *essentials of artistic interpretation* to show listeners where the action crests and reposes, to communicate mood, and to let phrases breathe. Like a storyteller, you lead an audience through the narrative of a piece. Without appreciation for compositional design, a performer might overlay grandiose inflections that have little to do with a piece's syntax. "Vanity is indeed the archenemy of the interpreter," wrote conductor Erich Leinsdorf, "because it interferes with his ability to receive messages from other minds."[9] Become a more egoless interpreter: Build your aptitude at recognizing and responding to form. Consult your teacher if formal construction is new to you.

Although the framework here will help you flesh out your interpretative insights, its effectiveness rests on your musical and technical skills. That is, you have to be able to perceive compositional content and also execute expressive gestures with your instrument or voice. Both musicianship and technique receive attention in chapter 5, but you can heighten your perceptiveness right away through critical listening (p. 98). So, regularly peruse landmark recordings—with scores in hand—and scrutinize how performers exploit the seven *essentials*. Then, when you make music, live by the advice of cellist Pablo Casals: "Don't give notes," he once exhorted a student. "Give the meaning of the notes."[10]

Mental Imaging

> When I sit in Paris in a café, surrounded by people, I don't sit casually—I go over a certain sonata in my head and discover new things all the time.
>
> —Arthur Rubinstein, pianist

The upcoming practice methods incorporate the technique of mental imaging as a fundamental tool for learning, memorizing, and performing music. This section describes mental imaging and provides an introductory exercise.

Like Arthur Rubinstein, myriad performers use imaging to rehearse compositions in their minds. They'll internally "hear" a piece of music, feel the sensations of executing it, and mentally hone their interpretations. However, imaging isn't a trick reserved solely for elite musicians; everyone uses imaging in daily life. For example, suppose that you're reading a book, and then you decide to exit the room you're in. What's the likelihood that you would accidentally walk into a wall? Nil, I hope. When you enter a room, you detect where you are with respect to the door. When you leave, you move in relation to your mental map of the space.

Just as people form mental maps to guide their walking, expert musicians depend on inner maps to steer their performances. While playing or singing, they know where they are in a composition, where they've been, and where they're going.

Performers construct their musical maps through shrewd practice. To learn a new piece, let's say, savvy practicers first get an overview of the music and then carve it into sections. Next, as chapter 3 explains, they progressively map the interpretive and technical elements. With clear mental maps established, musicians play or sing with abandon, knowing that they can't get lost. Unprepared performers rely on spotty maps that send them fishtailing out of control. The gaps in their awareness provoke one wrong turn after another.

By working with the practice methods to come, you'll discover how mental imaging can speed up the learning process and liberate your artistry. As a preface, try the following exercise—it calls for a metronome and a piano or electronic keyboard.

Mental Imaging Exercise

In this exercise, you image playing a simple passage on a keyboard, and then you actually play the passage. During your actual playing, you use imaging to lead your execution.

1. Imaging

   a. Sit in front of a piano keyboard, and locate the keys needed to play example 2.17 (p. 36). Play a G (sol) to get the pitch in your ear, and then switch on your metronome.

   b. Keeping your eyes on the music, repeatedly sing the example while you imagine playing it—vocalize note names, and playfully move your right-hand fingers in the air.

Example 2.17. Mental imaging exercise.

   c. Create a vibrant, multisensory experience: Feel your fingers depress the imaginary keys, mentally hear the sound of a piano, perceive the spatial layout of the keyboard, and soak in the emotion of the dynamics.

   d. Image the example at least three times. Aim to register fresh, more realistic sensations with each recap.

2. Imaging and executing

   a. Place your right hand on the keyboard, and sense how you'll execute the first measure of the example. With your metronome ticking, prepare to play by counting aloud: "1 and 2 and."

   b. As you begin to play, image one measure ahead of the one that you're playing. When executing the ascending scale, sense the descending scale; as you execute the descending scale, sense the last two notes; as you play the final notes, sense the ascending scale, and so on.

   c. Execute unselfconsciously. Instead of micromanaging your movements, trust your mental map, be playful, and allow accuracy to occur without being obsessed with correctness.

   d. Repeat several times. Sing along using note names during your first time through; thereafter, cease using your voice, and mentally sing note names. With each repeat, withdraw effort.

When you employ imaging to practice and perform music, you harness your mind in these two ways. First, to aid in learning and memorizing a piece, you simulate playing or singing to imprint a lucid mental map. Then, as you execute, you image ahead so that your music making is secure and spontaneous.

In *The Inner Game of Tennis*, Timothy Gallwey depicts two exercises that underscore the power of imaging coupled with unselfconscious execution.[11] In both exercises, a can is placed in the corner of a tennis court. Then, standing on the opposite baseline, a player attempts to hit the can with a ball. First, the player focuses on technique—she thinks about racket angle, swing, and so forth. She tries hard to do things "correctly." In the second instance, the player gives up that sort of forced trying. She notes the location of the can, imagines the ball traveling from racket to target, and then swings the racket naturally—without self-judging. In which exercise do you envision yourself having more fun and being more accurate?

To perform music with abandon, you have to sense imminent phrases with the clarity of a tennis player who knows the location of that can. Still, your mastery must be such that it's as though the can is an arm's length away, and you can't miss it. You gain that degree of musical clarity by selecting accessible material and forging robust mental maps in practice. Nonetheless, keen imaging skills take time to develop. In due course, you'll image so easily that you'll be able to learn and rehearse music while riding a bus or sitting in a café. If you're on tour, for example, and spending hours in transit before an event, you'll use imaging to practice mentally, and your confidence will grow rather than fade. Then, when you step on stage, your awareness of your material will anchor your control and set your creativity free.

Warming Up

If you warm up in the right way, all your practicing and playing will have a sense of completeness and integration.

—William Pleeth, cellist

Like sensuous opening ceremonies, warm-ups prepare the body, mind, and spirit for making music. On the physical side, warm-ups increase blood flow to the muscles, encourage lubrication in the joints, and, for singers, limber up the vocal mechanism. Mentally, they focus the attention; spiritu-ally, they inspire excitement for music. If you bypass warming up, though, you not only make playing or singing more difficult but

> **Warm-Up Fundamentals**
> 1. Breathe, move, and center
> 2. Specify goals
> 3. Mindfully set up and tune
> 4. Begin moderately
> 5. Mix it up
> 6. Finish in 10–15 minutes

also multiply your risk of injury because cold muscles are prone to fatigue and tearing. Added to that, a scattered mind can neither learn deeply nor create uplifting music. The guidelines here will help you devise warm-ups that nourish both your music making and your well-being.

1. Breathe, move, and center

To transition from your everyday existence to the lofty spheres of music, allocate a few minutes to do some breathing, moving, and centering before you sing or play. For instance, in a standing position, you might circle your arms overhead as you inhale and then lower them as you exhale (p. 76). You could also roll your shoulders a number of times. While you move and breathe, achieve a centered presence: Affirm the significance of music in your life, let go of extraneous concerns, and restore inner balance.

Also, fit your movements to your circumstances. In cool settings, put on layers of clothing, and move vigorously enough to bump up your body temperature; when you feel sluggish, opt for energizers like jumping jacks. If you're unsure what sorts of movements might suit you, check with your teacher, an athletic trainer, or a physical therapist. Additional resources are available via *musiciansway.com*.

2. Specify goals

Next, turn your thoughts toward specific goals. When preparing for a practice session, clarify what items you'll work on, and organize your materials. Envision how you'll proceed; maybe jot down a plan. When getting ready for a performance, connect with the expressive substance of your repertoire along with your desire to commune with listeners—see *backstage techniques* (p. 162) for preparatory routines to use before a show.

3. Mindfully set up and tune

For most instrumentalists, the first act of playing revolves around unpacking an instrument, assuming playing position, and tuning. And how musicians do those things can bolster or weaken their creative mindsets. If you play an instrument that requires tuning, use a consistent tuning protocol, and make precise intonation central to your aesthetic. Whatever your musical specialty, though, carry out your preparatory regimen efficiently, easefully, and with a mindful reverence that reinforces your artistic aims.

4. Begin moderately

The physical aspect of your warm-up serves one main purpose: to draw blood to your music-making muscles and render them warm and supple. Therefore, begin to play or vocalize at moderate speed and intensity. Avoid any hard-driving material until your muscles are permeated with heat. (Singers: See *voice care*, p. 268, for added tips.)

Is there an ideal warm-up procedure? Probably not. You aren't the same each day, so you should adapt your warm-up patterns in response to how you feel. You can get going with material from any practice zone, including improvised material, as long as it's undemanding. "When warming up, what you play isn't as important as how you play it," writes violinist Julie Lyonn Lieberman.[12]

Whether you commence with an exercise or a favorite melody, image ahead, and embody the mastery, integration, and transcendence that underpin deep practice. Be open to whatever you experience and adjust as needed. Some days things will seem fluid and natural; other times, you'll need to select elementary material and steadily reintegrate your faculties. Either way, saturate your warm-up with *habits of excellence* (p. 20).

5. Mix it up

With any warm-up, mix in a range of techniques to reinstate broad-based control. You might review some scales, arpeggios, diction exercises, and part of a beloved piece at an easygoing tempo. Consult your teacher for warm-up strategies tailored to your individual needs, and continually look for creative ways to kick off your music making.

6. Finish in 10–15 minutes

Efficiency is vital to both practice and warming up. An efficient warm-up preserves practice time and promptly readies the musician. An overlong warm-up might drain energies such that a performer would tire partway through a rehearsal or concert.

By and large, once you start to play or sing, complete your warm-up in 10–15 minutes so that you're well prepared but unfatigued. Still, don't be too strict with time limits. Some musicians warm up more gradually than others. Plus, warm-ups should be more extended on tough days or prior to brief performances such as auditions. Be systematic, but also bring flexibility and inventiveness to any warm-up plan.

3

Practicing Deeply, II

In this chapter:

- The three practice activities
- Starting new material
- Bringing life to repetition
- Solving problems

The Craftsmanship of Practice

Without craftsmanship, inspiration is a mere reed shaken in the wind.

—Johannes Brahms, composer

This chapter delves into strategies for starting on a new piece and advancing it from the *new material* zone into the *developing material* one (p. 6). To review how those zones operate, with fresh repertoire, you begin learning at a moderate tempo and in sections, gradually knitting sections together. Once you can play or sing an intact composition at a preliminary tempo, it graduates to *developing* status. Practice maneuvers for the *developing material* zone are covered in the next chapter.

The first stages of working on a piece set the foundation upon which future performance is built. Even so, I've found that students often lack explicit means for approaching unfamiliar material; many pick up inaccurate and unmusical habits. Therefore, I'm devoting quite a few pages to describing the initial phases of learning so that you'll be equipped to close any gaps in your practice skills. Given the extent of the discussion, as a preview, I'd like to share a story about a pianist named Tara.

Tara was a 20-something musician who accompanied dance classes, performed occasional recitals, and taught privately. She sought me out for help with what she believed was a memorization problem. "I've been plagued by memory slips since I was a kid," she said. "Every time I play solo, I'm on the edge."

At our first lesson, she played part of a Beethoven sonata and, as predicted, her memory hiccupped repeatedly.

"How did you first learn this piece?" I asked.

"I'm not sure," she replied. "I guess I played through it several times; then I'd play each page over, sometimes slow, sometimes fast."

"How did you work out the expressive ideas and the fingerings?"

"I just let them come to me as I played," she said.

"And to memorize it," I inquired, "what did you do?"

"I kind of played it until I didn't need the music anymore."

"Well," I said, "I think we've found the cause of your troubles."

I took out an easy piece by Bartók and guided Tara through a process of mastering it. Here's a summary of that process.

I played the piece for Tara to get the sound in her ear. Then, dividing it into eight-measure sections, I asked how she might interpret the opening section in her own way. She hummed bits of the melody as she notated dynamics and articulations in the score. Next, I adjusted a metronome to a slowish tempo and invited her to vocalize the rhythm of the section. Using counting syllables, she sensitively sang the rhythm of the melody while moving her body in sync with the pulse.

With a visceral feel for the music established, Tara was set to apply her musical ideas to the piano. I asked her to discover fingerings for the section, but without touching the keys. Moving her fingers in the air, she envisioned the keyboard and, in a matter of seconds, devised fingerings that matched the musical shapes. She scribbled some finger numbers in the score and was ready to play.

But before turning her loose on the keyboard, I had her image playing the section, miming the playing motions with her hands as she expressively sang the tune—that is, she played mentally (see *mental imaging,* p. 34). With the metronome clicking, she did three mental run-throughs, refining her interpretation with each pass.

Having plotted the music's expressive and technical components, she then played the section on the piano and did so with such ease and spirit that we both laughed. I switched off the metronome and asked her to play it twice more, continually tweaking her interpretation in a playful way. It took her 15 minutes to learn the remaining sections of the piece and link them together. Throughout the process, she never played a wrong note or rhythm. Everything felt simple.

To commit the music to memory, I steered her through a similar routine. Section by section, without looking at the score, she played mentally three times, and then she repeated on the keys, fine-tuning her interpretation with every recap. Before our lesson finished, she performed the piece beautifully from memory, free of the glitches that had pervaded her Beethoven.

The Three Practice Activities
• Discovery
• Repetition
• Evaluation

Tara realized that day that, when we musicians practice, we do essentially three activities: We discover, repeat, and evaluate. We first discover a composition's musical and technical content. Then, repetition builds security so that the music flows according to our will. All the while, to ensure quality, we evaluate our work. That, in a nutshell, is the craftsmanship of practice.

Tara was able to sail through the Bartók because she fashioned a vivid image of how she wanted the music to sound and feel. When she had previously practiced the Beethoven, however, she repeated large swaths of the piece from the start, bypassing discovery and evaluation. As a result, her repetitions spawned a hodgepodge of mental impulses. It was those muddled signals that led to her iffy memorization and on-edge performances. "We get messed up," wrote pianist Eloise Ristad, "because we don't have a clear image . . . and thereby give ourselves too many conflicting messages about how to play."[1]

For you to become an accomplished practicer, you, too, have to develop facility with discovery, repetition, and evaluation. And you need a practice method that will adapt to your learning style and enable you to master music efficiently. The next section proposes such a method.

Starting New Material

I suppose that when I play in public it looks easy, but before I ever came on the concert stage I worked very hard. And I do yet—but always putting the two things together, mental work and physical work.

—Jascha Heifetz, violinist

When a new piece enters your life, it's something of a romance, and you're brimming with excitement. Nonetheless, the outset of learning is also when you instill enduring habits because the brain and body tend to imprint. That is, you begin with a clean inner slate, yet whatever you inscribe at first resists being erased. So it's crucial that you not only enjoy a new piece but also learn it deeply from square one by combining the mental and physical work to which Jascha Heifetz refers.

The process outlined here for learning new material is designed to deepen your awareness of a composition while fostering your romance with it. As Tara's experience with mastering the Bartók shows, this process centers on the discovery of artistic and technical components before executing. The aim is for you to be accurate and creative and also cultivate easeful, expressive execution.

The general strategy starts with getting an overview of a piece and continues with map- ping an interpretation—a step that includes the vocalization of rhythm. The next phase entails forming a technical map; you then execute your map. The more capably you complete each phase, the more efficient and artistic your prac- tice will be.

Starting New Material
1. Get an overview
2. Map an interpretation
3. Map the technique
4. Execute your map

To try out the following ideas, select a brief, elementary solo that you've never played or sung in the past; the piece should be simple enough to allow you to progress fluently through the learning stages. Then, read the upcom- ing concepts under "Get an overview," apply the procedures to your selec- tion, and move on to phase two of the learning process.

1. Get an overview

Getting an overview of a piece involves discovering aspects of the composi- tion itself and of the printed edition that you're working with. Your three main tasks are:

a. Establish an aural model.

b. Research background information.

c. Prepare the score.

a. Establish an aural model

Until you acquire the expertise to look at a score and mentally hear the music, the most straightforward route to establishing an aural model of a piece is to listen to recordings. Still, you don't want to mimic other musicians. With the exception of conductor-led pieces, you're going to flesh out your own inter- pretations. So peruse several audio or video recordings, with score in hand, to prevent one performance from sticking in your ear. As you listen, connect with the emotional fabric of the piece: Unleash your imagination, and let the music inspire feelings, scenes, or storylines.

When recordings aren't available, the primary avenue to gaining an aural model is to sight-read. However, doing so is a risky proposition for inexpert readers because they're vulnerable to embedding imprecise habits if they fumble through alien music—it can be like trying to assemble a complex de- vice without studying the instructions. Seasoned musicians, in contrast, can read novel material and not ingrain errors. On the whole, unless you're an

adept sight-reader, minimize executing untried music until you form interpretive and technical maps. When read-throughs are necessary, go forward
at moderate tempos and in manageable portions so that confused habits
don't take hold. Nonkeyboardists often benefit from using pianos to do preparatory readings.

b. Research background information

Every piece of music represents a particular time and civilization. When you
research a composition's background and, with vocal music, reflect on a text,
you bond with both the composer and the culture surrounding the music's
creation. Enhance your overview by answering these questions:

- When was the music written? Was it composed for a purpose, perhaps
  as a commission or to commemorate an event?
- What stylistic traditions does it spring from, and how does it compare
  with other compositions of its day?
- Where does it fall within the composer's output? Is it a student work,
  for instance, or a mature one?
- Singers and vocal accompanists: What's the meaning of a song's text?
  If you're preparing music for a dramatic production, what's the gist of
  the story? When a text is in a foreign language that you don't fully understand, print out a translation and transcribe it into your score; you
  might also write in pronunciation guides.

c. Prepare the score

A well-prepared score expedites learning. Here are five steps to carry out
with every notated composition that comes your way:

i. *Translate any text.* Here I'm referring to foreign-language text other
   than the song text just mentioned. Most scores contain text that sheds
   light on a composer's style. To decode unfamiliar terms, use an online
   or print dictionary, and then pencil in your translations.

ii. *Number the measures.* When an edition lacks measure numbers,
    number the first measure of each line. This allows you to communicate
    crisply with fellow musicians during rehearsals and, when you listen to
    a self-recording, makes it easy to write concise notes: "Measure 42,
    beat 2, out of tune." Be sure that you and your coperformers agree on
    your numbering rules. For example, the first measure of a piece begins
    at the first downbeat—incomplete pickup measures aren't numbered.

When dealing with first and second endings, either number the measures consecutively or give them matching numbers, that is, if the first ending starts with measure 72, you could assign the initial measure of the second ending number 72 as well.

iii. *Delineate sections.* To avoid overloading your learning capacity, it's best to practice pieces in digestible sections. Size your sections according to the music's complexity—the more intricate the material, the shorter the sections should be (a single piece might incorporate sections of varying lengths). If you like, denote the onset of a section with a capital letter in a box.

iv. *Identify difficulties.* As you carve out sections, identify tricky spots. By tracking the locations of difficulties, you can tackle them promptly.

v. *Estimate the final tempo.* Knowing the final tempo equips you to choose fingerings, breaths, and so on that will be effective both at a preliminary tempo and as the tempo increases. Jot down an approximate metronome setting on your score, and stay open to the prospect of revising it later.

2. Map an interpretation

Building on your overview, map out a basic interpretation that gives you a context for making technical choices. "Once you have a clear musical intention," says pianist Leon Fleischer, "then you can set up some kind of physical choreography."[2] Begin by analyzing and marking the score; then, to internalize your interpretation of a section, vocalize the rhythm.

a. Analyze and mark the score

Craft your interpretive map using the *essentials of artistic interpretation* described in chapter 2:

i. Capture the mood, style, and tempo
ii. Shape the dynamics
iii. Color the tone
iv. Mold the articulation
v. Contour the meter
vi. Drive the rhythm
vii. Express the form

To begin, look over the entire piece, and clarify any indistinct aspects of the mood, style, and form (you've already set a tempo). Then, do as eloquent an analysis of the compositional design as your abilities permit. With your aural model echoing in your mind, grasp patterns of melody, harmony, and rhythm; locate phrase boundaries and dramatic peaks; take in how the action unfurls across the grand scale.

Next, turn your attention to the first section. Observe any expression markings, and mull over additional options for sculpting the sound: Mentally hear the music, hum or vocalize softly, and toy with expressive possibilities; write in breath marks and expressive cues as you go. Instrumentalists should minimize playing at this stage because a technical plan hasn't yet been formed. However, both singers and instrumentalists may want to use a piano to illuminate harmonies and melodies.

b. Vocalize the rhythm

To instill the feel of your interpretive map and to spotlight the rhythmic framework, vocalize the rhythm of the one section that you just explored. Set your metronome to a comfortable tempo, and lightly sing or speak counting syllables (example 3.1).

Example 3.1. Vocalizing rhythm; from Franz Schubert, Sonata D. 821 for arpeggione and piano, third movement, measures 17–24.

Conduct the beat as you vocalize—use your arm or tap your foot—and express your interpretive map with your voice: Shape the dynamics, mold the articulation, drive the rhythm, and so forth. With multipart textures such as you find in keyboard and guitar pieces, either vocalize the rhythm of the principal part or express the composite feel of several parts. In any case, unless the music is rudimentary, vocalize the rhythm three times, and, with each repeat, heighten ease and expressiveness.

3. Map the technique

Now that you have an interpretive blueprint, it's time to figure out how to translate your sound-image into actual music. Here are separate guidelines for singers and instrumentalists to map technique. Apply these ideas to one section of your piece, and then go on to the execution phase.

Singers

i. *Speak text in rhythm.* To grasp how the words and rhythm fit together, expressively speak the text in rhythm. Once through may suffice because you counted the rhythm previously, but if anything feels uncertain, speak a section three times.

ii. *Polish diction and comprehension.* In *The Naked Voice,* W. Stephen Smith recommends that singers polish their diction and word-for-word comprehension of a text via a two- or three-part method, all done in free rhythm. For texts in languages that you understand well, you can carry out this procedure before speaking the text in rhythm. But if you don't know a language intimately, then by speaking in rhythm first you'll ensure that your accents line up correctly.

To start with, Smith advocates honing diction by speaking a text with minimal inflection. Then, for texts in foreign languages in which singers aren't fluent, he advises proceeding through the text phrase by phrase, speaking a passage in one's native tongue and then in the original language. Last, he proposes reciting the text in the original language "as if in a dramatic reading."[3]

iii. *Sing the melody on "ah."* With the rhythm, diction, and meaning clear, move on to mapping pitches. Using a piano, play the melody of a section to form a vibrant, in-tune sound-image. Following that, expressively sing the section on *ah* or by using other vowels. If any of the pitches don't ring true, review the relevant intervals, and then sing the section three times.

When a piece is going to be memorized, besides singing on *ah,* you may also profit from singing the melody with fixed-do solfège syllables, letter names, or scale degree numbers. Doing so fuels comprehension of melodic and harmonic structure. Depending on your learning style, it can also aid memorization. If you vocalize letters, however, when a sharp or flat is present, you could opt to sing plain letters and mentally perceive the sharp or flat so that vocalizing isn't cumbersome.

Instrumentalists

i. *Work systematically.* Bit by bit and in free rhythm, analyze how to execute a section with optimal ease and expressiveness. Then, pencil in fingerings, bowings, breaths, and other technical cues as needed.

ii. *Image and vocalize.* As you weigh up the technical prospects, refrain from excessive playing. When necessary, test various options on your instrument, but primarily image the act of playing to conserve energy and prevent the imprinting of unwelcome habits. In tandem, it's a good idea to vocalize the names of the notes that you're mapping—either sing fixed-do solfège syllables or letter names (unpitched percussion parts merit counting). Such vocalizing helps to merge all of your faculties into the mapping process. For many performers, it creates a more robust mental record of the music and aids memorization.

iii. *Convey your interpretation.* In assembling a technical map, keep your interpretive notions at the forefront. Align breaths or position shifts, for example, in relation to the note grouping such that interruptions of sound coincide with expressive articulations. Also be mindful of the final tempo. If you'll execute at a slow pace initially, envision the way things will operate at concert speed so that your technical choices will suit higher velocities.

4. Execute your map

With your interpretive and technical maps in place, you're ready to make music. Here are strategies pertinent to both singers and instrumentalists.

> **Execute Your Map**
>
> a. Work with digestible portions
> b. Manage the tempo
> c. Image ahead
> d. Be artistic yet detached
> e. Execute three times
> f. Link sections together

a. Work with digestible portions

Although the basic unit of mapping is a section, to execute, you should work with readily digestible portions of music, and these will frequently be smaller than sections.

b. Manage the tempo

Choose a preliminary tempo that permits you to execute with ease and awareness. Use a metronome to keep your pulse steady, but don't automatically leave the metronome ticking on each repeat. When you're working at a slow tempo but your final one will be swift, relate your slower execution to how it will feel to perform at a brisk pace. That is, if a note group will later be tossed off quickly, conceive of it as a whole entity and not as a series of separate bits. Otherwise, as pianist Abby Whiteside warns, "Slow practice can establish habits that are completely unrelated to the coordination demanded for speed."[4] Suggestions for increasing tempo are listed later in this chapter and in chapter 4.

c. Image ahead (p. 34)

As you execute one note group, listen intently, but also image the ensuing group. "The mind always has to anticipate the physical action that is to be taken and then to send the command for its execution," advised violin teacher Ivan Galamian.[5] If you're an instrumentalist, while executing one musical gesture, experience the sound, meaning, and tactile sensations of the gesture to come. If you're singing, when delivering one group of words, mentally perceive the upcoming word group.

d. Be artistic yet detached

Bring the music to life, but don't get swallowed up by passion. Create gripping lines while you image ahead, release tension, and coolly assess the quality of your execution.

e. Execute three times

At a steady tempo, execute three consecutive, accurate statements of a portion or section, boosting ease and expressiveness with each recap (challenging portions may merit five runs). If your first two attempts are solid and your third one cracks, start over at zero. Assuming that your material fits your level, your mapping is thorough, and your tempo is slow enough, you should be assured right away. If any section gives you trouble, though, isolate and unravel the problems before running the section again (pointers for solving problems appear in the coming pages). After finishing three runs of a section, map and execute another section.

- Instrumentalists: As with Tara, executing at this stage could include two parts: imaging, followed by playing. In general, image a portion or section one to three times at an easygoing tempo, and then play three times. Vocalize as you image, and mime the playing motions in miniature—you don't have to act out inclusive movements; just move enough to register the sensations of playing (some musicians image without moving at all). Regarding what to vocalize while imaging, be flexible: Expressively sing note names, counting syllables, or finger numbers, whichever needs clearing up or seems the most compelling. If a piece contains multiple lines, as in a keyboard work, vocalize the principal line, usually the melody, or sing a different voice with each repeat.

f. Link sections together

  i. *Overlap sections.* To guarantee that portions or sections will join up seamlessly, slightly overlap them: When imaging or executing section A, for example, proceed through the opening pitches of section B before stopping to repeat.
  ii. *Create larger structures.* To link sections into larger structures, here's one of many viable strategies: If a piece is made up of 32 sections, learn sections A and B individually, and then execute the chunk A–B one to

three times. Learn C, then D, run C–D one to three times, and, if all's well, execute A–B–C–D once. If anything isn't secure, solve the problems, repeat the troublesome section, and then run A–B–C–D again. Learn the next four sections in a parallel manner, and then run all eight sections one to three times. Follow the same line of attack for the subsequent eight-section area; then, link the two eight-section areas, executing the 16-section span once or more. Practice the second half of the piece similarly, and then join the two halves.

iii. *Balance working on small portions and large spans.* After groups of sections are connected, build the rhythmic continuity needed on stage by executing multisection spans, and make sure to either sit or stand in line with how you'll perform. Then debug trouble spots separately.

iv. *Maintain a consistent tempo.* As you repeat, reduce effort rather than letting the tempo accelerate. You'll step up the pace later, when the piece reaches the *developing material* zone.

v. *Record.* Record yourself playing or singing multisection areas to verify that your execution is on track.

vi. *Set limits, rest, and review.* Work efficiently, but don't try to assimilate too much at once. If you overdo it, everything you take in during a practice session could become jumbled in your mind. Slot in practice breaks (p. 75), and get ample sleep to allow your brain to consolidate what you've learned. Also, keep freshly learned material sturdy by reviewing it regularly, either through imaging, executing, or both.

The four-stage process described here represents a model of how you might begin mastering a piece, but it's not a strict recipe. It's up to you to implement these concepts in agreement with your skill level, learning style, and the repertoire in front of you. For example, musicians with limited sight-reading prowess will need to spend more time vocalizing rhythms and mapping interpretations than the performers who can immediately distinguish rhythmic and expressive nuances. Also consider that the abovementioned procedure for linking sections proceeds sequentially. Sequential modes are highly effective, especially with shorter compositions. However, longer pieces might be easier to absorb by targeting difficulties and learning nonadjoining sections concurrently. That is, you could adopt a more holist slant and stitch a composition together from several directions. Neither the sequential nor the holist mode outperforms the other, but I encourage you to use features of both and to invent your own approaches for working with new material so that your practice strategies become as versatile as possible.

Finally, if, like Tara with her Beethoven, your repertoire includes pieces with entrenched problems, you may want to let those pieces go and not attempt to refurbish them. I've found that, for students to achieve breakthroughs with their practice and performance skills, they're more successful learning fresh music than striving to renovate older compositions. If your practice habits need revamping, set your well-worn pieces aside, at least for a time, and collaborate with your teacher to pick new, accessible titles. Then have a great time mastering them.

Managing Repetition

Practice perfects only the elements in use. Why not consistently practice using the complete tools needed for an arresting performance?

—Abby Whiteside, pianist and teacher

Repetition in practice can either amplify your artistry or, when managed poorly, drain your spirit dry. What's more, there's no escaping the consequence of repetition: habits. When you repeat, you must take care to instill the "complete tools" that Abby Whiteside refers to and not habits like tension or sloppiness, which undermine creativity. This section, therefore, presents four principles of artistic repetition.

Principles of Artistic Repetition
1. Insist on excellence
2. Reject mindless repetition
3. Aim for growth rather than sameness
4. Evaluate continuously

1. Insist on excellence

Whenever you repeat, emphasize the *habits of excellence* introduced in chapter 2. Then excellence will resonate in every phrase that you play or sing. As a reminder, those seven habits are:

  i. Ease
 ii. Expressiveness
iii. Accuracy
 iv. Rhythmic vitality
  v. Beautiful tone
 vi. Focused attention
vii. Positive attitude

If, as you practice, your tone frays, your focus drifts, or you otherwise can't sustain excellence, take a break. Musicians who repeat without excellence marinate in mediocrity.

2. Reject mindless repetition

Naïve practicers might repeat a passage profusely and make error after error. Then, on the eleventh try, when it finally comes out right, they say, "There, I've got it," and move on to something else. But ten dubious repetitions plus a single accurate one don't equal security. Quite the opposite.

Repetition inevitably begets habits. If musicians squander ten garbled recaps while deciphering how to execute a passage, they've ingested chaotic tendencies that don't disappear after the passage is understood. In effect, the confused run-throughs implant mixed-up mental patterns that can be replaced only with tedious work. Added to that, excessive repetition overworks the body and is a prime cause of injury.

Always devise interpretive and technical maps before repeating. Then use the three-times formula proposed earlier: Execute a section of music three times consecutively without slips, learn another section, and progressively join the sections into larger structures (complex passages may warrant five runs). Above all, steer clear of repeated, imprecise run-throughs. If your first shot at a passage isn't trouble free, isolate and solve the problems instead of running the entire passage again.

As you commit to mindful repetitions, be unafraid of errors. Mistakes will happen. Handled intelligently, miscues feed your evolution because they alert you to faults in your mental maps. In fact, as discussed below, errors and problems can be your most valuable teachers. But repeating mistakes is foolish. If you ever catch yourself in a whirl of hazy repetition, stop what you're doing and regroup.

3. Aim for growth rather than sameness

Over the course of your life in music, you're going to do a lot of repeating. There will be standard repertoire that you'll perform for years, and you'll revisit exercises to keep your technical abilities strong. On top of that, new pieces will be streaming down the pipe, and repetition will be the driver of your learning process. Whatever the material, your repetitions should lead somewhere meaningful—to greater ease, higher beauty, and deeper feeling— and not to a dreary sameness where nothing changes.

Think of it this way: The main purpose of repetition is to form easeful habits so that you can be secure and artistic in performance. Smart repetitions engender ease because they reinforce the mental pathways through which you direct your execution. As adept repetitions add up, the pathways become more inbuilt, and you expend less mental energy to attain control.

The keys to growth are:

- Build ease and awareness with each recap.
- Cultivate a reserve of mental and physical capacity.
- Tap your surplus capacity to enhance your expressiveness.

To bring off nourishing repetitions, set specific goals before executing, but also be open to shaping phrases in impromptu ways. For instance, after one pristine statement of a passage, for your second pass, you might fatten your tone and loosen your shoulders; for the third run, you could shore up your previous objectives while you also smooth out your legato and image ahead more vividly. Each run should distill your interpretive and technical maps so that you can readily control and modify your execution. And when, through repetition, you practice being inventive and playful, your concerts will resound with those same spontaneous traits.

4. Evaluate continuously

Evaluation isn't done solely at the end of practicing a passage; it takes place continuously: As you play or sing, you ceaselessly listen to yourself and any coperformers and fine-tune your execution. Students with dormant evaluation skills slog robotically through their pieces: "I guess it's coming along," they say and then grind out another useless recap. But repetition leads to growth only when musicians can pick up how they're doing from moment to moment. If musicians can't assess the quality of their repetitions—for example, if they don't hear themselves accurately—then they can't improve their abilities. If they rashly hack through their material, they develop shoddy habits that take them further and further from the proficiency they crave.

During any repetition, gauge your sound and internal experience against the benchmarks of excellence: Is your expression compelling, your tone full, and your rhythm vibrant? Are you achieving optimal ease? Shrewd evaluation transforms repetition from drudgery into a white-hot fire of musical refinement. You can then mold your music and yourself, and your practice becomes a true creative act.

Solving Problems

When a problem is complex, you become tense, but when you break it down into basic components, you can approach each element without stress.

—Yo-Yo Ma, cellist

No matter how musically advanced you become, you'll encounter passages that defy easy mastery. Some will push your technical limits; others will challenge you artistically. Performers label those passages "problem spots," but in spite of that ominous name, all musicians need such spots. By tackling them, you exit familiar territory and climb to new levels of competence. And when you acquire the means to untangle predicaments creatively, problem solving will be among the most rewarding aspects of your practice, as was the case with Duke Ellington: "My biggest kick in music—playing or writing—is when I have a problem," he said. "Without a problem to solve, how much interest do you take in anything?"[6]

Students often mistakenly believe that mature artists don't run into vexing problems. But what makes professionals like Ma and Ellington stand out is that they're masters at morphing dilemmas into art. The following will help you become a fleet problem-solver, too—first, by looking at ways to think about problems and, second, by chronicling a problem-solving process.

Thinking about Problems

Creative problem solving requires creative thinking. Nevertheless, the style of thinking that's commonly taught in schools may not serve your needs in the practice room when artistic quandaries loom. That is, a subject such as basic math nurtures a convergent thinking that zeroes in on single solutions, but such reasoning works only with linear problems, where one correct answer exists. If you're dealing with a mechanical malfunction, let's say, convergent thinking might fit the bill:

- "Why is that weird sound coming out of the piano?" A pencil fell on the strings.
- "Why won't the guitar play in tune?" The strings are old and should be replaced.

Artistic problems, however, cry out for a more adventurous sort of thinking, one that can engage difficulties from disparate angles and generate many promising solutions. That's where divergent thinking comes in. When you let your thoughts diverge, you perceive problems from compound viewpoints. You leave conventional categories behind and hunt for ideas by posing open-ended questions. "What if I tried it this way?" you wonder, unlike convergent thinkers, who thirst for "the right answers."

Actually, divergent thinking is more about asking questions than finding answers. With clever questioning, solutions to problems reveal themselves. Still, formulating questions can be the stickiest part of problem solving. In the midst of a predicament, the inspired notions that you seek aren't marked with signs; they're hidden, so you can't just ask how to reach them.

To question your way to gold, you have to concoct pointed queries that illuminate subtle distinctions. The more incisively you probe, the more likely it is that you'll score a triumph. Later, if need be, you might brainstorm, but when first-round questions are inexact, they can overwhelm your mind and emotions.

As an example, if a four-note passage isn't sounding clean, then an unwieldy question would be "Why is this so hard?" The answer: "I don't know." The result: frustration. Precise questions infiltrate a problem's outer walls: "What if I focus on the first two notes and sound the initial one four times—then would the transition between the two notes be clear?"

By highlighting two notes instead of four and taking a divergent "What if?" tack, the impenetrable four-note fragment converts into a series of simple two-note ones. Then, the problems are laid bare, and you can close in on solutions. "Making the simple complicated is commonplace," said bassist and composer Charles Mingus; "making the complicated simple, awesomely simple, that's creativity."[7]

Last of all, if divergent thinking forms the cutting edge of problem solving, emotional intelligence is the whetstone that keeps that edge sharp. Thoughts and feelings interact; they can't be totally separated. If you regard a problem with curiosity and as the portal to progress that it is, your positive outlook will ignite your enthusiasm. "A problem?" you'll say. "Great, let me at it."

Musicians who become distressed by dilemmas often dodge practicing, or they repeat furiously. Either way, their negative emotions cancel their creativity. Psychologist John Gottman claims, "Even more than IQ, your emotional awareness and ability to handle feelings will determine your success in all walks of life."[8] When a problem plops down on your path, attend to your emotional response, and uphold an inquisitive, playful attitude. You can fuel that playfulness by arming yourself with an agile problem-solving process.

The Problem-Solving Process

Problem solving has three main parts: (1) recognizing when a problem exists; (2) isolating and defining the problem; (3) applying problem-solving tactics.

Here I'll examine each part. For help
with memorization problems, see p. 82.

1. Recognize a problem

If problem recognition strikes you as an
easy step, think again. "Creativity can be

The Problem-Solving Process
1. Recognize a problem
2. Isolate and define the problem
3. Apply problem-solving tactics

as much a process of finding problems as solving them," wrote creativity consultant Ken Robinson.[9] For example, recall attending a subpar performance,
and ask yourself this: Did the musicians know in advance that their execution was weak or that their phrasing seemed clumsy? Surely not. If they
did, they would have polished things before appearing in public. Problems
abounded as they practiced, but they failed to notice them, so their creativity suffered, and their listeners did, too.

To recognize problems, musicians need keen perceptual skills. Yet perceptions are fallible. Anyone is likely to conclude that no problems exist
when in fact various defects are circling beneath the radar. Worse still, if
musicians believe that their perceptions are impeccable, they may turn away
from noticing faults to avoid upsetting their glorified self-images.

Problem recognition begins with humility, with acceptance of the fact
that you might be missing something. Assuming that flagrant flaws already
set off your alarms, you now need ways to detect less-obvious weaknesses
in your music making, ones that you could overlook if you weren't attuned
to fine details. Start with an open mind and a can-do attitude, and then employ questions such as these to assess for excellence (see *habits of excellence*,
p. 20).

- *Ease:* Are you imaging ahead distinctly and directing your movements
  with a minimum of effort? If something doesn't feel right, stop and
  ferret out the source of discomfort.

- *Expressiveness:* Are you creating alluring musical landscapes? For instance, are your dynamic contrasts voluptuous, or do they seem too
  slight? Listen to a self-recording, and rework any passage that doesn't
  meet your standards.

- *Accuracy:* Do your lines flow, or are there interruptions? What about
  intonation, timing, and articulation—do they flash with precision?

- *Rhythmic vitality:* Do your rhythm and meter transcend accuracy by
  incorporating varied emphasis and supple forward motion?

- *Beautiful tone:* Are you producing sufficient density of sound to project
  beyond the footlights? Are you varying your tone to complement the
  emotional arc of phrases?

When assessing for excellence, if you discern major shortcomings in every measure, then you should acknowledge the bigger issue: The music is too demanding. As the section *choosing new material* (p. 14) explains, to promote artistry, the repertoire you select has to be within your capacity. Students who wrestle with overly demanding music ingrain detrimental habits, among them, performance anxiety, distorted rhythm, and pain-inducing tension. Choose suitable material and a thorough practice plan so that your problem-spotting powers—and all of your aptitudes—mature rapidly.

2. Isolate and define the problem

With a problem pinging on your radar screen, you've crossed out of the sea of ignorance. If you stop there, however, your music and spirit will sink. "I'll practice my part, but I doubt that it will do any good," gripe the musicians who recognize problems but can't bring them into focus. They then lurch repeatedly through blurry phrases, and the problem-causing elements remain concealed, torpedoing each run.

To send a problem packing, you have to stop lavishing attention on a lengthy phrase and instead pinpoint where a glitch is occurring and clarify its nature. Then, when a trouble-making ingredient has nowhere to hide, a solution can be found.

The following is a two-part technique to bring problems into the light. The first part, isolating, entails knowing exactly *where* the problem is; then, defining classifies *what* sort of snag is tripping you up.

a. Isolate the problem in brackets

- When a problem turns up, isolate the troublesome notes in brackets on your score; if any pesky pitches stand out, circle them (example 3.2).

Example 3.2. From Fritz Kreisler, Liebesfreud for violin and piano, measures 1–5.

b. Define the problem

- *Be specific.* Does the trouble involve ease, expressiveness, accuracy, rhythm, or tone? If it's an accuracy problem, register what kind— intonation, diction, flubbed fingering, and so on.

- *Be objective.* Treat discoveries as neutral information. As opposed to thinking "Measure four is awful," calmly make a written or mental memo: "The G# and B in measure four are out of tune."

3. Apply problem-solving tactics

Straightforward problems will often surrender when isolated and defined. For instance, if you hear a misaligned chord during a quartet rehearsal, and you realize that it arose because you miscounted a rest, then victory is yours: Count differently. Many obstacles, though, can be overcome only with meticulous work. Suppose that you've pinned down a shaky spot, but you don't know why you tend to bungle it. Or perhaps you're stymied by a swift passage that won't come together at concert speed. With an arsenal of problem-solving tactics, you can cut through to the causes and attain supremacy.

Below are seven problem-solving tactics that both instrumentalists and singers can employ in solo practice. All of them require a divergent-thinking mindset. With a problem before you, choose a tactic by wondering "What if?" Then draw on two or more tactics to gain multidimensional control of problem areas. When working with these tactics, by and large, keep a metronome handy, begin at an unhurried tempo, and gradually step up the speed across a number of practice sessions.

Each tactic is illustrated with a music example. However, it takes ingenuity to apply these tactics to diverse musical and technical circumstances. So think broadly about the principles demonstrated here, and then consider how you might harness these concepts to prevail over problems in the compositions and exercises that you're learning.

Problem-Solving Tactics
a. Vary rhythms
b. Work from the end
c. Modify the rate of change
d. Focus on components
e. Omit, then reinsert pitches
f. Reconstruct
g. Edit

a. Vary rhythms

Practicing a passage in varied rhythms is a classic tactic to use when you're having trouble executing easily, accurately, or rapidly. Example 3.3 is an excerpt from a typical speed-building etude. Either sing the excerpt or play it on any instrument.

Allegretto

Example 3.3. From Emilio Pujol, Etude no. 1, from *Escuela razonada de la guitarra,* book II, measures 1–3.

To boost your facility with this type of passage, you could execute rhythmic variations that form progressively larger note groups (examples 3.4–3.8). After completing the variations, you'd return to the original passage. Consciously image ahead when using this or any tactic: Hear and feel the upcoming note groups before you execute them.

Step 1a

Step 1b

Example 3.4. Two-note groups.

Step 2a

Step 2b

Example 3.5. Three-note groups.

Step 3a

Step 3b

Example 3.6. Four-note groups.

Step 4

Example 3.7. Five-note groups.

Step 5

Example 3.8. Whole-measure groups.

When practicing in varied rhythms, or anytime that you're honing a passage, it's often worthwhile to halt the forward motion and deliberately image note groups prior to executing them. Examples 3.9–3.10 will help you increase fluency with the above five-note and whole-measure groups.

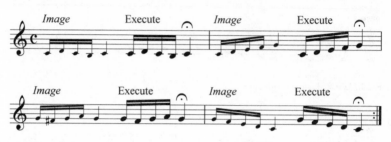

Example 3.9.

After repeating example 3.9, play or sing Step 4 again, and consciously image one note group ahead of the one that you're executing. Then, carry on with example 3.10.

Example 3.10.

When you're comfortable with example 3.10, revisit Step 5, and then execute the original passage (example 3.3). Experiment with brisk tempos, and strive to image one measure ahead.

b. Work from the end

This tactic can help make speedy or complex music feel effortless. In example 3.11, the thirty-second notes in the bracketed passage need special attention if they're to be as easy to bring off as the material that surrounds them.

Andante cantabile

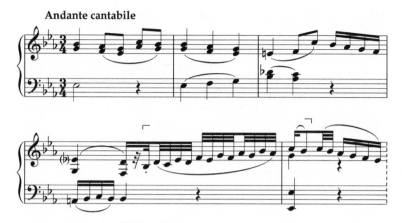

Example 3.11. From W. A. Mozart, Sonata K. 333 for piano, second movement, measures 1–5.

In the following steps, the bracketed passage is tackled in stages, starting with its concluding note group (example 3.12). Whenever you use this tactic, image before playing, and then execute each step two or three times.

Step 1

Example 3.12.

Next, tack on the preceding note group (example 3.13).

Step 2

Example 3.13.

Third, go over the opening note group (example 3.14).

Step 3

Example 3.14.

Fourth, image and then execute the entire passage (example 3.15).

Example 3.15.

Finally, play from the beginning of the measure (example 3.16).

Example 3.16.

If you encounter problems in the final step, focus on the note group that causes you to stumble, and maybe repeat it using varied rhythms. As a rule, when one tactic doesn't yield sufficient mastery, incorporate other tactics.

c. Modify the rate of change

To play example 3.17 on a keyboard, you have to cross your left hand back and forth over your right at a quick pace.

Example 3.17. From J. S. Bach, Partita no. 1, BWV 825 for harpsichord, measures 45–47.

Modifying the rate that pitches and harmonies change gives you the physical and mental space necessary to prepare your execution without obliging you to slow the tempo excessively. First, you might increase the time between each left-hand shift (example 3.18).

Example 3.18.

Second, you could reduce the time between the shifts by one beat (example 3.19).

Example 3.19.

Third, you might execute the shifts in pairs and add time in between (example 3.20).

Example 3.20.

Fourth, you could pair the shifts in the reverse order of Step 3 (example 3.21).

Example 3.21.

To finish, you'd execute as originally written, while conceiving of the left-hand shifts in pairs and imaging one measure beyond the one that you're playing (example 3.22).

Final step

Example 3.22.

d. Focus on components

Many difficulties can't be resolved unless you take them apart and focus on their components. For instance, depending on the situation, a musician might vocalize or clap rhythms, speak text, buzz on a mouthpiece, play hands alone, or separately execute the voices from a multivoice piece.

In example 3.23, an intonation problem is marked in brackets.

Example 3.23. From Fritz Kreisler, Liebesfreud for violin and piano, measures 1–5.

Examples 3.24–3.26 depict the way a violinist might surmount this hurdle by focusing on individual voices from the problematic measure. In each step, the musician would need to employ fingerings and bowings that correspond with the original passage. Notice that the rate of change is modified by repeating pitches; rhythmic variation is also exploited.

Step 1

Example 3.24.

Step 2

Example 3.25.

Step 3

Example 3.26.

Upon finishing the third step, the violinist would put the extracted measure back in context (example 3.27).

Final step

Example 3.27.

e. Omit, then reinsert pitches

Example 3.28 is the sort of passage where running sixteenth notes combine with a fast tempo to make execution tricky. Play the passage on a keyboard or guitar, or just vocalize or play the melody.

Example 3.28. From Mauro Giuliani, Sonatina, op. 71, no. 3 for guitar, fourth movement, measures 100–103.

By strategically omitting and then reinserting certain pitches you can reassemble the passage, mastering it in the process (be sure to use consistent fingerings). One maneuver would be to omit the pick-up notes and some arpeggio tones (example 3.29).

Step 1

Example 3.29.

Then, the omitted pitches could be reinserted, but without some of the notes played previously (example 3.30).

Example 3.30.

Third, you'd reinsert more pitches (example 3.31).

Example 3.31.

When you're confident executing Step 3, play or sing the intact excerpt (example 3.28).

f. Reconstruct

Many passages that seem intimidating become simple when you reconstruct them from their basic elements. Consider, for instance, example 3.32, which comes from Handel's *Messiah*. In the original, the passage is sung by the basses on a single word: rage, as in "Why do the nations rage?" Such a passage would present both singers and instrumentalists with similar challenges—to execute easily, smoothly, and in tune.

Example 3.32. From G. F. Handel, Messiah, Air 2.17B, measures 50–52.

Examples 3.33–3.37 show how voice teacher W. Stephen Smith, in his book *The Naked Voice*, reconstructs this passage.[10] When singers use the following method, Smith advises them to vocalize on an open vowel, such as *eh*, before singing the pitches and text combined. Execute the steps in any octave two or three times, either with your voice or on an instrument.

Step 1

Example 3.33.

Step 2

Example 3.34.

Step 3

Example 3.35.

Step 4

Example 3.36.

Final step

Example 3.37.

Before performing the third and fourth steps, you may want to insert preparatory stages where you distinctly image each note group before executing it
(examples 3.38–3.39).

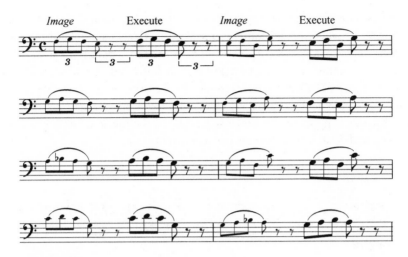

Example 3.38.

As soon as you complete example 3.38, execute Step 3, and consciously image one note group ahead. After that, continue with example 3.39.

Example 3.39.

When example 3.39 feels secure, return to Step 4 and image ahead in undivided note groups. Then, execute the final step while imaging two beats ahead.

g. Edit

Editorial revision is the secret weapon that performers use in exceptional cases to make awkward passages sound fluid. Editing is most apropos when a composer or an arranger has written something impractical, as in the next example, or when a page contains a misprint. It's also a standard practice among accompanists who are pressed for time to prepare their parts—for instance, a pianist or guitarist might facilitate left-hand execution in a song accompaniment by leaving out some doubled chord tones. The goal of editing is to implement the smallest change that will tailor a passage to your needs while supporting the expressive intent of the music. In example 3.40, editing makes an unmanageable passage trouble free.

Example 3.40. From Richard Rodney Bennett, Impromptu no. 2 for guitar, measures 32–35.

These seven tactics have abundant uses; however, the examples provide only a glimpse into the near-infinite ways that you can approach problem solving. When you come upon a thorny passage, isolate and define it, and then playfully explore its inner qualities—turn it this way and that using assorted tactics. When you're stumped, ask a teacher or colleague for help. But whatever musical difficulties you face, bear in mind that confronting them is what takes you beyond your current limitations and toward your genuine potential.

Practicing Deeply, III

In this chapter:

- Maturing pieces to concert level
- Taking breaks
- Memorization concepts
- Memorization strategies

Ripening Your Repertoire

People so often do not know what they are striving for in their practice. One should hunger after the whole concept, the whole mood, what the music stands for.

—William Pleeth, cellist

This chapter mainly examines strategies for practicing pieces in the *developing* and *performance material* zones (p. 6). To recap how those zones function, a new piece graduates to *developing* status when you can securely proceed all the way through it at a preliminary tempo. When the music becomes concert ready, it ascends to the *performance material* zone.

With developing pieces, your main practice tasks are to refine your interpretive ideas, increase tempo, and, when applicable, memorize. In this section you'll read about methods to upgrade interpretation and boost tempo. Memorization is sorted out in the sections ahead. With performance pieces, you practice performing—a subject covered in part II of this book—and, as discussed in the coming pages, you amplify your creativity by means of renewal and innovation.

> **Ripen Your Repertoire**
>
> 1. Refine interpretation
> 2. Increase tempo
> 3. Renew and innovate

1. Refine interpretation

When you began working on a new piece, you established an interpretive blueprint and then did your utmost to execute expressively. Now, as the music progresses through the *developing material* zone, it's time to lift your interpretation to concert rank. Here are six ways to do so:

a. *Record yourself.* Self-recording provides an express route to excellence. To assess your interpretation of a developing piece, record yourself playing or singing it at a comfortable tempo; then listen to the recording with an analytical ear.

- Is each passage and phrase doing its part to dramatize the musical landscape?

- Does your performance embody the *essentials of artistic interpretation* (p. 24)?

b. *Listen to professional recordings and performances.* Take in recordings and performances not to copy them but to hear disparate interpretations and to spur your imagination. If you listened to recordings back when getting an overview of a piece, check out those tracks again and use your more seasoned ear to pick up further details.

c. *Study the score.* When learning an ensemble part, delve into the full score: Mentally hear the music, sing other musicians' lines, observe the interplay between the parts, and explore the compositional terrain. If you're polishing a solo piece, comb the score to glean substance that you may have overlooked before. For instance, review the articulation, dynamic, and expression markings; scrutinize the melodic and harmonic design. With a vocal piece, reflect on how the composer treats particular words to enhance imagery and convey feelings. Whatever the composition, look for ways to generate drama.

d. *Deepen emotional connections.* Ask the following sorts of questions, and do additional research, to deepen your emotional connections to a piece:

- What images, feelings, or storylines does the music evoke?

- What do you suppose that listeners might feel as you perform?

- Can you articulate, in a personal way, what William Pleeth calls "the whole concept, the whole mood, what the music stands for"?

e. *Experiment.* To break out of your customary interpretive style, playfully experiment with turning phrases in atypical ways: Exaggerate the dynamics, toy with the timing, and otherwise push the boundaries of convention. Collect a variety of ideas, and then distill them into a co-hesive interpretation.

f. *Schedule coaching sessions.* Veteran musicians are gold mines of artistic insight. You might be learning a piece for the first time, but you can access performers and teachers who have studied a composition for years. When a piece enters the *developing material* zone, do a moderate-tempo run-through for your teacher (with your recorder switched on, of course). You might also perform for senior colleagues or arrange coaching sessions with artist-educators outside of your school.

2. Increase tempo

To escalate the tempo of newly learned material, you first have to reduce the effort required to play or sing it at your initial tempo, so maintain a deliberate pace until you achieve profound ease. Then employ these maneuvers to heighten velocity without sacrificing control:

a. *Isolate and solve problems.* Shrewd problem-solving skills are pivotal to rapid execution. Pinpoint passages that challenge you at faster tempos, and then apply problem-solving tactics (p. 58) to surmount difficulties.

b. *Step up by degrees.* Verify your intended final tempo, and note the fastest metronome setting at which you can execute the thorniest parts of a piece. Practice problem spots daily, using assorted tactics, and step up your tempo by degrees rather than abruptly hiking it (to track upticks in your fluency, pencil metronome settings and dates in your music). For example, to speed up a tough passage, you could do a couple of runs at a moderate tempo with the metronome ticking. For two more recaps, you'd steadily increase the pulse; for a fifth run, you might test your tempo limit. The next day you'd practice the passage again. You might keep to the same tempo pattern, or you could begin and end your five runs at a slightly faster pace. To foster surplus security, work toward speeds somewhat swifter than your target tempo.

c. *Image ahead in larger chunks.* If you conceived of smallish note groups in the early rounds of learning, you must now form larger mental chunks that fit a quicker tempo. For instance, musicians executing running sixteenth notes in common time might have felt ahead in one-beat units to start with, but to ripple along smoothly, they'll need to sense chunks of two or more beats. (Mental imaging is explained on page 34.)

d. *Simplify your technical choreography.* Although you began the learning process with technical choices that you believed would work at your final tempo, you may realize that adaptations are necessary to reach your ultimate speed. Be flexible. When appropriate, revise fingerings, bowings, breaths, and so on.

e. *Invent exercises.* When a technique trips you up at higher velocities, concoct relevant exercises. If a violinist gets tangled on a bowing, let's say, she should integrate allied bowing drills into her daily technique work.

f. *Balance working on small portions and large spans.* To instill the rhythmic continuity required on stage, do trial runs of multisection spans of a piece. Then isolate trouble spots, and, after the problems are solved, merge extracted segments back into the greater context. Occasionally record and evaluate a complete run-through.

g. *Manage repetition.* Take care to regulate repetition so that you work efficiently and you don't repeat any material excessively (p. 51). You might revisit a passage several times in one day—doing some repetitions mentally—but never hammer away relentlessly. Most of all, be patient, and, with daunting excerpts, ask a teacher or colleague for help.

3. Renew and innovate

Once a composition earns a place in your *performance material* zone, you and the music may spend substantial time together. Some titles, in fact, will inhabit your repertoire for years. How do you keep music up to performance level and yet dodge staleness? You inspire renewal and innovation using strategies such as the following:

a. *Rekindle affection for your repertoire.* The pieces in your repertoire are like friends with whom you preserve lasting relationships. To rekindle affection for a long-standing piece, consider these questions:

- What originally drew you to the music?
- What does it offer that no other music can?
- Why do listeners enjoy hearing it?

Then, whenever you practice or perform a composition, celebrate its unique message. Feel the excitement of listening to the music for the first time.

b. *Review in detail.* Meticulous review enhances control and aids in detecting new angles for interpretation. In addition to focusing on tricky passages, periodically recondition an entire piece by dropping it into the *new material* zone and then reripening it: Slow the tempo, work in sections, and go over component elements to make the music more vibrant than ever.

c. *Make meaning.* Every worthy composition is suffused with veins of meaning for you to mine. Even in pieces that you've known for years, there will be new things to discover and express. As you practice, be playful; question your interpretive patterns, and try out new ones. Continually rouse fresh thoughts and emotions.

d. *Implement a practice rotation.* Cycle your well-learned pieces through your practice schedule to give some titles a rest now and then. Also, be sure that your *performance material* zone includes plenty of undemanding compositions—assemble a cache of pieces that you can perform without needing to practice at length.

e. *Schedule performances.* Nothing sparks innovation better than an opportunity to share music with an audience. Study part II of this book, and then, when you're ready, set up appearances in an array of venues. With each concert, create something novel. Pianist Vladimir Horowitz said, "A work should never be played the same way. I never do. I may play the same program from one recital to the next, but I will play it differently. And because it is always different, it is always new."[1]

Taking Breaks

I never solved a major mechanical or interpretive problem at the keyboard, only away from it.

—Jorge Bolet, pianist

Breaks are as vital to musicians as they are to athletes. And breathers don't merely recharge your energies and help prevent injuries. As Jorge Bolet conveys, well-timed practice breaks can fortify your problem-solving powers.

In general, rest about 10 minutes of each hour that you spend in the practice room. Preferably, play or sing no more than 25–30 minutes in solo practice before pausing for a 5-minute respite; sometimes you might want to take breaks of 2–3 minutes every 15 minutes. At large-group rehearsals, when working on straightforward material, your ensemble might rest for 10 minutes after practicing for 50, although high-intensity music making calls for more frequent pauses.

Three Types of Breaks
1. Active
2. Diverting
3. Restorative

No less important than how you time your breaks are the activities that you do during your breathers. So, for the remainder of this section, I describe three types of breaks and offer suggestions for cooling down at the close of practice sessions.

1. Active breaks

On an active break, you rest your playing or singing muscles but otherwise stay engaged with your music. For example, a brass player practicing alone might set her instrument down for a few minutes and then vocalize rhythms from a piece that she's learning. Similarly, a singer or pianist memorizing a solo might move dancelike around the practice room as he mentally reviews a page of music. Such interludes fit best in the earlier part of practice sessions, when you're freshest, but take one whenever you need to clarify your musical intentions. Some musicians mix many brief, active breaks into each hour of practice.

2. Diverting breaks

Diverting breaks take you out of the practice room and get your mind off what you're doing. Examples include going for a walk or having a snack. These timeouts are apt when you're working for an extended period and can serve as rewards after you finish practice tasks. Be mindful, though, that your breathers aren't overlong, and ensure that your music-making muscles get a rest: Instrumentalists should avoid hand-intensive tasks such as typing or text messaging; singers should sip water and regulate speech. Also, adopt postures that contrast with those that you use in practice. If you've been sitting, stand or take a stroll; to offset standing, lounge in a chair. Opt for quiet environments, too, to give your ears relief (see *hearing conservation*, p. 277).

3. Restorative breaks

During a restorative break, you either rest or do gentle movements. These respites are ideal for centering the mind, revitalizing the body, and counteracting the effects of asymmetrical playing positions. For instance, a violinist on a restorative break might circle his arms (figure 4.1); a singer who has been rehearsing a taxing role could choose to lie on the floor, close her eyes, and breathe (figure 4.5). Six restorative poses and movements are depicted here—a musician taking a break might do one, two, or all of them.

Restorative Poses and Movements
a. Arm circles
b. Arms overhead
c. Arms behind back
d. Forward bend
e. Constructive rest
f. Total rest

a. Arm circles (figure 4.1)

   i. Stand with your feet hip-width apart.

   ii. Gently contract your abdominal and gluteus muscles to lengthen your lower back (p. 256).

Figure 4.1. Arm circles.

    iii. Inhale through your nose as you slowly raise one arm overhead; exhale through your mouth as the arm descends.

    iv. Spread your fingers as your arm rises; release them as your arm lowers.

    v. Complete three circles; then reverse the direction, and do three more. Repeat with the other arm.

b. Arms overhead (figure 4.2)

    i. Stand with your feet hip-width or wider apart, and gently contract your abdominal and gluteus muscles.

    ii. Interlace your fingers in front of you, and then exhale as you extend your arms overhead.

    iii. Without straining, keep lengthening your arms for 10–20 seconds. Move your arms back toward your ears, breathe normally through your nose, and release tension in your neck and face.

    iv. Lower your arms, swing them loosely, and then repeat, switching the interlacing of your fingers (if your left thumb was initially on top of the right, move all of the fingers so that, when you repeat the movement, your right thumb is atop the left).

Figure 4.2. Arms overhead.

Figure 4.3. Arms behind back.

c. Arms behind back (figure 4.3)

   i. Stand with your feet hip-width apart. Contract your abdominal and gluteus muscles, and tilt your head somewhat downward.

  ii. Clasp your hands behind your lower back, with wrists straight and palms touching. Exhale as you raise your arms.

 iii. Maintain straight wrists and the downward tilt of your head; breathe normally through your nose; release the muscles in your chest.

 iv. Without forcing, continue in the pose for 10–20 seconds. Then lower your arms, swing them loosely, and repeat, switching the interlacing of your fingers.

d. Forward bend (figure 4.4)

   i. Stand with your feet about hip-width apart, and bend your knees a bit.

  ii. Exhale as you hinge forward at the hips. Let your head and arms dangle; shift your weight toward the balls of your feet. Breathe normally.

 iii. Without bouncing or straining, release your hamstring muscles. If your hamstrings feel tight, bend your knees further; for an added stretch,

Figure 4.4. Forward bend with knees bent.

move your knees toward a straighter alignment, but don't push your limits. You should experience a pleasant stretch and no stabbing pain. If you feel persistent pain when doing this or any other restorative technique, stop and seek guidance.

iv. Remain in the pose for 20–30 seconds. To return to a standing position, exhale as you unhinge at the hips and unroll your spine. Bring your head up last. Repeat.

e. Constructive rest (figure 4.5)

Known in the Alexander technique tradition as "constructive rest," this pose releases muscle tension, especially in the neck, shoulders, and back.

i. Lie on the floor with your head elevated on one or more books such that your neck is neither tilted back nor bent forward.

ii. Place your feet flat on the floor, wider than your hips, with your knees aiming skyward and your toes pointing away from your head. Rest your hands, palms down, on your abdomen or lower ribs.

iii. Close your eyes, let go of tension, and breathe naturally. Feel your body sink into the earth.

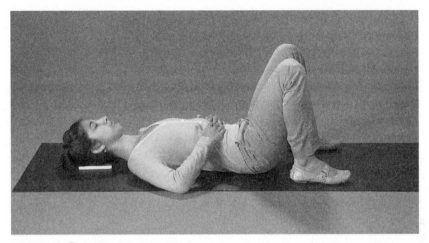

Figure 4.5. Constructive rest.

   iv. Stay in this position for several minutes to 10 minutes. Come out of the pose by rolling to one side.

f. Total rest (figure 4.6)

   i. Lie on the floor with your head either resting on the floor or somewhat elevated on a book or a cushion.

   ii. Position your feet wider than your hips, and flop your feet outward. Lay your hands palms up at your sides.

   iii. Close your eyes, release tension, and breathe naturally. Melt into the floor.

   iv. Continue for 5–10 minutes, and then come out of the pose slowly, deepening your breath and rolling to one side.

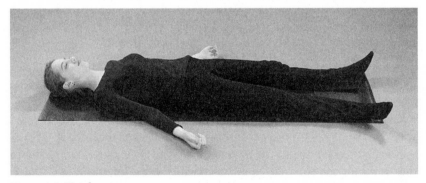

Figure 4.6. Total rest.

These examples supply a basis for you to integrate restorative techniques into your practice, but countless other moves are possible as well. In addition, certain movements are better suited to some musicians than others due to differences in performers' health histories and musical activities. To learn movements matched to your needs, consult a physical therapist or an athletic trainer. You can also find supplemental information and images via links at *musiciansway.com*.

Finally, to top off a practice session, allot 5–10 minutes to cool down. Just as athletes walk and stretch after jogging to hasten recovery and defend against muscle stiffness, musicians can benefit from gentle postpractice playing or vocalizing along with some mild stretching. You might cool down with easygoing scales, sighs, or lip trills; you could follow these with some restorative movements. After that, set the goals for your next practice session, and curb hand or vocal use, thereby allowing your body to recuperate. Much like you use warm-ups to prepare for music making, enlist cool-downs to transition back to worldly life.

Memorization Concepts

I'm very mistrustful of tactile memory. I think it's the first thing that goes.

—André Watts, pianist

- A vocalist performs a song that she has known for years but is shocked when she forgets some of the words.
- A piano student plays a sonata flawlessly in practice but fumbles in recital. He has no clue why his memory blinked.
- A clarinetist will perform a concerto in a month, yet she has little experience playing without music in front of her. She worries that her memory will fail but doesn't know how to prevent memory slips.

Performing from memory can be a beautiful thing. When you memorize deeply, you gain maximal freedom on stage and enjoy unfettered communion with listeners. Memorizing is also an exacting business. Performers who are unaware of comprehensive memorization techniques risk facing dilemmas like the three musicians above. By working with the ideas here, however, you can take strides toward becoming an accomplished memorizer.

The first concept to grasp is that memorization styles differ—an approach that works for one musician could be of limited use to another. For instance, performers who are conversant with music theory can employ harmonic analysis to bolster their memory of pieces, whereas students without knowledge of theory cannot do so. Therefore, you're going to have to experiment with the upcoming recommendations until you discover your own memorization preferences. Keep in mind, too, that your methods will evolve over time as your musical proficiency grows.

To begin, this section presents a four-stage model of the memorization process. The next section offers memorization strategies.

The Four Stages of Memorization

Memorization basically entails storage and recall. Nevertheless, it's useful to think of the storage process as having three stages—perception, ingraining, and maintenance—while recall serves as the culminating stage of your memorization plan. That is, when you're confronted with a new piece to memorize, you first perceive its musical and technical content; second, you draw on procedures to ingrain it in your mind; third, to avert forgetting, you review. When each phase of storage is thorough, recall can be glitch free. Here's a summary of how the stages function.

Stages of Memorization
1. Perception
2. Ingraining
3. Maintenance
4. Recall

1. Perception

Expert memorizers don't just memorize better than novices; they do so differently. And that distinction doesn't pertain to musicians alone. When researchers compared the memory skills of expert versus novice chess players, they found that, when chess pieces were arranged on a board as they might be in a match, the experts displayed vastly superior memories of where the pieces were located. When pieces were positioned randomly, though, the experts and novices showed comparable recall.[2]

Such a finding indicates that, for one, accomplished memorizers perceive information in meaningful ways that facilitate remembering. It also confirms that memory skills are task specific and that capable memorizers have acquired particular knacks.

High-level musicians exhibit perceptual agility similar to that of chess masters. When violinist and researcher Susan Hallam compared the practice habits of professional performers with those of students, she saw that the professionals promptly took in the whole picture of a composition's structure. The students tended to ignore issues of musical structure and had less awareness of their practice strategies. Overall, the professionals formed richer conceptions of their material, and their perceptual abilities enabled them to learn and memorize more effectively.[3]

Whatever your level of musical development, you already use perceptual tricks to aid memory in daily life. For instance, if you want to memorize a 10-digit phone number, you'll probably perceive it in multinumber chunks as opposed to thinking of it as a series of single digits. Compare 1, 8, 5, 3, 4, 2, 7, 9, 6, 0 with 185–342–7960. Likewise, a sequence of unrelated words is harder to memorize than a sentence. When you plan to recall words, you conceive of them in groups that correspond to thoughts or images. Contrast these:

- fence the a jumps cat over
- A cat jumps over the fence.

All told, for you to memorize music like a pro, your perceptions of a piece have to resonate with meaning.

2. Ingraining

Ingraining is the most procedural part of memorization. Its object is to implant a composition vividly and lastingly in your mind, and both of those qualities are supported when you adopt a versatile approach that brings various types of memory into play.

For example, an adept memorizer won't merely create a sonic template of a piece using aural memory but will also exploit conceptual memory to internalize a composition's design. Tactile and movement sensations will be lodged, too, and visual and spatial information will get taken into account— for instance, a musician might register the look of a passage on a page or log the distance of an interval on a keyboard. In total, the brain will store such an opulent representation of the music and its execution that the performer not only recalls the music with assurance but can also vary every performance.

Musicians who ingrain in unthinking ways sow an automated kind of learning that withers under pressure. One example is the musician who repeats a piece mindlessly in practice and then can't hold things together on stage. Another is the student who, in preparing for a lesson, runs through a composition numerous times and believes it to be memorized, only to have it fall apart in front of the teacher.

Memorized pieces crumble for such musicians because mindless learning depends on an unconscious recall that doesn't work except under pristine conditions. When musicians who memorize mindlessly feel unsettled, they can't get into the state needed for their fragile recall to succeed. As they perform, they might try to fill in their memory rifts by thinking about imminent phrases, but there won't be any mental guideposts for them to latch onto because none were ingrained. Interpretation, fingering, text, and so on were stored unconsciously, so the conscious mind can't retrieve them. It's not surprising that their memories aren't trustworthy or that they're jittery in concerts.

For you to perform securely from memory, your ingraining processes have to instill potent records that you can recall no matter how you feel.

3. Maintenance

After you ingrain music in your memory, if you leave it there unattended, it's unlikely to stay intact. When the brain cells that you enlist to memorize are neglected, they take off for more pressing tasks, and that leaves your stored material riddled with holes. You undoubtedly know the feeling: You memorize a piece, set it aside, and, when you come back to it months later, countless ingredients have slipped away.

Memorized music requires skillful maintenance. But casually running through a memorized piece won't preserve a mental map; actually, it's more of a highway to memory disintegration. To appreciate why, consider that, when you ingrain a composition, you soak up a fertile assortment of details. You can then recall the music fluently, without losing any fine points. If you don't refresh those fine points, and casual run-throughs don't, then you're in for two kinds of trouble.

First, to manipulate the music artistically, you need an awareness of the details. Without renewing a piece's interpretive and technical particulars, you won't be able to modify those features spontaneously, and your performances will become dull. Second, when crucial elements fade, your mental map will decay into a mindless format known among instrumentalists as muscle memory, tactile memory, or finger memory; and performers agree that there's no memory more tenuous: "I think probably the least reliable, in terms of public performance, is finger memory," says pianist Leon Fleischer, "because it's the finger that deserts one first."[4]

Such memory decay, however, isn't exclusive to instrumentalists. Think of the vocalist mentioned earlier who forgot the words to a long-memorized song. What was the cause of her bungled recall? Poor memory maintenance. She took her memory for granted and didn't uphold her mental storage of the text, so the words drifted into an unconscious backwater. For you to avoid such pitfalls, your maintenance methods must keep the details strong.

4. Recall

Perception, ingraining, and maintenance make up the storage side of the memorization process, but the purpose of storage is failsafe recall. And you can be confident that your recall is as failsafe as possible when it's lucid, multidimensional, and flexible.

Lucid recall allows you to image ahead easily (see *mental imaging,* p. 34). In the practice room, you can start from anywhere in a piece. When performing, you expend little effort to conjure up the music from your mind—even a stressful situation can't blur your mental record.

With multidimensional recall, interlocking components unite to form a robust awareness. Musical structure and meaning, technique, and interpretation—they're all incorporated. Such recall also equips you to execute constituent elements out of context. For instance, pianists with multidimensional recall can play hands separately; vocalists are able to recite text without singing.

Flexible recall permits you to change tempo, articulation, tone, or any other interpretive facet at will. When you recall a piece flexibly, you recreate it. The music is born afresh, and you infuse it with impromptu ideas.

On the opposite end of the recall spectrum lurks the musician's archnemesis: mindless, muscle memory. Unlike failsafe recall, the mindless type is hazy, narrowly conceived, and inflexible. Musicians who put their faith in mindless recall find that things shatter with minimal interference. Even if they can evade breakdown, they perform on the verge of collapse.

In sum, if you intend to develop failsafe recall, you have to shun mindless learning schemes and instead build up conscious memorization strategies.

Memorization Strategies

Memory is the most meaningful measure of attention.
—Ellen Langer, psychologist and author

The following strategies are organized under the four stages of memorization just described: perception, ingraining, maintenance, and recall. In many ways, these strategies parallel the recommendations from chapter 3 for learning new material. They combine mental imagining with actual playing or singing, plus they advocate forming interpretive and technical awareness, working in sections, and managing repetition. They're also fairly detailed, in keeping with the exacting nature of memorized performance.

Before getting under way, there's a vital question to address: At what point on the route to mastering a new piece should deliberate memorization begin? Given the diversity of memorization styles, there's no one answer. Some musicians memorize early on; others hold off until a piece graduates from *new* to *developing* status (that is, until they can execute an entire composition at a preliminary tempo). Then there are those who wait until a piece is mature. If you test memorizing at various phases of learning, you'll discover what works for you.

As a general rule, though, defer memorizing until your interpretive and technical maps are in place. If you memorize when you're fuzzy about musical structure, diction, or fingering, you could ingrain errors and bland expression. Still, I suspect that it's best for many students to memorize relatively soon in the course of ripening a piece—perhaps on the cusp between the *new* and *developing material* zones—so that habits of memorized execution become established. Otherwise, an extended period of working from score could habituate a musician to reading. Then, depending on the person, memorized performance might feel foreign, and an arduous memorization process would be needed to reprogram inbuilt habits.

Regardless of when you prefer to memorize, before starting on a new piece, be sure that you know whether you'll memorize it or not. In that way, you register the intention to memorize from the outset, and your memory work can commence as promptly as you wish. For now, to try out these strategies, prepare a new, elementary composition to the *developing* level. Then apply the perception strategies to your selection, and similarly proceed through the subsequent stages. Take your time at first. Later, using a different piece, quicken your memorization pace.

Perception Strategies

Your perceptions should spawn a rich, multilayered notion of a piece. Then, ingraining and maintenance are streamlined, and recall becomes a cinch. Launch your memorization process by studying the score and reflecting on these topics:

> **Perception Strategies**
>
> 1. Reexamine the musical structure
> 2. Review your interpretive map
> 3. Go over your technical map

1. Reexamine the musical structure

a. What is the overall form? For instance, a Classical or Romantic sonata will typically have three main sections; a folksong might consist of several verses with a chorus after each one. When you know the form before you ingrain, then, as you work, you'll sense where you are in the piece, like a jogger who knows her position on an oval track.

b. Where do phrases begin and end? If phrase breaks aren't obvious to you, mark them on the page.

c. Is there repetition of phrases? Do you detect rhythmic, harmonic, or melodic patterns?

d. What key or keys does the music venture through?

2. Review your interpretive map

   a. What emotions does the piece suggest? If it's a vocal work, what's the substance of the text? The more profound your emotional connection, the more enduring your memory is likely to be.

   b. How will you convey the musical architecture and the emotional energy? Review where phrases climax and repose, and pencil in guides such as dynamic and articulation signs.

3. Go over your technical map

   a. Is your execution precise? Confirm that fingerings, bowings, diction, and so on are clear and that problems are solved.

   b. When you play or sing from score, can you confidently image ahead (p. 34)? If you feel on edge, then the material is too difficult, the tempo too fast, or further groundwork is needed.

Ingraining Strategies

Ingraining is the step-by-step means whereby you lay down tracks in your memory. For your memory tracks to be durable, however, they must be forged with heartfelt meaning. Then, sizeable areas of your brain become involved, and the memory gets a firm foothold. Conversely, to ingrain mechanical notes would be akin to memorizing a poem by the sounds of the words without knowing what those words mean. Starved of significance, such rote memorization splinters on stage. But durability isn't the only issue; efficiency of learning is critical as well. Ingraining is swiftest when tackled in an ordered manner.

> **Ingraining Strategies**
> 1. Start with a plan
> 2. Image, then execute
> 3. Use multiple memory types

1. Start with a plan

   a. Schedule memorization sessions in advance so that you enter the practice room primed to memorize. Arrange frequent, concise sessions, and allocate how much material you'll assimilate in one sitting. You might ingrain the opening sections of a piece first, or you could begin elsewhere. For example, in the case of a three-verse song, a singer might initially memorize the concluding verse.

   b. Identify digestible segments. Here, a "segment" refers to a cohesive portion of music that you'll ingrain as a unit. Contingent on the intricacy of a piece, a segment could be as small as a measure or as big as a phrase or two.

c. Balance work and rest. Work intently, take breaks, and get sufficient overnight sleep. "Sleep is important for making memories stable and strong," counsels memory researcher Jeffrey Ellenbogen.[5]

d. Avoid trying to take in too much at once. Your brain can store only a finite amount at a time. If you exceed your threshold, everything you memorize in a session could become scrambled. To fend off memory overload, set viable goals, and cease ingraining before you grow fatigued.

2. Image, then execute

a. At an easygoing tempo, without looking at the music, accurately image a segment one to three times, and then play or sing one to three times. If anything isn't clear on your first attempt at imaging, refer to the score, and image the segment once or twice while reading. Then, image and execute without the music.

- Instrumentalists: As you image, vocalize note names, counting syllables, or tonguings, and mime playing motions in miniature. Do your best to sing melodies exactly in tune.

- Singers: When first learning a song, you sort through the elements of text and melody separately. To ingrain, however, you're probably best off absorbing them as one: "Memorizing words and melody together appears to be a more effective approach than memorizing them separately," writes singer and researcher Jane Ginsborg.[6] So, as you image, hum or silently mouth words as you internally hear the collective text, melody, and accompaniment. Be mindful to use your voice gently to avert overuse. For staged productions, also act out theatrical aspects in miniature. Even for nonstaged pieces, opera singer and voice teacher Marion Pratnicki advises vocalists to incorporate expressive gestures into the ingraining process.[7]

b. Link segments. First, as you ingrain single segments, overlap them a bit so that they join up smoothly: When imaging or executing segment A, proceed through the first few notes of segment B before stopping to repeat. Then, to merge the segments into larger structures, here's one of many options:

After ingraining segments A and B individually, execute A–B once. Next, ingrain segments C and D; run C–D once; and then execute A–B–C–D one to three times. If clarity is lacking, reingrain the stubborn segment, and repeat A–B–C–D. Learn the next four segments in a parallel manner, and then run all eight. Follow the same line of attack for the subsequent eight-segment area, and then execute the 16-segment span once or more. Continue assembling eight- or 16-segment spans until the complete piece is memorized. After that, review by imaging and executing both small and large portions. If memory gaps arise, though, reingrain segments in isolation.

c. Maintain a steady tempo as you repeat. Later, when extended spans become secure, step up the tempo, as appropriate.

d. Emphasize *habits of excellence* (p. 20). Make each repetition easier and more expressive than the last. Also ensure that your mental focus is sharp whenever you memorize.

3. Use multiple memory types

a. As you ingrain, engage your mind, emotions, and senses to create a multidimensional representation of the music.

- Use aural memory to construct an expansive sonic template. Whether you're imaging or executing, always hear ahead, preparing the next phrase in your mind. Perceive both your part and any accompaniment.

- Marshal conceptual memory to correlate each segment with its place in the compositional framework.

- Awaken tactile and movement senses to direct your technical execution—relish the feel of each impending passage.

- Register any visual or spatial information that draws your interest. To grab hold of a slippery passage, for instance, some musicians find that it helps to summon up how the passage looks on the score.

- Savor the emotional essence of phrases such that each layer you ingrain vibrates with meaning.

b. Highlight components. To support diverse memory types, explore components of the music and its execution.

- To underscore aural memory, when imaging, vocalize not only the melody of a piece but also mix in aspects of its accompaniment.

- Conceptual memory thrives when you sing melodies using note names, scale degree numbers, or counting syllables, as well as when you do harmonic and structural analyses.

- Keyboardists and string players can heighten memory of touch and movement by imaging or playing hands individually.

- By writing out your material, you brighten both visual and conceptual memory. Notating is most apt with thorny excerpts or in preparation for high-stakes performances. For example, when violist William Primrose was preparing to give the world premiere of the Viola Concerto by William Walton with the Philadelphia Orchestra, he wrote out his complete solo part from memory—not once but several times.[8]

Maintenance Strategies

The purpose of maintenance isn't just to keep memorized music stable. Your memory will shine brightest when it's also invigorated by new artistic and technical discoveries. Some musicians might argue that such enhancements could threaten an ingrained memory program, but when you learn with awareness, memorized

Maintenance Strategies
1. Do mental rehearsals
2. Practice performing
3. Review components

music isn't frail. You can tweak your interpretive and technical maps, and security is enriched rather than compromised. The following are memory-maintenance strategies essential to high-level performance:

1. Do mental rehearsals

a. Mentally perform an entire piece as well as selected sections from different areas of a piece. Experiment with slow, moderate, and final tempos.

- Instrumentalists: Vocalize softly, and mime playing motions in miniature.
- Singers: Image silently to conserve your voice, but, if you like, mouth words, and act out any theatrical gestures.

b. Are your interpretive and technical maps unmistakable? As you run the music in your mind, do you vividly hear any accompaniment and also sense where you are in the large-scale structure? Reingrain any vague segments.

2. Practice performing (p. 199)

a. During a practice performance, were you able to image ahead distinctly, or were some areas sketchy? Don't let hazy passages squeak by uncorrected; reingrain them.

b. Was your execution on target? Did you feel a spontaneous spark? Rethink any sections that don't seem technically comfortable and emotionally authentic.

3. Review components

    a. To enliven your memory and thwart decay, isolate sections and, without the score, play hands separately, recite the text of a song, buzz on a mouthpiece, sing lines using note names, or expressively count rhythms. If you can't retrieve an element from your memory, take out the score and ingrain anew.

    b. When reviewing components, discern their connection to the whole. For instance, if a pianist plays the left hand singly, he should mentally hear and feel how it ties in with the right.

    c. Study the score and any text to retrace the form and content of a composition. Hunt for new dramatic possibilities to integrate into your interpretation.

Recall Strategies

Maintenance procedures will help you rejuvenate stored music and assess your recall; use them regularly to confirm that your memory is failsafe. Then, harness these strategies to facilitate your recall in performance situations:

> **Recall Strategies**
> 1. Prepare yourself
> 2. Image ahead
> 3. Withdraw effort
> 4. Keep going

1. Prepare yourself

    a. Your recall operates best when you're calm and alert. To bring yourself into performance-ready condition, rely on the backstage techniques described on page 162.

    b. Trust in your practice habits. Before performing, acknowledge that you've learned your material deeply.

2. Image ahead

    a. As you perform, image ahead in lucid chunks. Create the next chunk in your mind before executing it.

    b. Track your place in the musical landscape, and imbue each phrase with emotion so that everything you recall exists in a context.

3. Withdraw effort

    a. Release physical and psychological tension, and steadfastly direct yourself with an inner conductor.

b. As you withdraw effort, stay positive and immersed in musical expression so that the channels of recall stay open. Negativity, in contrast, triggers recall shutdown.

4. Keep going

a. If your memory hiccups, maintain the forward flow of the music, come what may. See *dealing with errors* (p. 190) for techniques to cope with memory lapses.

b. If nervousness hampers your memory, improve your performance skills according to the guidelines in part II. Without those skills, performance stress will hijack much of the mental bandwidth that you need to recall music securely.

In closing, there's one last question to resolve: Should you invariably perform solo concerts from memory? I think not. On stage, artistry and security matter most. Memorization can encourage artistic freedom and promote communication with listeners, but every audience prefers an exquisite performance from score over a mediocre one from memory, more so when a soloist's music is handled unobtrusively (p. 175). If your recall in practice doesn't reach failsafe standing, you should enthusiastically perform from music. In other words, a piece is either thoroughly memorized, or it's not memorized at all.

Practicing Deeply, IV

Building Technique

The purpose of technique is to free the unconscious.

—David Mamet, author

Technique represents the interface between imagination and creation. When you develop robust technical skills, you can close the gap between what you feel and what you're able to express through your instrument or voice.

For you to assemble an inclusive technique, however, you need a plan. Proficiency isn't likely to mature from studying repertoire alone because the components of technique are many, and they need individual attention if they're to flourish. Hence, in the five-zone model for organizing practice (p. 6), technique gets a zone all to itself.

This section lays out concepts for working effectively in the *technique* zone. It doesn't scour the idiosyncrasies of instruments, as those are beyond the reach of this book. But the following three-part strategy provides a platform for any musician to build up consciousness-freeing technical skills.

> **Building Technique**
>
> 1. Organize a regimen
> 2. Emphasize excellence
> 3. Delve into details

1. Organize a regimen

For the musician, technique is the means of producing musical ideas, and it functions as a storehouse of instrumental or vocal ingredients. To improve your abilities, you have to sort out the technical ingredients that are inherent to your specialty and recognize which ones you possess and which you lack. Then, with your teacher's support, you can organize a regimen to overcome weaknesses.

In my experience, few students arrive at college with comprehensive technical preparation—almost all of them need to do groundwork to remedy deficiencies. Ask your teacher to appraise your skills, and then devote yourself to constructing a solid technical foundation so that your artistic growth can proceed unhindered. Here's how to get your technical-improvement plan under way.

a. *Synchronize goals, materials, and strategies.* Begin by listing technical categories on a practice sheet (see page 9 for a basic design). Your categories should include universal items, such as scales, arpeggios, and etudes, as well as crucial technical ingredients: position shifts, diction, tone production, breathing, and so on. Then, gather materials to upgrade your aptitude in each area, and set attainable, short-term goals.

For example, to enhance velocity, an instrumentalist might single out some scale etudes and aim for small upticks in speed every couple of days. A singer, looking to groom tone and intonation, might practice a pair of eight-measure exercises for several minutes twice a day. Get help from your teacher to ensure that your categories are complete, your goals are realistic, and your materials and practice strategies are apt.

b. *Follow a schedule.*
- *Practice consistently.* Technical ingredients are perishable. Regular practice allows your established skills to remain vibrant and your emerging ones to sprout quickly.
- *Range widely.* Keep a broad set of ingredients sturdy by reviewing multiple techniques in each practice session.
- *Set limits.* Technique practice uses select muscles repeatedly. To avoid exhaustion or injury, regulate how much you work on any exercise. Some techniques need only minutes of daily review, whereas others are best practiced on alternate days.

2. Emphasize excellence

By integrating *habits of excellence* (p. 20) into your technique practice, you assimilate professional standards of execution.

a. *Ease:* When practicing technical material, no goal ranks higher than ease. To create ease, however, you must go to the core of the way you produce music. In essence, easeful technique flows from efficiency of thought and action; it depends on clear self-directions and the dissolving of useless tension. As you practice an exercise, image ahead (p. 34), and use your awareness to withdraw effort. Also enliven your senses of touch, movement, and posture to simplify the physical elements of your execution: Minimize pressure, strive for a feeling of weightlessness in your limbs, and balance supply as you sit or stand (p. 250).

b. *Expressiveness:* With an expressive technique at your command, you're able to hear musical nuances in your mind and simultaneously perceive how to execute them. As a result, you can be both secure and flexible on stage. To promote expressiveness, bring meaning to all that you practice—shape your lines no matter how modest the material. Musicians who ignore expressiveness in their technical work implant habits of blandness that can infect every phrase they perform.

c. *Accuracy:* Aim for accuracy that surpasses "correct" and ascends toward the sublime. Execute timing with atomic precision; tune your intervals until they shimmer. Choose short enough segments of material and slow enough tempos that you instill all-embracing exactness.

d. *Rhythmic vitality:* Generate lively forward motion and a terrain of undulating emphasis. Even when you're repeating a three-note morsel, initiate a pulse, and steer one note into the next. With scales, enlist your metronome, and group pitches meaningfully, often driving toward downbeats (p. 31).

e. *Beautiful tone:* Tone, maybe more than any other feature, drenches music with emotion. By insisting on beauty of sound in your technique practice, you'll find that your tone becomes exquisite by default. Craft a primary tone that's powerful and rich, and then experiment with diverse tonal hues until you amass a palette of colors to complement any composition. Over time, draw on exercises and etudes that traverse the full range of your voice or instrument, thereby enabling you to burnish your tone at all registers and volume levels.

f. *Focused attention:* When you integrate multilayered objectives into technique work, practice becomes engrossing. And by focusing on small, definite tasks, you can efficiently accomplish your goals. In contrast, the musicians who mindlessly run through exercises ingrain lax mental habits that suffocate artistry and sap motivation.

g. *Positive attitude:* Technical progress can't be rushed. Like the greenery in a garden, you can nurture your technique, but the flowers will bloom in their own time. Infuse your practice with patient optimism. If your technical skills aren't as advanced as you'd like, carry on, confident that your agility will improve and the music you produce will add beauty to the world.

3. Delve into details

It may seem that top-notch performers were born with bravura techniques, but elite musicians, like pianist Bill Evans, have all labored diligently to carve out their skills: "I didn't have the kind of facile talent that a lot of people have," Evans said, "the ability just to listen and transfer something to my instrument. I had to go through a terribly hard analytical and building process. In the end, I came out ahead in a sense because I knew what I was doing in a more thorough way."[1] To put together your own technique, like Evans, you have to delve into details.

a. *Use your whole self.* Unity of body, mind, and spirit lies at the center of artistic music making. You don't sing only with your voice, nor do you play an instrument merely with your head and hands; you perform with your whole self. Therefore, attend to your total use as you practice— be mindful of your posture, breath, movements, and mental focus. The more adept you become at using yourself in an integrated way, the more effortless your technique will be.

b. *Dissect your exercises.* No technical exercise is of value on its own. However, exercises can be gold mines of refinement if you extract and polish the principles embedded within them. Probe the minutiae of your exercises, and home in on things that don't feel easy to execute; such blips alert you to ingredients that are missing in your technical lineup.

c. *Target your quirks.* All musicians and classes of instruments have technical peculiarities. By identifying your foibles and the oddities of your instrument, you can select materials and devise original exercises that target those areas. If you fail to zero in on technical impediments, your quirks will continue to haunt you.

d. *Tap technology.* Both low- and high-tech gadgetry can boost your dexterity. On the low-tech end, nothing beats a mirror. Cheap and abundant, mirrors aid you to assess many technical habits. Video recording, though, lets you go further. For instance, violinist Kathryn Lucktenberg recommends that string players who want to hone their vibrato technique should zoom in on their left hands and then replay their videos at half-speed, scrutinizing every movement.[2] Audio recording offers a comparable opportunity for lucid self-assessment. Biofeedback, neurofeedback, and motion analysis are more costly tools that help musicians reduce tension and heighten coordination; if you hit a technical barrier, it will be worth checking to see whether your school has such services available. As new technologies appear, musical applications will mushroom, so drop by *musiciansway.com* now and again to monitor innovations.

Upgrading Musicianship

I think I was first awakened to musical exploration by Dizzy Gillespie and Bird. It was through their work that I began to learn about musical structures and the more theoretical aspects of music.

—John Coltrane, saxophonist and composer

The practice that you do in the *musicianship* zone increases your knowledge of music theory, elevates your sight-reading and improvisation skills, and quickens your artistic intelligence. And as your musicianship abilities ripen, you become not only a better artist but also a more employable one. For example, on the artistic side, through the study of theory, you glean awareness of musical architecture that equips you to grasp the expressive bones of a piece. Employment-wise, when you're a nimble sight-reader, you can accept the last-minute gigs and land the studio work that poor readers can't manage. To expand your musicianship, mix the following subjects into your practice and study routines.

> **Upgrading Musicianship**
>
> 1. Become a perceptive listener
> 2. Sight-read
> 3. Improvise
> 4. Study general music topics
> 5. Feed your artistry

1. Become a perceptive listener

It's likely that you can recall hearing music that left you cold initially but later attracted your interest. That is, something within you changed, and you were able to appreciate musical content that you had previously overlooked. What was at the crux of that transformation? Your listening skills evolved, and you became more perceptive.

Perceptive listening entails facility with the aural grammar of music; and distinct musical styles communicate in their own languages. Once you internalize the syntax of a style as a listener, you possess the background to perform that style convincingly. In the reverse situation, when musicians with scant listening experience try to play or sing repertoire from unfamiliar genres, they produce the musical equivalent of a clumsy accent.

For you to perform with native inflection, you have to listen and listen until you break through to the soul of a style. You need to be able to hear the gestures that composers write and the spin that performers add. To reach that point, regularly peruse recordings and catch numerous live performances. Listen to an array of titles, and also size up different performers interpreting the same pieces. But don't take in the repertoire just for your instrument; if you're a string player drawn to compositions by Bach, submerge yourself in some of his vocal music. Get to know the wider scope of a composer's musical personality.

Also branch out beyond your genre—be a musical polyglot who's receptive to disparate styles. Boundaries between genres continue to blur, so musicians today can probably use more stylistic versatility than those of past eras. Nevertheless, whether you focus on one tradition or opt to diversify, keen listening skills will leave you with fertile soil in which to mature your artistry as a performer.

2. Sight-read

Here, "sight-reading" refers to the performance of untried music at first sight with no more than a minute or two to scan. Expertise with sight-reading belongs at the top of your list of priorities because, without it, you'll be fated to slow-paced learning and restricted job options. As an example of how sight-reading skills play out in the professional world, here's oboist and studio musician John Ellis, who has performed on the soundtracks of nearly 400 films, speaking about the requirements of being a studio wind player: "You have to have a background in the standard symphonic literature," he says, "and you have to sight-read—you never get the music ahead of time. They just put it on your music stand, and you play."[3]

Whether you hope to be a studio performer or not, make sight-reading practice a daily custom. At minimum, allocate 10 minutes per day. If your reading skills need major improvement, ramp up to 20 minutes or more. Here are practice guidelines:

a. *Select varied, accessible material.* Your material can make or break your sight-reading practice. Start with hyperaccessible music that bolsters your fluency. For instance, you could open a reading session by vocalizing rhythm exercises; then you might play or sing elementary melodies. When you become confident reading rudimentary material, move on to scores that span assorted keys, rhythms, registers, and styles; you might additionally want to practice transposing at sight. To locate material, query your teacher; also visit libraries, retailers, and online forums.

b. *Practice alone and with others.* Solitary practice is vital for covering the breadth of your instrument and genre, but group rehearsal solidifies your skills. If you don't already meet with a reading ensemble, try to gather weekly with one or more colleagues.

c. *Reinforce basic skills.* The musicians who excel at sight-reading didn't get that way by practicing haphazardly; on the contrary, they rehearsed the following basic skills until those skills became habitual.

Basic Sight-Reading Skills
i. Scan first
ii. Count mentally
iii. Look ahead
iv. Keep going
v. Express the music
vi. Withdraw effort

  i. *Scan first.* (See below.)

  ii. *Count mentally.* Use a metronome in practice, and, as you play or sing, silently count in agreement with the musical context.

  iii. *Look ahead.* When you read music or text, your eyes don't pass smoothly across a page; they fix in chunks called "fixation units." As an illustration, reread the previous few sentences, and notice how your eyes fix.

   Now, at a laid-back pace, read the preceding sentence aloud, and go on to the end of this sentence, making sure that your eyes see one or two units in front of the unit that you're speaking.

   Your eyes and execution should operate comparably when you read music: You take in an entire unit before executing it, and you look at least one unit beyond the one that you're playing or singing. You should see sufficiently far ahead that you have ample time to understand and eloquently execute the music; you might even glance around at various places on a score to determine what's coming next. Still, your eyes shouldn't travel so far afield that you forget a passage before the time comes to perform it.

   Expert readers look farther ahead than beginners, but not to a superhuman extent. They also tend to fix on larger units, although the size of those units fluctuates in relation to phrase structure. Researchers Sam Thompson and Andreas Lehmann report that, when reading straightforward melodies, adept musicians "read around six or seven notes ahead, while novices read only two or three notes ahead."[4] If you choose accessible material to practice sight-reading, however, you can quickly learn to see ahead like a pro.

   Tally your visual units with the note grouping so that you capture a composition's dramatic language (example 5.1). If the note grouping isn't apparent to you, fix on units of one or more beats, depending on the music's complexity—greater complexity calls for units of shorter duration. When reading in an ensemble, in addition to moving your eyes ahead, stay aware of your colleagues or director via your peripheral vision, and look up from your score often. In reality, eye movements during sight-reading can be quite elaborate; see *musiciansway.com* for more information.

iv. *Keep going.* Rhythmic continuity is paramount when you sight-read, so disregard errors, and never backtrack to correct flubs. If you come upon an ornate segment that outstrips your ability, one ploy is to perform the notes on the main beats and let the florid ones go; alternatively, you might drop out for a beat and then reenter. Whatever you do, keep on counting and looking ahead.

  If you frequently lose your place when sight-reading, opt for simpler material and slower tempos. Should troubles persist, get help from a teacher. Also consider scheduling a vision exam.

v. *Express the music.* Respond to expression markings with the same fidelity as rhythms and pitches. When a score lacks markings, sculpt phrases in line with your sense of the compositional layout.

vi. *Withdraw effort.* As you sight-read, release physical and emotional tension. Even when the going gets rough, breathe and be positive.

d. *Master the preperformance scan.* The following scanning procedure enables you to pick up decisive musical content before you sight-read. If you're a novice at scanning, then, in practice, scan music without hurrying. As your abilities grow, accelerate your scanning speed until you can digest these components in seconds and more or less together.

  i. *Grasp the framework.* Discern these facets of a piece's design:

  - title, tempo, time signature, form, character—including, for vocal music, the gist of a text
  - prevalent rhythms and expression marks, plus the nature of any intricate rhythms
  - locations of repeats and other navigation signs

  ii. *Form a pitch map.* Your pitch map spotlights melodic and harmonic traits, and it alerts you to where on your instrument or voice the music will lie. Scan a composition for the following aspects either in tandem with or after scanning the framework:

  - key signature and key(s)
  - melodic and harmonic features—especially notated sharps, flats, or naturals—and the makeup of any tricky passages
  - range

Example 5.1 provides a sample melody for applying sight-reading concepts. The brackets inserted in the music indicate suggested fixation units suited to less experienced sight-readers playing at a slow tempo (more experienced readers might prefer to execute at a faster tempo and fix on larger units). Scan the example, and then, using a keyboard or other instrument, sight-read with a metronome ticking at an easygoing pace, perhaps quarter note = 66. As you execute, mentally count "1 and 2 and," create legato phrases, and perceive the musical content one or two units beyond the one that you're playing. After one read-through, tackle the example again, and experiment with a faster tempo and with looking somewhat farther ahead.

Example 5.1. From Franz Schubert, Sonata D. 821 for arpeggione and piano, third movement, measures 1–40.

3. Improvise

Improvisation is the most playful way that you can make music, and it's also one of the most fulfilling: "It's very gratifying to improvise in front of people," says guitarist Jim Hall. "I feel I'm including them in what I'm doing, taking them someplace they might like to go and haven't been before."[5]

But improvisation isn't the exclusive domain of jazz specialists like Hall. Although it may have leaked out of the classical mainstream, if you're a classical musician, improvisation doesn't need to be absent from your aesthetic universe. In fact, it shouldn't be, for both artistic and practical reasons. In the case of a classical clarinetist, let's say, moderate competence at improvisation, coupled with agility in playing symphonic and chamber music repertoire, would outfit her to perform in classical ensembles and in a mix of combos—jazz, klezmer, world music, and so forth. She could then contribute broadly to her community, take pleasure in impromptu performances, and enlarge her income. Weighed against the musicians who can perform only from notation, her career has a more eclectic potential.

Nonetheless, eclecticism isn't for everyone. For the classical musicians who don't resonate with other styles, an improvisational vocabulary arms them to handle memory slips and to perform avant-garde pieces that call for spontaneity. Plus, the playfulness of improvisation provides an unmatched outlet for artistic expression, whatever the genre.

If improvisation is new to you, you can get your feet wet through self-study. Your best bet for learning fundamentals, though, may be to enroll in a class or workshop. In a classroom setting, you acquire a background that you can flesh out independently, and you meet colleagues with whom to practice.

To keep the improvisational juices flowing during your individual practice, improvise a bit each day, even if you come up with just a variation on a scale exercise. For a more in-depth session, you might get together with fellow musicians, or you could ad-lib to the audio materials from an improvisation method. Either way, have fun when you improvise; let improvisation be a vehicle for expressing your true self.

4. Study general music topics

General music topics commonly consist of music theory, ear training, keyboard, music history and literature, world music, and composition. Studying these areas impacts your artistry in a wealth of dimensions. For example, in combination with theory, familiarity with ear training and music literature enables you to soak up the syntax of a piece at first sight. Keyboard skills are advantageous for composing, teaching, understanding harmony, and learning new material.

With regard to composing, I encourage you to invent original music. If you've never cooked up a melody, try concocting exercises for honing technical skills, or devise material for use as warm-ups. More substantially, if you can, enroll in a composition class geared to performers.

These topics have proven so valuable that most are incorporated into music curricula. Despite that, general music courses will stoke your development only if you integrate their content into your practice. Aside from taking classes, do some self-study. You might explore theory concepts by tinkering with chord voicings on a keyboard; you could augment your appreciation for a composer you're studying in a world music class by improvising in the composer's style. Music is a field so vast that no one person can comprehend more than a slice of its totality. Even so, pledge yourself to a lifelong quest for encompassing musical literacy.

5. Feed your artistry

Your musical personality springs from your inner artistic landscape. That landscape, however, wasn't inborn—it grew out of your upbringing and the circumstances of your life. Now it's up to you to engineer the conditions in which your creativity will prosper.

Among the constellation of ways to boost artistry, collaboration may be the greatest of all. Choreographer Robby Barnett, cofounder of Pilobolus Dance Theater, speaks of the "biodiversity of collaboration," that is, the ways in which partnerships fortify artists' creative ecosystems.[6] He underscores that, although communal activity isn't simple, the interplay of teamwork can spark otherwise inconceivable innovations. Therefore, partake of collaborative opportunities whenever your schedule permits.

Reading and writing also feed artistry. Art-nourishing texts include poetry, musicians' biographies, practical guidebooks, and treatises on musical style. Beneficial writing could comprise journaling, penning a music column for a newspaper, or exchanging letters.

In the realm of movement education, Dalcroze eurhythmics trains musicians to express rhythm, meter, and emotion through body movement; it helps many to infuse their performances with vitality. The Alexander technique and the Feldenkrais method educate musicians to move with integration and awareness (see *musiciansway.com*). You may also find that dance, yoga, or tai chi classes enhance your strength, body consciousness, and centering power. Similarly, lessons in meditation could raise your capacity to focus in practice and calm yourself in performance.

Participating in workshops and festivals will also extend your artistic sphere, as will attending varied arts events. Besides concerts, check out plays, art exhibits, and dance performances, and then reflect on how different disciplines create drama. Singer-songwriter Bob Dylan said, "In writing songs, I've learned as much from Cézanne as I have from Woody Guthrie."[7] Whatever styles of music you prefer, stepping away from your everyday environment stirs your imagination, and widening your arts network may prompt collaborative adventures that you can't now foresee.

Fueling Motivation

My strength is my enthusiasm.

—Plácido Domingo, tenor

Motivation is the engine that drives your musical growth. But motivation isn't a lone entity; it basically has two sides: internal and external. Internal motivation stems from the urge for personal expression and achievement. When you practice purely for the love of music or you improve a skill for its own sake, it's your internal motivation that opens the creative spigot. External motivation comes into play when you learn a part for a school ensemble, you gig for a paycheck, or you otherwise work toward a deadline.

The two types of motivation act in chorus to promote musical progress. For instance, a piano student named Jennifer, whom you'll meet in chapter 14, was an expert self-motivator. To jump-start her learning of a solo program, she scheduled a recital at a church so that her internal desire to play the music would be supported by the external incentive of a looming concert date. The result was intense practice and a performance so brilliant that it launched a tour.

What about the musicians who let motivation slide? In the words of Andrew Carnegie, "People who are unable to motivate themselves must be content with mediocrity, no matter how impressive their other talents."[8] For you to excel today and tomorrow, you need strategies that fuel both internal and external motivation. Here are some suggestions.

Fueling Internal Motivation

Productive artists are brimming with enthusiasm. Whatever life throws in their path, whether good or bad, they channel it into art. When Duke Ellington felt glum, for example, he wouldn't let melancholy stay his pen: "I merely took the energy it takes to pout," he said, "and wrote some blues."[9]

With a reservoir of internal motivation, you, too, can make art amid the vagaries of life. Yet motivation doesn't fall benevolently from the sky. You have to foster it day by day with maneuvers such as these.

> **Fueling Internal Motivation**
>
> 1. Clarify goals
> 2. Kindle devotion
> 3. Inspire yourself
> 4. Master basic skills
> 5. Be productive

1. Clarify goals

Compelling goals whip up torrents of motivation. To pin down your long-term aims, mull over the pointers in chapter 14 for drafting a career plan

(p. 300). Use those ideals, as well as your teacher's advice, to set near-term goals in the five practice zones. Then, before turning in each night, review the next day's practice agenda so that you get up in the morning primed to work.

2. Kindle devotion

Tenor Luciano Pavarotti said, "People think I am disciplined. It is not discipline, it is devotion. There is a great difference."[10] By kindling your devotion to music, your heart will steer you toward practice. Still, it can be tough to do the work that needs to be done. You're a person, not a machine, and you're going to encounter ups and downs. One way to heighten devotion is to use affirmations—self-statements that revive zeal and cancel negativity. Try these sample affirmations, and then think up some of your own.

Affirmations to generate practice energy

- When your alarm clock sounds, and a part of you negotiates for more sleep, tell yourself, "Music, not sleep, feeds my soul." Then get up and prepare for the day's practice.
- If your practice time approaches and a procrastinating voice within you grumbles, dispute it: "Music never lets me down."
- After a subpar performance, if your eagerness ebbs, annihilate your angst with the likes of "I'm a student; I'm here to learn. Mistakes don't threaten me."
- If you feel blasé before a practice session, remind yourself: "Few people get the chance to make music. I'm grateful for the privilege."

When life's currents threaten to push you off track, call up affirmations. And if you ever catch yourself saying discouraging things like "I'm not talented enough" or "There's too much competition," discuss your self-talk patterns with your teacher and a counselor. As psychologists Paul Salmon and Robert Meyer wrote in *Notes from the Green Room*, "Self-talk can be positive, negative, or neutral, but it almost always has some influence on our behavior."[11]

3. Inspire yourself

Practicing a new piece of music is like starting a love affair; there's no end to your motivation. That headiness doesn't last, though, unless you continually rouse your relationship with music. So routinely do things that inspire you: Listen to recordings, improvise, and attend concerts and festivals. Also take up sensible habits of self-care. If your health seeps away, inspiration won't be far behind.

4. Master basic skills

Nothing motivates better than success. When you pour your soul into a piece of music and perform it without a hitch, the magical feeling leaves you craving more. Conversely, what could be a wetter blanket than inscrutable problems? By getting hold of the fundamentals covered in this book, you outfit yourself with the tools of a competent music maker, and your proficiency spurs you on.

For example, your internal motivation to practice will be strongest when the music you work on uplifts you and is within your reach, and you know how to learn it thoroughly. Without the means to choose suitable material (chapter 1), practice it deeply (chapters 2–4), and solve problems (chapter 3), your motivation gets dampened. Therefore, review these chapters often, and work with your teacher to get the basics under your control. Then your facility will nourish your spirit, and you'll have the knack, like Ellington, to translate emotions into sound.

5. Be productive

Some musicians think that they can't be productive unless they're already motivated. Then, owing to their convictions, instead of practicing, they languish in coffee shops, lazily awaiting their muse. But productivity and motivation fuel each other. Besides, in case you were wondering, there's no muse out there coming to motivate you. You have to do the motivating yourself.

Productivity begets motivation because the satisfaction of mastering one piece unleashes momentum that propels you onward. In due course, when your *performance material* zone burgeons with music, you never lack for compositions that you're eager to perform. Accruing a sizable repertoire, however, requires both efficient practice skills and the ability to work consistently. So abide by your practice schedule, and keep your productivity rolling. What if your practice time arrives and you don't have any burning insights to express? Warm up and get started anyway. In the words of author Anne Lamott, "Take the action and the insight will follow."[12]

Fueling External Motivation

It might seem that external motivation would be a lesser sibling of the internal variety, but, for musicians, the two types of motivation function as equal partners. Actually, the external sort will give direction to your creativity because, to perform, you need an audience, and audiences don't materialize randomly; an event has to be organized. With a commitment on your calendar, your practice becomes targeted toward an exhilarating purpose.

Most professional music making happens due to external commitments: A recital date is set; a recording studio gets booked. Such obligations are catalysts that unite energy and ideas to form viable works of art. Songwriter Cole Porter crystallized that notion: "All the inspiration I ever needed was a phone call from a producer."[13] Here are four ways to ensure that your motivational phone rings nonstop.

> **Fueling External Motivation**
>
> 1. Book performances
> 2. Be generous
> 3. Set deadlines
> 4. Collaborate

1. Book performances

Performances are unrivaled motivators, but they have a positive effect only when your musical responsibilities lie within your capacity. If repertoire is too intricate or preparation time is too short, anxiety—more than motivation—will be triggered. Correspondingly, if a performance doesn't excite you, it will feel more like a burden than a joy. Check with your teacher to identify appropriate bookings, and then pick titles that you'll be thrilled to perform. The following are motivating engagements that fit students of assorted levels.

- performances in master classes, workshops, and coaching sessions
- concerts in community venues such as churches, museums, and synagogues
- competitions and auditions
- recitals at music schools and summer festivals
- recording sessions
- gigs at pubs, coffee shops, and reception halls

2. Be generous

At this stage in your education, you've probably stockpiled considerable musical ability. And through your music, you can be part of something larger than yourself: your community. With that in mind, on top of arranging formal appearances, contribute in other ways. Maybe spread a little cheer at a nursing home or children's hospital. The more you share music with others, the more relevance your art has in the broader culture. The benefits that you give to your community are then redoubled in terms of your personal fulfillment and ongoing motivation.

3. Set deadlines

Whether you have an event on the horizon or not, structure your practice with deadlines. For starters, consult with your teacher so that your lesson and studio class offer a stream of weekly objectives. Also, link up with peers to initiate a performance-development group (p. 199), and then agree to present pieces on fixed dates. Deadlines, like concerts, invigorate your practice with goals.

4. Collaborate

Musicians with mutual plans motivate each other. When you play or sing with an ensemble, you commit to preparing your parts, to rehearsing regularly, and to molding a team culture. Casual improvisation sessions, too, supply a context whereby musicians can buoy their creativity. However, collaboration can be complex, so study chapter 6 before instigating any joint enterprise.

As you tend to your motivation, be mindful to harmonize the two sides. If you take on too many external obligations, your internal zest may flag from overwork and a scarcity of time to explore personal interests. On the other hand, if you dodge external prospects, you could wind up starved for a creative outlet. Strive for a balance, but beware of remaining too long in a comfort zone. Keep stoking the fires of internal motivation with new repertoire and inspiring challenges. All the while, grab hold of projects that take you out of your typical surroundings or put you under deadlines. "A ship in port is safe," said Admiral Grace Murray Hopper, "but that is not what ships are built for."[14] Likewise, rich artistic futures await the musicians who are unafraid to cut loose from predictable moorings.

Committing to the Creative Process

The real essence of art turned out to be not something high up and far off; it was right inside my ordinary daily self.
> —Shinichi Suzuki, violinist and teacher

This and the preceding chapters have combed strategies to help you organize your practice and work effectively in the five practice zones that are outlined in chapter 1. If you've read from the beginning, then you've taken in bundles of information, so it would be reasonable to ask, "What's the best way to absorb these concepts?" The answer is to apply them again and again—for instance, by mastering one accessible piece after another—and via that process to cultivate your skills and forge a secure practice style.

The key word here is *process*. When you fell in love with music and started to sing or to play an instrument, you activated a process that goes on without end because being a musician isn't about pursuing some nirvana of artistic enlightenment; it's about endless refinement and discovery. Along the way, you'll have triumphs and setbacks, and you need them both to see which routes lead forward. Such is the nature of the creative process. The route has twists and potholes; and it isn't clearly marked—you chart much of it on your own in the solitude of a practice room. How do you endure the many difficulties? You commit to the process itself and acknowledge that it's on this often-bumpy road that your music making occurs.

Sticking with the creative process, though, calls for both self-motivation and a kind of detachment. That is, rather than getting wrapped up in every little thing that goes right or wrong, you have to maintain an objective stance toward your work so that you can evaluate your strengths and weaknesses even-handedly. That's not easy to do, but a commitment to process acts as an inner GPS. You can carry on through successes and dilemmas without emotional extremes knocking you off course.

With a process orientation, when you run into a technical problem in practice, you don't sulk in frustration; instead, you proceed with gusto to unpack the impasse. Similarly, if you botch a phrase in concert, you go over that phrase the next day, conscious that it contains something you need to learn. Like the athlete who drops the ball, you analyze what went wrong, make corrections, and jump back in the game. You treat the slip-up as information for use in bettering your art, not as a test of your talent or personal worth. With patient enthusiasm, you practice, advancing on your path.

If musicians forsake detachment, however, and align their self-esteem with each note, they release art-crushing emotions. "You fool!" they might silently rage after missing an entrance in rehearsal. Instead of surmounting troubles, they may avoid practice out of shame or aggravation. They say, "I'm untalented," as opposed to "What can I do to solve this?" They lament, "Other people have it easier," rather than asserting, "I can figure out how to move ahead." Such perfectionist beliefs undermine countless musicians. But committing to the creative process neutralizes perfectionism, as a singer named Kaci found out.

Kaci's passion was opera and musical theater. She also sat in occasionally with a blues band. A year after graduating from college, to prepare for some auditions, she signed up for voice lessons with a new teacher. Her teacher then referred her to me because he saw that Kaci had a long-standing habit that was blocking her growth.

Kaci came to my studio, and I asked her to sing an excerpt. She let loose a B. B. King–style version of "Every Day I Have the Blues," and her spirit filled the room. She was a formidable artist. Before I voiced my opinion, however, I wanted to hear her thoughts.

"How'd that go?" I asked, after she sang a couple of verses.

"Crummy," she replied.

"Why's that?"

"I got shrill," she complained.

"How do your audiences at the club respond to your singing?"

"They like anything," came the reply. "They don't care."

As Kaci spoke, her perfectionist outlook pierced every sentence. In her mind, if artists weren't "great," like her idol, Sarah Vaughn, they were worthless. Any flaw in her singing she saw as proof that she didn't have what it takes. She couldn't see that the "essence of art," as Shinichi Suzuki put it, was already within her, and she was blind to the process-centered truth that underpins creative work. So she harbored a brutal, self-defeating attitude.

I countered with an inventory of the aspects of her singing that had struck me. She seemed surprised as I listed the numerous skills, such as subtle control of rhythm and tone color, that she had displayed. I explained that neither great artists nor their performances are flawless and that adherence to perfectionist myths leeches away at musicians' dreams. To prove my point, I pulled out quotations from top-tier performers.

One quote that struck her was from tenor Luciano Pavarotti. "I try to overcome my limitations and to be the best I can," he told an interviewer. "In my life I don't consider myself to be perfect; I think I could do better. But on stage, I do everything possible to be the best." I recounted what Pavarotti had once said in a master class concerning the way that he memorized opera roles. He claimed that, compared to his peers, he learned slowly, but once he mastered a role, he never forgot it. Clearly, he had found a learning process that worked for him, and he had committed to that process.

With the understanding that her mindset was stifling her evolution, Kaci resolved to give herself over to the beauty of music, value her talents, and renounce self-condemnation. She began to engage with the issues in her singing that she wanted to improve and stopped chastising herself for them. She also ceased viewing slight flaws as gargantuan gaffes—she saw that they had no bearing on a performance's impact. She would enjoy each musical moment and give her all, and that would be enough. In fact, it was more than enough. With her teacher's guidance, she won a string of auditions; in less than a year, she was singing full time.

All accomplished musicians craft processes for preparing performances and then trust in those processes. They grant that, over the span of a show, some things won't turn out as intended. But they accept their human shortcomings, and instead of lamenting their humanity, they celebrate it. They recognize that a perfect performance can't occur because music is the offspring of emotion, for which the term "perfect" has no meaning. Even when every pitch, rhythm, and nuance falls into place, there's always room for interpretive breakthroughs. What's more, artistic performance demands spontaneity, so there can't be a consummate rendition of any piece. At each concert, music is created anew, according to a performer's imagination.

For you to achieve your musical potential, you have to commit to the creative process, take risks, and follow your heart. Inevitably, some of your work won't be as high in quality as you'd like. Nonetheless, only by experimenting with ideas that don't bear fruit will you be able to find ones that will.

In sum, musical excellence arises not only from artistic sensitivity but also from resiliency and perseverance. Therefore, make the finest music that you can, but when you miss the mark, react with curiosity, not worry. Combine your mistakes and your triumphs, stir them into the pot of artistic progress, and then savor what bubbles up.

To help you assess your proficiency with practice processes, table 5.1 presents a self-evaluation that compiles 32 true/false statements derived from subjects explored in this chapter and the previous four. Read each statement, and then circle your response. Any statement that you can't respond to in the affirmative indicates an area that needs your attention. To patch up deficiencies, study this book, confer with your teacher, and then return to table 5.1 to monitor improvements.

Table 5.1 **General Evaluation of Practice Development**

1. My practice is deeply meaningful to me; I seldom feel bored.	T or F
2. I keep to a regular practice schedule.	T or F
3. My practice space is fully equipped with the things I need.	T or F
4. I set detailed goals before beginning to practice.	T or F
5. I typically feel a sense of accomplishment after practicing.	T or F
6. I'm able to maintain mental focus as I practice.	T or F
7. I commonly record portions of my practice, and then I appraise my recordings.	T or F
8. I assess my practice objectively and rarely become upset by difficulties.	T or F
9. I use a metronome in practice.	T or F
10. I consistently warm up before practicing.	T or F

Table 5.1 (*Continued*)

11. I intersperse practice sessions with regular breaks and I stop practicing if I become tired.	T or F
12. I can learn accessible music securely and efficiently.	T or F
13. I have plenty of accessible pieces in my repertoire.	T or F
14. At the outset of learning a piece, I develop a basic interpretation before making technical decisions.	T or F
15. I'm able to shape dramatic musical interpretations that move listeners.	T or F
16. When learning a new piece, I expressively vocalize rhythm.	T or F
17. I use specific strategies to solve musical and technical problems.	T or F
18. I manage repetition so that I neither repeat errors nor drill passages to the point of fatigue.	T or F
19. I use mental imaging (p. 34) to aid my learning and memorizing of music.	T or F
20. I consciously image ahead as I play or sing.	T or F
21. I'm satisfied with the tactics that I use to increase the tempos of pieces.	T or F
22. I'm confident of my ability to memorize music and to perform from memory.	T or F
23. I have a broad-based plan to polish my technique, and I practice technique daily.	T or F
24. I routinely practice sight-reading.	T or F
25. I can improvise melodies over straightforward chord progressions.	T or F
26. I review my favorite pieces in detail so that the expressive and technical components stay vibrant.	T or F
27. I listen to a range of recorded music, and I regularly attend live music performances.	T or F
28. I'm advancing my knowledge of music theory, ear training, and other general music topics.	T or F
29. I take deliberate steps to fuel my motivation to practice and to counter procrastination.	T or F
30. When I make errors in practice, I view them as instructive and not as indicative of failure.	T or F
31. I understand how to practice such that I can perform confidently and artistically.	T or F
32. As I practice, I embody *habits of excellence:* ease, expressiveness, accuracy, rhythmic vitality, beautiful tone, focused attention, and positive attitude.	T or F

6

Musical Collaboration

In this chapter:

- The four elements of professionalism
- Interacting in rehearsal
- Correlating solitary and group practice
- Six ways to ignite synergy in an ensemble
- Forming a musical group

Musical Collaboration

> *We just got together and just ran on some few things and just played, just played. And it was a swingin' thing. We had a ball.*
>
> —Art Blakey, drummer

Collaborative music making is one of life's true joys, but it can also present thorny challenges. Whenever musicians work together, there exists the potential for both synergy and friction. This chapter offers guidelines for crafting group situations that ignite synergy, minimize friction, and encourage positive relationships among performers.

The preceding pages have plumbed ways to upgrade your individual musicianship. In groups, however, your artistic success rests on three things aside from you and your partners' musical abilities: your group culture, your interpersonal skills, and your rehearsal strategies. All three are examined here, beginning with the central theme of ensemble culture: professionalism.

Professionalism

As a member of a quartet, you come to realize that you're responsible for other people's reputations and livelihoods as well as your own.
—Michael Tree, violist

- A student string quartet disbands. One of the musicians was seldom prepared for rehearsals, so the other players threw up their hands in disgust.
- A trio delivers a lackluster performance. The group members have been arguing so much in rehearsals that they can barely tolerate each other's company, even on stage.
- A jazz combo cancels a concert. The group leader hasn't paid his colleagues for two previous gigs, so the musicians refused to play.

Few occasions in life are more hopeful than when musicians team up to form ensembles. All too often, though, a group's promise is scuttled due to circumstances like those in the above examples. However, when musicians commit to professionalism, dysfunctional behaviors don't easily take hold.

Professionalism underpins the culture in any productive ensemble, large or small, because it allows performers to build trust and make music without chafing.

The Elements of Professionalism
1. Punctuality
2. Preparation
3. Courtesy
4. Integrity

In fact, a musician's reputation is shaped as much by consistent professionalism (or the lack thereof) as it is by artistry. Here I distill professionalism into four elements: punctuality, preparation, courtesy, and integrity.

1. Punctuality

Professionals don't show up on time for rehearsals; they arrive *early*. If a practice session is slated for noon, the first downbeat happens at noon. Before then, all of the musicians will be set up and ready to begin.

Adopt this same always-early habit, and you'll start rehearsals warm and performing at your best. Plus, you'll earn a name for reliability. Be punctual at the outset of sessions, and also stick to your group's schedule for pacing, taking breaks, and concluding. To meet your goals within the allotted time, stay on task, avoid irrelevant conversation, and savor the privilege of cooperative music making.

2. Preparation

Veteran performers systematically prepare for each engagement. They know that their careers depend on how they perform day in and day out, and excellence is what everyone expects.

Embrace an equally rigorous benchmark by meticulously practicing your part between rehearsals. Never shirk your preparation and turn up for a rehearsal underprepared. If an illness or other unforeseen incident foils your practice, convey the news ahead of your group session so that rehearsal plans can be adjusted.

In addition, thorough preparation entails more than knowing your part; it also involves familiarity with an entire composition and the way your part fits within the whole. When possible, listen to recordings of the pieces that you're preparing, and study complete scores. If you're performing with an egalitarian group, as opposed to a leader-run ensemble, come to rehearsals with interpretive ideas brewing. Your groundwork will stimulate everyone's creativity.

3. Courtesy

Refined courtesy will solidify your standing as a performer that other musicians want to work with. To fashion a courteous rehearsal environment, employ task-oriented, businesslike manners, and move things along at an efficient pace. When you discuss musical issues, speak precisely and listen attentively, but limit verbal exchanges, thereby preserving a music-centered culture.

In egalitarian groups, provide ample opportunities for experimentation. If someone suggests a phrasing or rehearsal tactic, try it; be receptive to whatever a colleague comes up with. Even if you believe that a phrasing won't fly, give an ensemble partner the chance to test her ideas.

When you rehearse with conductor-led groups and you share a music stand, make sure that both your own and your stand partner's needs for space and viewing are met. And if you mark a shared score, do so neatly. Also relate constructively with your directors—take in their interpretive concepts, exhibit positive body language, and make frequent eye contact. Mold an atmosphere where mutual respect is the norm.

The courtesy side of professionalism also extends beyond the rehearsal setting. For one, courtesy is indispensable to ensemble communications. When ensemble-related messages land in your inbox, reply right away, and consult all of the members before anyone makes decisions that affect the group.

4. Integrity

Integrity among group members permits a culture of trust and openness to flourish. Demonstrate your integrity by speaking truthfully, honoring your word, and carrying out your responsibilities. When you oversee finances, for instance, log records and distribute payments promptly.

Cellist Steven Pologe of the Oregon String Quartet further counsels that, in any collaborative enterprise, one of your duties is to help your colleagues feel successful.[1] Let your fellow musicians know that you have a high regard for their talents, and head off any disparaging talk about a peer. Your commitment to integrity—in combination with courtesy, preparation, and punctuality—will enable your ensemble to stay on course through whatever challenges you may face.

Interacting in Rehearsal

A good quartet is like a good conversation among friends interacting to each other's ideas.

—Stan Getz, saxophonist and bandleader

Even when collaborating musicians act professionally and get along well, they still need plenty of know-how to cope with team dynamics. Arnold Steinhardt, first violinist of the Guarneri String Quartet, explains: "In developing a quartet, personal qualities play as important a role as musicianship; the two can't be easily separated. Each of us has to be strong enough to exert his leadership, strong enough to endure the constant criticism of his colleagues, and strong enough to let go of cherished ideas when they don't coincide with the majority opinion."[2] Steinhardt's insights apply not only to string quartets but also to all egalitarian groups.

This section focuses on four collaborative situations that almost every egalitarian ensemble encounters at one time or another. Managed competently, these types of episodes can strengthen a group's cohesion. Treated carelessly, they can incite a group to implode. Nimble interpersonal skills will equip you to handle these situations with confidence.

Situation 1: "No way! It goes like this."

How can group members reconcile conflicting interpretations? Typically, egalitarian ensembles form interpretations via the discovery process. That is, musicians will turn a phrase in varied ways and collectively pick a style. Still, preferences can diverge sharply.

As mentioned previously, if someone proposes a tempo or phrasing that you deem unsuitable, let your primary response be to attempt it and not criticize. Interpretive notions are like opinions—people have different ones, and musicians should know that their outlooks are welcome. Added to that, you stimulate creativity when you foster a culture that promotes experimentation and free expression.

When you volunteer interpretive changes, speak conditionally, often using questions that start with "What if?" or "How would it sound if?" Then, request feedback right after your group tries out your suggestion. For example, when your colleagues release a tied chord sooner than you'd like, you might stop and ask, "What if we held the tie a little longer?" Similarly, if a crescendo seems overblown, you could inquire, "How would it sound if we did a subtler increase in volume?"

After surveying diverse approaches, if unanimity seems elusive, work on other music for a while, and then return to the earlier material to see whether perspectives converge. At least compromise to where you select one interpretation for an impending performance and a different reading for another. Try to engineer a consensus rather than voting. When a solo part has the lead, however, defer to the soloist's choice.

For any musician, balancing compromise with contribution is an ongoing operation. If you tend to cling to your views, let go more; if you rarely state your preferences, assert yourself more. Compromise that's one-sided isn't compromise.

Situation 2: "So what? I was a little late."

Suppose that a normally responsible musician in your ensemble lags in keeping up his obligations, and the group suffers as a result. What constructive steps could you take? The short answer is to deal evenhandedly with behaviors and not criticize anyone personally.

As an example, imagine that a member of your ensemble traipses in 15 minutes late for a rehearsal, devoid of a legitimate excuse. He apologizes, and you get to work, but the loss of time means that you can't meet all of your practice goals. The following week, he's late once more. In the professional world of leader-run groups, such tardiness could result in dismissal. In egalitarian groups, more diplomatic actions are called for.

Let's say that, instead of reacting sensitively, you were to hurl an accusation at the latecomer: "You're being unprofessional!" What would be the likely effect? You'd escalate tension and strain your relationship because, although the words may seem accurate, they assail your colleague's character in lieu of addressing the punctuality issue.

A savvier comeback would be to offset lax behavior with polished courtesy. And the most courteous way that you can express yourself is with an "I" statement in place of a judgmental "you" statement. For instance, you could say, "I get frustrated when we can't begin on time. Should we rethink our schedule?"

Sincere words like those could spur a lapsing but loyal group member to turn things around. In private, you might ask your colleague whether he needs your assistance. If sloppy behaviors persist, though, arrange a group meeting. After that, if a musician still won't abide by professional standards of conduct, then it's time for him to move on.

Situation 3: "You expect me to play *that?*"

How do you react when your colleagues want to perform music that you dislike? Your professionalism obliges you to share in decision making, so rather than abruptly rejecting a repertoire suggestion, pose questions that let you empathize with your partners' feelings. You could ask, "How long have you wanted to perform that music?" Performing it might be someone's lifelong ambition, or it could be a passing whim. Probe deeper: "What do you like most about it?"

If a group member expresses an enduring wish to program a composition, and learning the music wouldn't be arduous, you wouldn't deny her the chance to fulfill that wish, would you? In that case, it's probably best to withhold your opinion. But if your comrades aren't intent on performing the music, articulate your view in a conditional way, using courteous "I" statements: "I know that many people love that music," you might say in an upbeat tone, "but I've never been attracted to it. Maybe I should listen to it again."

For accomplished performers, liking or disliking any one piece is often of little concern. Expert musicians breathe life into a composition whether they personally resonate with it or not; like actors, they give themselves over to the music's character. That doesn't mean, though, that you should sacrifice who you are when settling on repertoire. Be yourself, but also be open and generous.

When agreement on a title isn't immediate, make it your group's practice to postpone deciding. Set a date to reach a conclusion, and then carry on with other business. If the choosing of music commonly presents an obstacle for your ensemble, try proposing material by email: Swap lists of preferred pieces, and then meet outside of rehearsals to sift through your views.

Situation 4: "You're rushing!"

Musical collaborators come together out of a shared passion for music, and intense feelings about art can stir up ardent criticisms. How can musicians harmonize the critical give-and-take that's so integral to working in groups?

When it comes to receiving criticism in ensemble rehearsals, you'll hear words spanning the gamut from tactful to coarse. Critiques won't upset you, however, if you enlist a cooperative approach to listening and communicating. For example, let's say that at your inaugural rehearsal with a student quartet, a colleague turns to you and huffily exclaims, "You're rushing!" Instead of echoing back the hot emotion, demonstrate that you're interested in your partner's feedback. Set the rough tone aside for the moment, and calmly ask, "Where do you think the rushing began?" Review the relevant section; admit rushing, if you actually were; and proceed with your rehearsal. Later, perhaps during a breather, use an "I" statement to follow up on the harshness of the comment: "You were right to point out when my rhythm was off, but I felt like I was being attacked rather than informed."

That should be enough to prompt an ordinarily cordial person to recognize any lapse of courtesy and apologize. However, if the same musician heaves another gruff remark, you may want to reverse the order of your response: Coolly report how the remark makes you feel, and then get on with rehearsing. Stand up for professional norms of courtesy, but let the small stuff go, especially if you're working with less-experienced collaborators.

When you dole out critiques, use nonaccusing words that focus on musical matters. If you hear a timing error, halt your group, and say something like "We're not together. Let's figure out where our timing slipped." Then you can collectively tackle the problem, maybe by repeating an excerpt at a slower tempo in step with a metronome. If it becomes necessary to spotlight a flaw in someone's playing or singing, employ conditional questions: "Is it possible that the flute came in early at measure 40?"

When you put together your own groups, you can screen out musicians who bristle at criticism. As a student, though, you're frequently appointed to ensembles, so you could wind up partnering with people for whom any comments press delicate buttons. Therefore, at your initial rehearsal with a preassigned group, allocate a few minutes to affirm your desire to forge a professional team culture. Then periodically confer on how criticism is being offered and received (see *appreciating criticism,* p. 296).

Even among well-intentioned collaborators, some interpersonal turbulence is inevitable. When discord surfaces during a rehearsal, try to defuse it at once so that negative emotions don't smolder. At the same time, avoid sacrificing much practice time to talk. If debate is warranted, schedule a meeting, and, in the meantime, preclude speaking judgmentally behind anyone's back.

Most of all, be accepting of people's differences. Pianist John Lewis said that his group, the Modern Jazz Quartet, enjoyed a lasting career partly because "We're smart enough and clever enough to give each other room to live in, to have respect for each other's personalities."[3]

If you ever want advice on coping with problematic group members, consult a teacher or counselor. The energy you invest in forming healthy partnerships will pay rich dividends because you'll probably spend vast amounts of time working with others. The music and memories you create together may be among the defining aspects of your life.

Correlating Solitary and Group Practice

You adapt yourself to the contents of the paintbox.
—Paul Klee, painter

Like a painter dipping into a limited palette, a musician practicing an isolated part has to adapt to material that's incomplete. A part performed out of context may seem pale, but in an ensemble it will blend with the others to form a striking color and texture. The essential knack for the musician is to grasp the whole piece of music while working on an extracted line.

Have you ever felt artistically starved while practicing an ensemble part? Have you ever arrived at a group rehearsal to discover that you and your colleagues couldn't readily fit your parts together? If you answered "yes" to either question, you're not alone. To correlate solitary and group practice and to rehearse effectively within an ensemble, you have to accrue a formidable set of skills. The basic course of action is to mark parts and scores, master your part, and rehearse strategically.

1. Mark parts and scores

When you're in a leadership role, supply the musicians in your ensemble with more than mere parts; also give them access to recordings and full scores, perhaps by tapping online resources. Distribute music well ahead of your rehearsal, having marked the pages as follows:

a. Pencil in metronome settings that spell out both the estimated final tempo of a piece and the target tempo for your initial rehearsal.

b. Indicate interpretation with signs that show dynamics, timing, breaths, and articulations.

c. Write in decisive technical directions, for instance, bowings, diction, or cuing.

d. Number the first measure of each line (p. 44).

The effort you put into preparing music will heighten both expressiveness and efficiency in rehearsals because, when your colleagues practice individually, they'll incorporate matching tempos and interpretations that will mesh right away. Then, when you join forces, measure numbers will act as guide-posts so that you can swiftly locate corresponding places in your music.

2. Master your part

Rehearsals can't be fully productive unless all of the participating musicians have learned their parts. Here are crucial practice procedures:

    a. Prior to your first rehearsal, devise a solo practice agenda, and implement the general learning process described in chapter 3: Get an overview of the piece, map an interpretation, map the technique, and then execute your map (p. 43).

    b. Begin by listening to recordings and poring over any full score. Take in as much as you can about the musical structure and how the parts interweave. Pin down where you have solo passages, when you're doubling or imitating other lines, and, in egalitarian ensembles, where cues will be required (see *cuing,* below).

    c. As you play or sing in the solitude of your practice room, do your best to hear the inclusive sound. If the music is too complex for you to hear all of the parts mentally, sense one principal part, or perceive the overall feel of the music, especially at moments that cue your entrances.

    d. Picture your fellow musicians creating the music with you—make imaginary eye contact to accustom yourself to looking away from your stand.

    e. Position a metronome and a recorder at your side, and use them often. To verify your intonation, enlist a keyboard or an electronic tuner.

3. Rehearse strategically

The strategies involved in rehearsing ensemble music mirror those used to practice solo repertoire. That is, you progressively ripen pieces through the *new, developing,* and *performance material* zones (p. 6), working in sections, solving problems, refining interpretation, and steadily increasing tempo.

    a. When your group meets, adopt an organized but flexible rehearsal approach. Start each session with a verbal outline of how you'll proceed, but allow room in your timeline for unforeseen snags.

    b. Strike a balance between tackling small portions and executing multi-section spans. For instance, to identify problematic areas in a piece, your egalitarian group might run through a 32-measure span. Then, the group members would state which areas they found lacking, and you'd sort them out one after the other. You might practice tough bits sequentially, starting at the beginning of the span, or you could work on them in mixed order. To enhance efficiency, you might practice the less intricate passages before deconstructing the hardest spots. Another tack would be to start with segments that present rhythmic problems, followed by those that contain intonation challenges. At your subsequent rehearsal, however, invert the formula: Revisit the thorniest excerpts, and then execute the whole span. As large spans gel, do a trial run of the complete piece. When the music matures, schedule practice performances (p. 199).

c. Manage repetition as in solo practice (p. 51). If a phrase proves exceedingly tricky, rather than letting it consume your practice time, you may want to set it aside temporarily to work on other material. Then, to unravel the difficulties, instead of having everyone play or sing, try performing your parts in varied combinations: Listen to each other and share comments.

d. As interpretive developments unfold, mark your music. Keep a metronome handy as well, and regularly check your timing and tempos. It's also a good idea to record your rehearsals, and then make the recordings available for ensemble members to review.

e. Take breaks. If your repertoire isn't taxing, pause for a 10-minute breather after working for 50 minutes; with more intense material, stop for five minutes following 25 minutes of rehearsing. Also, be punctual about resuming work after timeouts—don't let breathers become occasions for long-winded socializing.

f. Finally, wrap up group sessions by discussing plans for upcoming rehearsals. Make sure that, before you disperse, everyone is clear about what, when, and where you'll rehearse next.

Igniting Synergy

Make the most seemingly insignificant part feel good for the rest of the ensemble.

—Wynton Marsalis, trumpeter and bandleader

Musical synergy ignites when collaborating musicians spark a creative fire that they could never kindle separately. Among egalitarian groups, the Beatles and the Guarneri String Quartet represent pinnacles of synergy. The Boston Symphony and the Count Basie Orchestra are models of synergistic leader-run groups. But you don't have to be a legendary musician to generate synergy in an ensemble. No matter how polished your group may be, the six topics explored here will help you lift your collective music making.

1. Set reachable goals

When you and your colleagues are driven to accomplish definite, near-term tasks, your rehearsals will crackle with intensity. So besides working toward a far-off ambition—such as a hoped-for concert tour—cook up smaller goals that test your abilities. Pick manageable music, delineate plans for each rehearsal, and arrange both formal and informal performances. The fusion of your inner musical zeal with tangible objectives will imbue your rehearsals with meaning.

> **Ignite Synergy**
>
> 1. Set reachable goals
> 2. Begin rehearsals with communal material
> 3. Balance leading with accompanying
> 4. Connect with a director
> 5. Transmit positive energy
> 6. Synchronize

2. Begin rehearsals with communal material

How you start rehearsals can facilitate or impede what follows. Getting under way with easy, communal material enables you and your partners to warm up, confirm your intonation, and renew your interlaced sound.

After tuning, you might play or sing unison scales or arpeggios, or you could run through a straightforward piece. As you do, blend your tone colors and timing, and set down a vibrant pulse. Even if you have scant rehearsal time and a full slate of music to cover, commence with routines that foster mindful attention, limber muscles, and heartfelt musical bonds.

3. Balance leading with accompanying

In most small-group situations, parts alternately play leading and accompanying roles. Think of a string quartet, for instance, performing music by Josef Haydn. The first violinist may often be in the lead, yet the other players will variably toss out responses to the violin, or they'll snatch the tune to drive the music onward. The same sorts of musical interactions occur in combos, vocal groups, and bands. Whatever the repertoire, collaborating musicians continually adjust their sounds to fit a composition's trajectory.

Immersing yourself in such musical interplay is an indescribable pleasure, and it's a cornerstone of synergy. As Wynton Marsalis says, one of your primary collaborative tasks is to make your part feel good for the other musicians in a group. Therefore, when you accompany, *listen* to your colleagues, and conform your tone, timing, volume, and vibrato to theirs. React in particular to the leader's sound, and become one with that person's phrasing. Then, when it's your turn to lead, show your partners the way. Only by being a strong leader and a receptive accompanist can you make ensemble music fly off the page.

4. Connect with a director

When working under a conductor or any group leader, your duty isn't merely to obey directions. Dynamic leader-run ensembles breathe life into music because the performers absorb a composition's content together with the director's interpretation.

To attain that apex of unity, on a practical level, maintain an unobstructed sightline, habitually look up at your conductor, and quickly assimilate instructions. If a cue or instruction isn't plain, politely ask for clarification. Artistically, let go of judgments about how you might shape a phrase differently and wholly engage with the music. In doing so, you'll draw the other ensemble members in and help inspire the attunement that makes synergy possible.

5. Transmit positive energy

Personal energy is contagious, more so in the close-knit setting of an ensemble. A glum player can bring a group down, and, conversely, a soulful musician can suffuse an ensemble with heart. If you become a beacon of creative strength, you can dispel negativity and uplift your colleagues.

To transmit positive emotions to your group, arrive early at rehearsals to warm up. Then restrict your warm-up material to either exercises or passages from the pieces that you're going to rehearse (it's discourteous and distracting to warm up with unrelated repertoire). As you rehearse, drench your part with spirit. Make the music so alive that your coperformers have no choice but to raise their games to your level.

Also keep up a sense of humor. Comedy writer Robert Orben said, "If you can laugh together, you can work together." Although collaborative music making is an intense activity, sprinkle in some good-natured quips. Your shared laughter will add to your musical relationship.

6. Synchronize

Ensemble performance centers on the synchronization of pitch, rhythm, and interpretation. Here I address two aspects of synchronizing: tuning and cuing.

Tuning

In instrumental ensembles, for the sake of efficiency, tune before the designated rehearsal start time. Have one instrument or tuning device give a reference pitch (typically an A-440), and let everyone tune to that same pitch. Then test your tuning intermittently throughout the rehearsal.

If you encounter intonation problems with any passages, apply focused solutions. "Good intonation is something one has to work for constantly," says cellist Yo-Yo Ma.[4] You might slow the tempo, repeat a brief segment, extract parts so that few musicians play or sing, or stop on a troublesome chord, sustain it, and then listen for which parts might be out of tune. It's also important to know how your part functions within a harmony, for instance, whether you have a chord tone or a dissonance and whether you're doubling another part. Prerehearsal score study will greatly help there. Take care, as well, to equalize your vibratos; if they conflict, even the most carefully tuned phrase can sound warped. Also experiment with tuning tough excerpts by reviewing them slowly without vibrato.

When you have access to a well-tuned piano, isolate difficult-to-tune parts, and assess them in unison with the keyboard. Alternatively, check intonation with an electronic tuner, but aim to hone your pitch sense such that your need for tuning support diminishes with time. Saxophonist Taimur Sullivan recommends using tuners that not only provide visual displays but also generate pitches.[5]

Last of all, a self-recorder is your most reliable intonation gauge. When you listen to a self-recording, you can pinpoint flaws that you might be missing as you execute. So record your rehearsals, as well as slices of your solo practice, and then listen with an analytical ear.

Cuing

With secure cuing skills, performers can communicate subtle musical gestures via precise body movements. For cuing to be effective, though, all of the musicians in an egalitarian group have to be proficient at cuing, and they need to know when cues are required in a composition and who will supply them.

To begin with, during your solo practice or in a preliminary group reading of a piece, identify the places where cues belong—cues are vital, for example, to line up entrances and cadences and to coordinate changes of tempo and meter. Then, in rehearsals, cooperatively decide who will cue each spot, and pencil reminders in your music.

When you lead a cue, connect with the music's tempo and mood, and inwardly hear how the parts will interact. Next, give a discreet but authoritative pulse by signaling with your body, your instrument, or both. Convey the spirit of the music through your body language, and make eye contact with your coperformers, if practical. When receiving a cue, look at the leader early, and harmonize your body movement. If a cue seems hard to follow, ask the cuing musician to count aloud and demonstrate how the rhythm and physical gestures correspond.

Fluency with cuing increases with practice, so rehearse cuing with your group and on your own. For instance, to brush up the cuing at a final cadence, your ensemble might repeat a closing phrase three times. Similarly, in your solitary practice, you could successively go over passages in which you lead cues. If cuing ever proves awkward, a mirror and video monitoring are potent learning aids. Also ask a teacher for help. Some rhythms are trickier to signal than others, and expert teachers know the secrets that untangle cuing dilemmas.

Forming a Musical Group

That was my gift, you know, having the ability to put certain guys together that would create a chemistry and then letting them go— letting them play what they knew, and above it.

—Miles Davis, trumpeter and bandleader

During your undergraduate years, most of the ensembles that you perform with are assembled by teachers. Nevertheless, students often create groups independently, and, upon graduating, many launch their own ensembles. This section, therefore, highlights strategies that will arm you to form successful groups both in and out of music school.

For starters, if you intend to found an ensemble, reflect on the following questions. Then discuss your plans with a teacher or mentor before you talk to prospective ensemble partners.

Questions for Prospective Collaborators

1. What are your individual goals as a musician, and how does your working with this group fit within your plans?
2. Will your ensemble exist for a finite term and then disband—perhaps as a student group—or will you and your colleagues collaborate indefinitely?
3. Will your ensemble be structured as an egalitarian or a leader-run group?
4. What styles of music will you perform, and how large a repertoire will you amass?
5. What levels of difficulty can you handle, and what titles might you learn first?
6. Where and when will you rehearse?
7. Where and how frequently will you perform?
8. Do you have commitments that could pose scheduling conflicts?
9. How will you meet any equipment needs?

10. How will you coordinate communications, transportation, and the various trappings of concert booking?

11. Will you arrange paying appearances, compose original material, or sell merchandise such as recordings? If so, how will your business affairs be managed (see below)?

12. What might your ensemble be named?

After you establish the parameters for a potential group, you're ready to single out musicians whose schedules, interests, and aptitudes are compatible with yours. To that end, before you and any peers seriously contemplate teaming up, verify that your calendars match, and then acquaint yourselves with each other's backgrounds; you might even exchange résumés and check out your respective references. If you haven't previously collaborated, set up some reading or improvisation sessions.

As you interact, be on the lookout for musical like-mindedness, professionalism, and behavioral red flags—bypass partnering with musicians who exhibit tardiness, underpreparation, rudeness, or dishonesty.

Once you've identified promising candidates, meet to determine whether you can arrive at a mutual vision of your future. Collectively review the preceding questions to clarify your aims and to sort through logistics. Confer long enough to make certain that all of the musicians concur with both the group's artistic intent and their individual duties. Future misunderstandings are bound to arise if it isn't made apparent at the outset who would be expected to do what.

Also, if you're attempting to form an egalitarian group but realize that the musicians you want to work with aren't prepared to shoulder nonmusical tasks, then you're probably better off creating a leader-run ensemble instead. Heading up a group, however, requires substantial administrative know-how. Unless you're a practiced leader, seek the counsel of a teacher or mentor before assuming directorship responsibilities.

With any fledgling ensemble, it's often worthwhile to stipulate a trial period during which the members consent to collaborate on an interim basis, maybe a single semester or season, after which they choose whether to continue their alliance. Such tryouts are routine with professional groups that phase in new members. For instance, a quartet planning to replace a departing member might hold auditions, hire a musician for a number of concerts, and then decide whether to invite that musician to become a permanent partner.

It's also imperative that collaborators address business matters. If your ensemble will produce income, recordings, musical arrangements, or compositions—or if you create a distinctive name or website—terms should be set down in a written agreement. Some performers may think that they don't need such documents, but if you neglect to detail your purpose, obligations, and rights, then you're asking for trouble.

For example, what if, six months into your partnership, one musician can't pull his weight? With an agreement, you'll have procedures on paper that state how a member could be asked to leave the group and what compensation, if any, he would receive. In another situation, suppose that you're part of a group that creates original arrangements or compositions: Who owns the rights to the material? Your agreement will spell that out. Otherwise, ownership won't be clear, and legal battles could be in your future over performance and recording rights, royalties, and more. Comparable disputes could emerge concerning the use of a group name or website.

It's far simpler to negotiate business terms at the founding of a partnership than at the end, when nerves can be raw. So get specialized advice to hammer things out—never execute contracts without expert guidance. You can obtain referrals for legal support from a mentor, a campus career office, the local musicians' union, an arts council, or a legal aid society such as California Lawyers for the Arts. Rather than sapping your artistry, an agreement will serve as the constitution of your ensemble's culture. It will help you do your best work.

The process of forming an ensemble draws on all of your musical, interpersonal, and professional skills. Then, once your coalition is born, you and your colleagues have to look after your culture to ensure that you thrive. Keep in mind, though, that group dynamics aren't easy to regulate, even among friends.

Many ensembles that start out amicably grow testy over time as one member ends up taking on more managerial tasks than anyone had predicted, another's musical tastes change, or an overeager performer tends to dominate rehearsals. If musicians don't discuss their feelings, resentments simmer and creativity dwindles. To ward off tensions in your ensemble, uphold professionalism, maintain open lines of communication, and see a teacher or mentor if you can't reconcile your differences. In that way, the musicians in your group can steer in a common direction.

Part II

Fearless Performance

Unmasking Performance Anxiety

In this chapter:

- The basic anxiety equation
- How anxiety affects musicians
- The three roots of performance anxiety
- Twelve strategies to craft confidence

Fearless Performance

You must play for the love of music. Perfect technique is not as important as making music from the heart.

—Mstislav Rostropovich, cellist and conductor

Envision yourself on stage, about to begin a performance. The audience falls silent; all eyes are on you. You launch your opening phrase and fill the space with music. As opposed to feeling edgy, you find that the concert setting focuses your mind and charges up your imagination. Your execution is exact; your sound radiates emotion. Both you and your listeners are transported.

Does that scenario depict your typical performance experience? If not, part II of *The Musician's Way* will set you on the path toward becoming a fearless, artistic performer. You'll see that confident performance isn't an elusive feat but involves knowledge and skills that any musician can learn. To get started, however, you first have to face up to the thing that chills the hearts of countless musicians: performance anxiety.

Unmasking Performance Anxiety

Nerves is a hard subject because nobody wants to talk about it.
—John Browning, pianist

- A singer walks on stage for a solo performance. Her mouth is dry, and her mind races with distracting thoughts. She fears that she might be unable to finish her song.
- A pianist starts to perform, but her hands shake so violently that she makes numerous errors. She's baffled because she played impeccably in the practice room.
- A trumpet player awaits his solo during an orchestra concert. "There's no way that I'll hit that high note," he tells himself. His entrance approaches, but he's so self-absorbed that he miscounts and comes in one measure early.

There's nothing like performing for a rapt audience. It can be one of the most magical experiences in a person's life. Or, as with the above three musicians, it can be fraught with angst. So although a musician's hard work can be most rewarded in a concert, in reality, almost every musician, at one time or another, has had run-ins with performance anxiety.

Still, not all performers grow to understand and master their nerves. Even among professionals, 25% claim to be impaired by stage fright.[1] To make matters worse, as John Browning suggests, many musicians add to their woes by refusing to confront the topic of performance anxiety at all.

This book doesn't turn away from the challenges or the enchantment of performing in public. On the contrary, I'll be asking you to reflect on the causes and effects of performance stress, and, most of all, develop countermeasures to anxiousness. Reading this chapter, you'll realize that you can figure out what activates your nerves and that you can prevail over difficulties. Then, in chapters 8–11, you'll find tools to help you become the self-assured performer that you're meant to be.

The Basic Anxiety Equation

The battle isn't with the instrument; it's with oneself.
—Vincent Cichowicz, trumpeter

Anxiety is a natural response to a perceived threat; it stems from the drive for self-preservation. For instance, when you walk across a road that's teeming with trucks and cars, you're in more danger than when you stroll through your living room. You aren't anxious in your home, but when crossing the busy street you become alert and cautious—your pulse accelerates, and your energy surges as you prepare to dodge the vehicles. Navigating the roadway makes you a bit anxious, and that innate response keeps you safe.

The arousal that erupts in the face of danger has a name: the fight-or-flight response. It originates in a primeval part of the brain and is wired to be set off quickly, without needing to be processed by thinking. When that response fires, adrenaline pours into your bloodstream. You're then ready to defend yourself vigorously or flee in a heartbeat.

The fight-or-flight response works wonders when you're standing on a sidewalk and a piano is falling from a building above. Someone yells, "Watch out!" and before you even know what's happening, you've leapt out of the way. The piano will need some attention, but you're unscathed. Your pounding heart and shaking limbs will settle down soon.

When a piano is poised safely on a stage, however, and you're about to meet it on friendlier terms to play a concert, then the fight-or-flight response can pose a problem. The part of your brain that instinctively protects you from danger doesn't discriminate. It sends out the adrenaline rush whenever you feel fear, irrespective of whether you're afraid of becoming a grill ornament on a truck or you're scared of performing badly.

Psychologist Stephen D. Curtis says, "The most important psychological contributor to the onset of performance anxiety is a performer's concern for, or fear of, the outcome of the performance: that is, the performer's thoughts become focused on an imagined negative outcome or failure."[2] If you're afraid at a concert, your fight-or-flight response will be joining you on stage. To reduce fight-or-flight activation, you have to manage fear. Adrenaline isn't all bad, though—a small jolt heightens the senses. Hence, musicians perform best when they're moderately keyed up. But if you cross the line that separates exhilaration from dread, then performing can turn into a battle. So, to distinguish the arousal that subverts performers from the types that bolster music making, in this book, the labels "performance anxiety" and "stage fright" refer to nervousness or distress that interferes with performing; performance *excitement* signifies arousal that aids performing.

That, however, is only the most straightforward part of the performance anxiety equation. Adrenaline-fueled jitters may strike on the day of a show, but other forms of anxiety can affect musicians before, during, and after a concert.

Anxiety's Effects

The devastation of stage fright is merciless. It leaves a wake of deso-lation, both physical and mental, not to talk of the horrors of artis-tic frustration.

—Kato Havas, violinist and teacher

Although anxiety is a normal part of life, the effects of performance anxiety vary widely among individuals. Whether you deal with mild uneasiness or you're trying to overcome a major handicap, it's useful to learn about the range of effects and pinpoint those that pertain to you. You'll then be primed to address current problems, and you can nip future ones in the bud.

I've found it useful to think of the effects of performance anxiety accord-ing to how they play out across three phases: preperformance, at-performance, and postperformance. During any of these phases, anxiety can disturb a musician's body, mind, emotions, and behaviors.

Preperformance Effects

Preperformance effects are those that occur in the days and weeks leading up to an event and also include those that plague musicians on an ongoing basis. The most obvious of these effects are behavioral. Anxious musicians often avoid practicing because heading to the practice room forces them to face their fears. Such procrastination is anxiety made plain. When avoidant per-formers have the chance to do something diverting, they don't hesitate; when the option comes to practice, they may decide that the dog needs a bath.

Some procrastinators display excessive busyness or disorganization be-cause the self-created maelstrom shields them from having to sort out their performance problems. Others act out by taking little action at all; they lazily watch TV, surf the Net, or otherwise accomplish nothing. They may feel fa-tigued but not know why. Some even turn to drugs and alcohol.

Plenty of musicians, however, don't put things off; instead, they practice obsessively. When a concert looms, they may disappear into practice rooms and emerge only when nature calls. Many push past their physical limits and wind up on the injured list.

Along with these behavioral effects, anxious performers endure mental and emotional consequences—such as worry and distorted thinking—that cause a concert's significance to be blown out of proportion. Troubled musi-cians might also grow depressed and then have difficulty focusing in practice. Others wrestle with stomach upset, loss of appetite, headaches, or insomnia. Music students who undergo such effects frequently find themselves in aca-

Table 7.1 **Preperformance Effects**

1. Avoidance of practice
2. Obsessive practice
3. Busyness/disorganization
4. Depression/fatigue/laziness
5. Worry/distorted thinking
6. Headaches
7. Insomnia
8. Difficulty focusing
9. Stomach upset/loss of appetite
10. Trouble with relationships
11. Academic decline
12. Substance abuse

demic jams as papers go unfinished or studying gets pushed aside. And when musicians become too distraught to relate positively with others, their relationships may crumble.

Selected preperformance effects are charted in table 7.1. Make check marks next to those that apply to you; add extra checks to the ones that affect you strongly. In the page margins, note any additional effects that might be impeding your creativity.

At-Performance Effects

At-performance effects are those that flare up shortly before a show begins and continue throughout a concert. They primarily surface backstage and on stage, but, for some musicians, these effects turn up anytime that performing crosses their minds. In this phase, the main culprit is the fight-or-flight response.

Most people recognize the physical effects of at-performance stress. From cold, shaking hands to a racing heart to a dry mouth, these reactions can travel throughout a performer's body. Musicians may also experience muscle tension, commonly in the neck and shoulders. Others sweat profusely. Many get butterflies, and, for a few, the butterfly effect is so pronounced that they vomit backstage. All in all, the physical effects don't make for a feeling of technical security.

Mental, behavioral, and emotional effects include confusion, agitation, and fear—especially fear of embarrassment—and these set the stage for memory lapses and negative self-talk. The fight-or-flight response also amplifies sensitivity, so nervous musicians might become distracted by bodily

Table 7.2 **At-Performance Effects**

Physical/Behavioral Effects	Mental/Emotional Effects
1. Trembling	1. Fear
2. Cold hands	2. Confusion
3. Racing heartbeat	3. Memory lapses
4. Heavy perspiration	4. Distorted thinking
5. Nausea/butterflies/wooziness	5. Agitation
6. Muscle tension	6. Hypersensitivity
7. Technical insecurity	7. Negative self-talk
8. Rapid or restricted breathing	8. Shame
9. Dry mouth	9. Anger
10. Urge to urinate	10. Panic

sensations: Shoes could suddenly seem too tight; a shirt may prompt an itch. One of the more sinister effects, though, is distorted thinking. Edgy musicians might make small errors and then interpret them as ruinous to a performance. Or, before going on stage, they may doubt their abilities and run mental movies of the catastrophes about to befall them. Shame, anger, and panic can then ensue.

Table 7.2 lists twenty at-performance effects. Again, mark those that you've felt, and log any others that you recall. Plenty of musicians will check all twenty items—not because something is wrong with them but because these are the routine repercussions of the fight-or-flight response. Remember that anxiousness in the face of danger is normal. When you develop the skills to cope with fear on stage, the disconcerting effects of anxiety will subside.

Postperformance Effects

After a concert ends, anxious musicians are seldom level headed in their evaluations. Distorted thinking takes center stage here as performers disparage themselves over minor imperfections. In their confusion, many misattribute the causes of their slips. For instance, instead of acknowledging that a memory gap arose due to an oversight in practice, flustered musicians will tell themselves that they're untalented and hopeless. As audience members come backstage to offer their congratulations, such performers might feel shame and maybe even anger and hostility.

Later, once they've cooled off, these frustrated performers may become depressed; some will numb their pain with drugs or alcohol. They may skirt practicing, thereby causing their insecurities to mount. As one concert recedes

Table 7.3 **Postperformance Effects**

1. Distorted thinking
2. Shame
3. Anger/hostility
4. Misattribution
5. Avoidance of practice
6. Depression/fatigue
7. Persistent insomnia
8. Trouble with relationships
9. Academic decline
10. Substance abuse

into memory and another appears on the horizon, the postperformance effects blend into the preperformance ones. The result is a chronic anxiousness that taints artistry and life in general.

Performance anxiety, therefore, isn't just about overt nervousness and the fight-or-flight response. When musicians lack methods to deal with anxiousness and when deficiencies in their practice and performance skills prevent them from preparing thoroughly for concerts, performance stress can undermine all aspects of their lives.

In table 7.3, check any of the postperformance effects that you've noticed in the hours, days, and weeks after you complete a show.

Although the abovementioned effects are prevalent, each nervous performer undergoes a personal constellation of symptoms. While one musician shakes and sweats on stage, another will avert physical instability but be racked by confusion and memory slips. Whatever the effects, when adrenaline combines with fear and a scarcity of skills to counter anxiousness, musicians find themselves in a bind. "One of the most troublesome features of anxiety," wrote psychologists Paul Salmon and Robert Meyer, "is the way it can spiral out of control in the absence of corrective, regulatory feedback."[3]

As you learn to recognize how anxiety manifests in your life, you can cultivate healthy responses. Then the electricity of preparing for and presenting performances will become a positive force that will power you to loftier heights of creativity. For example, if you know that one of your preperformance tendencies is to sidestep practice, then, when your practice time nears and you notice an odor coming from the dog, you can get busy with your artistic work rather than reaching for the canine shampoo. Musicians who don't offset their restlessness habitually feed their anxieties. Their dogs may smell fresh, but their productivity and happiness wane.

Knowing how performance stress affects you is a decisive step. But for you to conquer anxiousness, you need a deeper understanding of its causes. You might be bothered by a few effects or a cauldron of problems. In any event, to stop anxiety from getting in your way, you have to get to the root of any troubles.

The Roots of Performance Anxiety

No matter how much I rehearsed, I never felt ready for the stage. Instead, I felt like a deer stumbling into oncoming traffic on a dark road.

—Shannon Sexton, singer and writer

In *Psychology for Performing Artists,* Glenn Wilson traces the roots of performance anxiety to a three-pronged source: a person's nature, the task at hand, and the performance situation.[4] In essence, some people have personalities or histories that make them more prone to anxiety. Plus, the trickier any given material is for a musician to bring off, the more stressful it becomes to present that material in public. Third, some performance situations are inherently more demanding than others—an out-of-town audition, for instance, exerts greater pressure than a casual performance for friends.

Here, using Wilson's three-part framework, I've catalogued the primary instigators of performance anxiety. Included are causes cited by Wilson and other psychologists, as well as those that I've observed in music students.

> **The Roots of**
> **Performance Anxiety**
> • Person
> • Task
> • Situation

Personal Causes

1. *General anxiousness:* When musicians are anxious as a rule or if they have low arousal thresholds, they're usually rocked by performance nerves. Certain individuals are wired such that their fight-or-flight response is readily provoked. They have to acquire more antianxiety moves than the laid-back types, who aren't easily stirred up.

2. *Fear of evaluation:* Performance is a high-exposure setting in which listeners evaluate from moment to moment. Musicians who view evaluations as threatening will feel jeopardized when they play or sing, and

their brains will shift into fight-or-flight overdrive. Such performers can adjust their perceptions, however, so that performing becomes an occasion for sharing and not one tinged with judgment.

3. *History of stage nerves:* Musicians with histories of nervousness have anxious habits that follow them from one concert to the next. Compared to musicians with mostly positive performances behind them, long-anxious performers typically need to do more work to form reliable on-stage skills.

4. *Shyness:* Some people are gregarious and love to be with a crowd; others prefer to keep to themselves. Musicians who are less at ease in social situations may encounter higher levels and different kinds of performance stress than those with outgoing dispositions. Their coping strategies, therefore, must be tailored to their personalities. For example, they may need to do extra preconcert planning and curb backstage conversation.

Task-Related Causes

1. *Overly challenging repertoire:* If musicians select or receive music that's beyond their capacities, they've got a prescription for an on-stage dilemma. For musicians to develop confidence as performing artists, only manageable material will do.

2. *Insufficient practice:* When performers are handed music at the last minute or don't practice effectively, the shortage of preparation decreases their mastery and ratchets up their stress levels.

3. *Weak practice skills:* Practice habits, more than anything else, make performers who they are on stage. Without the expertise to learn music deeply, as described in part I, on-stage security eludes musicians. Then, no matter how simple the material, they won't possess the foundations to perform successfully.

4. *Lack of performance skills:* Similar to a deficit in practice skills, if musicians aren't polished at presenting themselves in concert or don't know how to allay the effects of the fight-or-flight response, performing can be grueling. When performance techniques are mastered, the thrill of being under the spotlights propels musicians to pinnacles of artistry.

Situational Causes

1. *Difficult circumstances:* If tour vans arrive late, heating fails, or weak lighting obscures performers' music, the trying circumstances multiply

performance stresses. Similarly, grumpy stand partners and belligerent conductors can make musicians jumpy. Nonetheless, musicians can nurture a skill set that allows them to adapt to virtually any situation.

2. *Public scrutiny:* Public performance opens musicians up to intense scrutiny. If they aren't prepared to take charge on stage, then contact with an attentive audience can make them unsteady.

3. *High degree of concern:* The greater the concern for the outcome of a performance, the more stressful the performance situation becomes. If prizes, esteem, or finances are at risk—say, at the likes of auditions, competitions, and recording sessions—nervousness is more likely. However, when musicians learn how to plan for high-stakes situations, they can practice and perform without anxiety setting them back.

4. *Poor self-care:* Those musicians who don't manage their preconcert rest, diet, and other personal needs unwittingly assemble the conditions for discomfort and underperformance. Adept performers take care of themselves so that they're brimming with energy and enthusiasm on stage.

To illustrate how a few of these causes and effects shape artists' lives, the next section recounts the stories of three musicians who sought my guidance to help them alleviate common sorts of performance anxiety.

Portraits of Anxious Performers

I don't have much of a feel for performing. When I think of performing, I think of being so nervous you want to throw up. That's what performing means to me.

—Art Garfunkel, singer

Portrait 1: Anxious avoidance

"I did everything the book said," Karen lamented, referring to her effort to apply the advice of a psychologist-author. "But when I got to the audition, none of it worked. I was as nervous as ever, I played badly, and I went home a wreck."

"Did any of the ideas help?" I asked.

"Let's see," she mused. "I flew in the day before, rehearsed at the audition site, and ate well. I tried to psych myself up with positive thoughts, but as I walked on stage, I felt shaky and tense—my mind was scurrying all over the place. I'd have to say that none of it helped at all."

"Why do you suppose that is?"

"I guess I need a different approach," she concluded. "Or maybe I should have given it more time."

"Given what more time?"

"The mental-training exercises in the book," she said. "Maybe I didn't do them long enough."

"Aren't you leaving something out?" I asked skeptically.

"I don't think so," she replied.

"You're talking about mental-skills training," I explained, "but you aren't saying a word about your musical preparation. How far in advance did you start learning the repertoire?"

"I'm busy," she said. "I never have much to time prepare. I began practicing in earnest ten days before the audition."

"Ten days?" I repeated. "Was that enough time to be in command of the material?"

"Not really. I guess I should've gotten to it sooner. But I'm always running around like crazy ahead of auditions. There never seems to be time to practice."

Karen, it appeared, would do anything to assuage her nerves except for the one thing that she knew would be effective: practice. Two years earlier, she had graduated with a master's degree from a top conservatory, and now she was supposedly striving to win a full-time orchestra position. The instant an audition date was set, however, she'd occupy herself with myriad projects, and practicing would move to the bottom of her list. Her procrastination guaranteed that she was never suitably prepared to play well.

I suggested that, to break the anxiety pattern, she had to make practice her first priority—for instance, by getting up early and keeping to a practice schedule. I also urged her to speak to a therapist to uncover the reasons for her avoidance. Rather than meeting her problem head-on, though, Karen chose to stop going to auditions and to pursue teaching and gardening instead. In the end, her unwillingness to confront her preperformance anxiety scuttled her orchestral career.

Portrait 2: Distorted thinking

"I'm dreading this concert," admitted Alex, a freshman music major getting ready for an end-of-year class recital. "Even though I've worked out most of my performance problems, this show has me worried."

"What makes this concert different?" I asked.

"My grandparents are coming," he said, "and they've never heard me play in a recital. They're not supportive of my decision to major in music; they were expecting me to go into engineering. But if they see me shine, they might help me pay for college."

Although Alex had a scholarship, his college fees were significant. Recently his parents had told him that, without supplemental financial aid, the family wouldn't be able to foot the bill for the coming year. Alex had now taken his family's financial plight upon himself. He believed that this one performance could make or break his education.

"Did your grandparents say that they'd pay the bills if you do well at this concert?" I asked.

"No, but if I impress them they might change their minds about me."

"One performance will cause your grandparents to change?"

"I see where you're going," he said. "I probably sound stupid."

"Not at all," I replied. "You're feeling acute financial pressure. Let's look at this from another angle. Do your grandparents go to concerts or play music themselves?"

"They never go to concerts," he claimed. "Maybe they hear music in church, but that's it."

"So will they know the difference whether you play brilliantly or you just have an average day?"

"I guess not."

"Even at your worst on stage, you can still keep going, right?"

"Sure," he said. "I can fake my way out of anything."

"Then assuming that you're poised as you play, the quality of your performance won't matter," I proposed. "Your grandparents will have the same experience regardless."

"I see what you mean," he concurred.

As we talked, Alex realized not only that his grandparents would enjoy rather than judge his concert but also that he couldn't change their opinions of the music profession any more than they could diminish his passion for music. Whether they assisted with his college fees was their decision. Neither this performance nor any other action he might take would sway them. At the upcoming recital, his role was to perform as well as he could, and what others thought was not under his control.

By clearing up the mental distortion, Alex let go of his inflated concerns, reversed the stressful situation that he had created for himself, and took pleasure in his final preparations. He delivered a solid performance, and the financial impasse was later resolved when his grandparents, seeing how happy he was, opted to chip in for his tuition costs.

Portrait 3: Lack of skills

Camille was a 19-year-old amateur pianist who excelled in school but was petrified to play in public. Her anxiety had surfaced in childhood, when she was compelled to play at her teacher's annual recital. At her first performance, when she was eight years old, she had two harrowing false starts but some-how got through her piece. In subsequent years, her hands, cold and shaking, would be too unruly to control. She would forget her music and occasionally couldn't finish a piece without breaking down.

After each concert, her tears would be met with cheering words, but by the time she turned 13, performing had become intolerable. She quit the piano until her junior year of high school, when she began playing informally on her own. In college, she majored in English, and, coincidentally, I was teach-ing at her university. She attended one of my performance seminars and then signed up to study with me privately.

How could a straight-A student like Camille fall victim to debilitating stage fright? As it turned out, the anxiety that had welled up at that initial recital was seeded by her unqualified instructor. Think about it: Camille per-formed once a year. Such a dearth of exposure to performance situations almost guarantees anxiety. Worse yet, she hadn't developed the rich prepa-ration skills that underpin secure performance; she merely repeated music mindlessly in practice until it came out by reflex.

In light of Camille's inadequate mastery of her material, her inexperience with performance situations, and her high-achieving personality, her anxi-ety wasn't surprising. That is, everyone expected her to perform admirably, yet she didn't have the requisite abilities to do so. Any performer in her shoes would be skittish. Sadly, like most students with her history, Camille mis-takenly thought that something was wrong with her and that it couldn't be fixed.

As a college student, however, Camille had access to the information that she needed. She began to practice deeply and memorize securely. Then, by playing simple pieces in my weekly performance class, she acquired on-stage skills: She learned to direct her mind and open her heart; she cultivated tech-niques to rein in fight-or-flight responses; she tamed a nagging perfectionism. Progressively, her hands stopped trembling, and her memory became reli-able. She grew into an expressive performer who could handle any remain-ing nerves. With her love of music rekindled, she enrolled in lessons with a piano professor and later graduated with a minor in piano performance.

These portraits offer glimpses into how anxiety can erode musicians' artistry, but such problems aren't exclusive to students and budding professionals. Some of history's best-known performers have been tormented by nerves. "Ever since I began to perform I have lived with stage fright," said cellist Pablo Casals. "I suffered when I was a child and I suffer even today when I must give a concert."[5] In the quotation that heads this section, Art Garfunkel attributes his anxiety to the absence of a "feel for performing," implying that nothing can be done and that anxiety is his fate.

No performers should resign themselves to debilitating anxiety. If you suffer from nerves, whether moderate or severe, don't surrender to any of the folklore about it being an incurable burden. You can triumph over its limiting effects and be the performer that you aspire to be. But it won't happen overnight.

Performance anxiety doesn't yield to band-aid solutions, nor does it abate on its own. It takes patient effort to reverse anxious habits, especially long-held ones, and replace them with secure knowledge and skill. Some students have the good fortune to study with teachers who supply them with essential know-how. Many don't. Other musicians, like Karen, need more than skills; they have unconscious anxieties that are best figured out with the support of a therapist. Whatever the case, all musicians can sift through their performance issues and come out the better for it—if they choose to do the work.

Crafting Confidence

Your central tasks are finding inner peace and strength, on the one hand, and being very well-prepared for your performances, on the other.

—Eric Maisel, author and psychologist

If you grapple with performance nerves, then I suspect that you've heard plenty of clichéd advice. "Just perform as much as you can," goes one refrain, "you'll get the hang of it." But as current research reveals, that conventional wisdom about beating stage fright doesn't ring true—approximately 25% of collegiate and professional musicians live with disabling performance anxiety; a larger percentage contend with less crippling but still unpleasant symptoms.[6] If you're looking to curtail nervous interference, then repeating what you've always done isn't going to bring new results.

To craft confidence, you need specific skills to generate the inner strength and thorough preparation that Eric Maisel refers to. Without such proficiency, you won't be equipped to be secure in concert. Author Frank R. Wilson echoes this point: "Confident performance is not a fluke, but the product of imaginative and consistent synthesis of technical and emotional work."[7]

This section provides an overview of 12 strategies for developing security on stage—four in each of the categories of person, task, and situation. Then, the ensuing chapters show how to enact these strategies. In other words, here I highlight what you need to do and why; the subsequent pages describe how to move forward. To wrap up this chapter, I touch on the subject of performance-anxiety medications and cite avenues for getting help with anxiety problems.

Personal Strategies

1. Develop positive responses to stress

Every musician needs a range of tactics to manage the causes and effects of performance stress. Whether you're affected before, during, or after a show, you have to get to know your issues and explore various responses until you have a fully stocked antianxiety toolkit. Then you can rid yourself of many anxious habits and trim the influence of others.

In contrast, musicians who ignore their anxieties are like carpenters whose only tools are hammers—problems get pounded into the subconscious background rather than being brought into the open and rebuilt. Such musicians put up with vulnerable interior construction. Even mild buffeting from stress can provoke a collapse.

2. Affirm meaning in performing

To get up in front of an audience and bare your soul, you must believe in the power of music and in your ability to perform eloquently. When you trust that your music making isn't merely adept but also makes a difference in your life and in the lives of others, you can celebrate your role as a performing artist. However, musicians who are conflicted about performing undercut themselves with ambivalence, which drains their confidence and makes soulful performance unlikely.

3. Refine your self-evaluation skills

To make prudent choices about how to prepare for concerts, musicians have to be keen self-evaluators. Not only does accurate evaluation lead to artistic and technical improvement, but psychologists Mitchell Robin and Rochelle Balter state, "Research has shown that people who think more clearly tend to experience less emotional disturbance than those who do not."[8] Your assessment skills, therefore, will impact your anxiety level. For instance, if you correctly determine that you fumbled during a solo performance because you started at too quick a tempo, you'll practice setting tempos more reliably, and your confidence will grow. Conversely, the musicians who misattribute the causes of their troubles make futile attempts to advance. Their abilities don't evolve, and their anxieties may even worsen.

4. Safeguard your health

Music making calls for mental, physical, and emotional vigor. To be an agile artist, you have to keep up wholesome practice habits and establish a self-care rhythm. At the same time, when health problems crop up, whether physical or psychological, you need to seek assistance promptly so that minor concerns don't escalate into dire predicaments. The statistics on musicians' wellness indicate that many performers don't excel in the self-care department. For you to reach your full potential, health maintenance needs to be front and center every day.

Task-Oriented Strategies

1. Choose accessible repertoire

Accessible repertoire is the rocket fuel of performance development. If you want to overcome nervousness and be masterful on stage, the music you perform must not overshoot your capacity. Accessible material leaves you with the mental, physical, and emotional space to experiment with performance techniques and forge secure habits.

By comparison, students who insist on excessively demanding music become inundated at concerts. With their brains maxed out by just getting the notes, they perform on the edge of a precipice. In place of building security, they shore up their anxieties.

2. Acquire comprehensive practice skills

When you're able to learn music deeply (see part I), your awareness creates a framework that's resistant to pressure. You can then trust in your preparation and spontaneously express yourself in performance. In fact, the excitement of a concert will aid you by releasing just enough adrenaline to uplift your spirits but not so much that it makes you jittery. Without inclusive preparation, musicians can't be cool in high-stakes situations.

3. Govern your practice schedule

Sensible preparation timelines, explained in chapter 11, will ensure that you have plenty of time for pieces to mature before you present them publicly. Also, as discussed in chapter 1, consistent practice yields the most dependable habits. It's vital, therefore, that you devise a practice schedule that optimizes your learning.

4. Reinforce performance habits

The habits that enable you to perform expressively in public can only be instilled through practice. So, whenever you make music, embody *habits of excellence* (p. 20). As hornist Philip Farkas wrote, "Our object is to *minimize* the contrast between studio practice and public performance."[9]

Even so, many students are cavalier about their practice customs. Some let their minds wander, while others emphasize mechanical repetition. It's no surprise, then, that mental focus eludes them on stage or they revert to sounding sterile when they're on the spot. Veteran performers reject such nonmusical habits—they correlate everything they do in practice with their creative intentions in concert.

Situational Strategies

1. Acclimate to performance settings

To perform a concert, you require much more than musical preparation. You also need skills to ready yourself backstage and to handle performing under bright lights and intense stares. By doing practice performances in diverse surroundings, you can accustom yourself to concert environments and feel at home on stage. The musicians who evade performing, however, are likely to be thrown off balance by the variability of performance situations.

2. Build up presentation skills

When you can project a robust presence from the stage, both you and your listeners will reap greater satisfaction from your performances. Public interaction will then inspire your creativity instead of making you uneasy.

3. Learn performance-enhancing techniques

The coming chapters outline ways to boost your self-assurance before the public. As you try out those techniques in practice performances, you'll discover how to stay centered, lessen fight-or-flight responses, and retain control. In time, the tactics you perfect will inoculate you to most situational pressures.

4. Get organized

Concerts, auditions, and recording sessions call for extensive planning. As chapter 8 demonstrates, tools such as preperformance inventories make it simpler to prepare without turmoil. Careful organization will also guarantee that you're rested and strong when the stage door opens. If musicians can't coordinate their preparations, however, performance situations become exceedingly stressful.

❦

On top of the preceding 12 strategies, some musicians have turned to a class of medications called beta blockers to alleviate anxious symptoms. Whatever you may have heard about beta blockers, be aware that they are potent prescription drugs that are usually taken for heart ailments, and they shouldn't be used except under the supervision of a medical doctor. They can have dangerous side effects, especially for people with asthma and diabetes. If an acquaintance offers you a beta blocker, don't accept it. Only a physician can determine whether such drugs are safe for you to use. Furthermore, it's illegal for prescription drugs to be distributed by anyone other than a licensed physician or pharmacist.

Beta blockers get their name from the fact that they block adrenaline from binding to beta receptors in the body. They prevent the physical effects and, therefore, some of the behavioral effects of the fight-or-flight response. They don't directly alter the mental and emotional consequences, although they can have a secondary impact. For instance, an anxious musician taking the beta blocker Inderal might be mentally agitated and find his thoughts racing, but, by and large, he won't have the shakes, a rapid heartbeat, or butterflies. In tandem, the easing of such physical symptoms may help him feel calmer.

Beta blockers are not appropriate for students who are just beginning to learn performance skills. Nor are they a substitute for addressing the underlying fears that cause fight-or-flight overload in the first place. For mature musicians, though, with intractable physical symptoms from performance anxiety or for those with extreme physical effects, many leading physicians find that beta blockers can be safe and effective.[10] I share that view. But as an educator, when working with college-age students, I regard the use of beta blockers more as a temporary aid or a last resort than as a core strategy. Additional facts concerning beta blockers are available at *musiciansway.com.*

Other drugs that mitigate persistent anxiety—for example, Xanax and Valium—are not recommended for performance problems and are hazardous if used improperly.[11] Doctors prescribe such medications to people with generalized anxiety conditions. Musicians should steer clear of those treatments unless a physician determines that they're necessary.

❦

Bear in mind that security in performance doesn't result from purging all nervous symptoms. It arises from knowing that you can perform well whether you feel jumpy or not. As you gain facility with performance skills, you should undergo less stress overall and be equipped to cope with any unrest that remains. Still, stress in life can't be eliminated. Actually, much of the time, stress itself isn't the issue. It's how you *react* to stress that determines whether its effect is positive or negative.

Expert performers understand what ignites their anxieties, and they always have coping mechanisms to call on. They experience arousal at a show, but it's largely of a constructive type that gets them fired up to perform. If detrimental effects emerge, they initiate countermoves that transform tension into enthusiasm. And when they need to offset pre- or postconcert worries, they take action and don't succumb.

You can be that competent in your own self-management, but you must uphold the conviction that anxiety troubles have solutions. Mild-to-moderate nervousness is commonplace under stressful circumstances and can ordinarily be toned down by using the techniques presented in this book. Musicians with more severe anxiety, however, will need further assistance.

If anxiousness sabotages your performances, act now. For help with task-related and situational skills, study the upcoming information, and consult a reputable music teacher. For guidance on personal matters, read the following chapters, and make an appointment with a licensed therapist. Therapists are available at campus health centers; physicians can also make referrals. Bring this book to your first session.

Many elite musicians have succeeded with the aid of therapists, among them pianist Claudio Arrau. "As a young man, I wasn't very sure of myself," Arrau said. "I had doubts about all sorts of things. So I went through analysis. I found an absolutely marvelous psychiatrist. Through analysis, I began to unfold and push aside my handicaps. . . . I was able to move forward with my playing and career."[12]

You can't rid yourself of the possibility of becoming anxious at a performance or in your everyday existence. But you can temper your anxiety and have multiple coping strategies standing by. In due course, with intelligent effort, performance anxiety and all of its effects can cease to be an inhibiting factor in your life. Public performance will then be one of your greatest pleasures.

8

Becoming a Performing Artist, I

In this chapter:

- Teaching and learning performance skills
- The five facets of performance preparation
- Preperformance routines
- Backstage techniques

Becoming a Performing Artist

Music is a performing art. . . . It isn't there in the score.

—Michael Tippett, composer

When you think about all that goes into preparing for a concert, performing can seem like a delicate skill, something akin to tightrope walking. I've found that many musicians think along those lines. But I'm convinced that performing can be as natural as having a conversation or sharing in a game. Even beginners can perform confidently, provided that the task is simple, the situation is friendly, and their intentions are wholesome.

For example, almost any novice pianist, in her initial lesson, is able to learn a four-measure melody involving three different pitches. Then, with her teacher as the audience, she can perform the tune. No pressure; no big deal. She enjoys expressing the music similar to the way she might take pleasure in tossing a ball.

That might seem like an obvious first-lesson format: The student learns an excerpt or an exercise and then performs. After all, it's a music teacher's job to teach music performance, so what else would you expect? Unfortunately, that's not how all lessons play out. Teachers may instead devote months to hand positions, scales, and score reading, deferring performance issues for later: "Once students are ready." What nonsense.

If performance is the goal of music study, and it is, then performance skills—such as how pieces are begun and concluded on stage—should be woven into every lesson. All music students should go into their teachers' studios knowing that what they're about to do relates to the big picture of connecting with listeners. When teachers deprive students of performance education, they do them a terrible disservice because the omission doesn't just create a knowledge gap; it also instills performance anxiety.

Anxiety takes hold because, if performance skills are ignored in lessons, then when a student eventually steps on stage, she won't have a clue how to maintain control, much less how to be an artistic communicator. As far as the student knows, she should be able to perform well. That's what everyone, including her teacher, seems to believe. But lacking familiarity with performance situations and with the allied personal and task-centered strategies discussed in chapter 7, the unprepared student becomes debilitated when her arousal escalates, and then nervous habits set in.

Her plight is analogous to that of an aspiring athlete who enrolls in private basketball training, never plays a game, and is suddenly called on to compete in a five-on-five tournament. No sensible coach would ever teach basketball that way, yet that's how multitudes of music educators run their studios. That is, unsuspecting students might attend music lessons for as much as a year, without any performance training or experience, and then they'll be pushed on stage for an annual recital where they get crushed by anxiety.

With the information that you pick up in this book, you can avoid being a perpetrator of such nonteaching. And if performance stress currently compromises your artistry, these pages will supply you with tools that will enable you to perform fearlessly.

This chapter looks into the nature of performing and sorts out the constituents of concert preparation. Chapter 9 offers ideas for crafting a stage presence and harnessing on-stage energy. Chapter 10 covers ways to deal with errors, practice performing, and evaluate your progress. Chapter 11 addresses the topics of programming, auditioning, recording, and more.

My aim is to help you cultivate the knowledge, skills, and attitudes you need to develop into an unhindered performing artist. No matter what your past performance experiences may have been, it's my conviction that, by taking the appropriate steps, you can acquire the ability to get up in front of people and unleash your musical soul.

The Heart of Performance

> *Every performance is different. That's the beauty of it.*
> —Van Morrison, singer-songwriter

To reach the heart of performance, let's start by defining what a performance is. Consider this: When you play or sing for someone else, you're performing, and when you're alone in a recording studio trying to lay down a clean track, you're performing then, too. The presence of an audience isn't the deciding factor in defining a performance. The difference between performing and other types of music making is that, in a performance situation, there are stakes involved in how well you play or sing. Those stakes may be personal or professional, but the higher the stakes become—for instance, when you're performing at a prestigious hall, auditioning for a lucrative job, or recording at a pricey studio—the greater the potential for stress and anxiety.

Here I focus on performing in what is arguably the highest-stake setting of all, the formal concert presented by either a soloist or a small ensemble. I zero in on concerts for two reasons. First, by learning the skills required to prepare for concerts and to perform on stage, you'll be equipped with the basics to perform anywhere. Second (and more important), a performance can occur with or without people listening, but the heart of performance is about sharing music with someone else.

Almost everyone feels the urge to share music. For example, when you discover an impressive recording, don't you want a friend to hear it, too? If you make a recording, isn't the point to set down music in a format that's easy to circulate? And what is it that drives you to spend all of those hours practicing anyway? The impulse to commune through music is so widespread that it seems innate. It burns strongly enough to cause musicians to practice for years, and it prompts listeners to endure expense and inconvenience to converge on performance venues.

A concert represents the summit of this yearning for musical communion. A concert hall is like a shrine that people turn to for something that they can't get anywhere else. It's a place where both performers and listeners can experience music in a way that's personal, communal, and unpredictable. The spontaneity and collective energy catch fire to a degree that some performances leave indelible memories.

You can learn to put on unforgettable concerts. First, however, you have to master a broad range of skills. A beginner may be able to perform casually in a lesson, but for you to achieve your promise as a performing artist, you need a profound understanding of performance preparation.

The Five Facets of Preparation

Elite performers plan assiduously and prepare in depth before, during, and after their performances.
—Shirlee Emmons and Alma Thomas, performance coaches

When you schedule a performance, it kicks your preparation into gear. That preparation will center on practicing, of course, but successful concerts aren't the product of practice alone. Many other details call for your attention as well: What pieces will you program? What will you wear? How will you set up the stage?

If you're unclear about any aspect of how to prepare or how to enlist help with your preparations, you create a breeding ground for anxiety and poor performance. For instance, when a musician's learning and organizational skills are inadequate, he can't complete the steps needed to succeed in performance. A concert date nears, and loose ends flap about: Pieces aren't up to tempo, his instrument is out of adjustment, and he becomes a nervous wreck. He has no idea whether his performance will come off well, but he knows for sure that things could fall apart.

Proficient artists recognize an alternative path, one that isn't teeming with chaos and worry. It's called *thorough preparation*. When you're thoroughly prepared for a concert, you've taken charge of the personal, task-oriented, and situational components of performing listed in chapter 7. Whether you're a novice or an old pro, you've chosen apt material, practiced deeply, worked on your fears, and managed the logistics. Your inclusive groundwork makes you self-assured, and you're then free to focus on musical expression. Herein lies the secret to artistry on the concert stage: Artistic performers are prepared performers.

This section proposes a five-sided model of performance preparation. The model also integrates the confidence-building strategies outlined in chapter 7. By weighing your aptitude in each area, you'll be able to sense your strengths and weaknesses. Then, the rest of part II will help you overcome deficiencies.

The Five Facets of Performance Preparation
1. Artistic
2. Technical
3. Mental/emotional
4. Physical
5. Organizational

1. Artistic preparation

Artistic preparation begins with programming. The music you choose has to be high in quality, within your capacity, and arranged in a lineup that excites listeners. Next, your practice skills must enable you to learn and interpret that music deeply, as described in chapters 1–6. Finally, your presentation style needs to be polished such that both you and your listeners look forward to being in each other's company.

2. Technical preparation

To hold sway on stage, your technical knowledge must span the gamut from instrumental or vocal proficiency to facility with setting up concert environments. Technical preparation is born in the practice room, where you establish the means to bring off your interpretive ideas. Your technical control should be such, however, that you retain mastery even when your arousal level mounts. If you've found that your security deteriorates in performance, then you require added technical resources, ones that don't easily degrade under pressure. Furthermore, to produce the sorts of shows that you envision, you need to be adept with on-stage customs and the ways in which venues operate so that you can adjust your manner and also modify performance sites to shape optimal experiences for you and your audiences.

3. Mental/emotional preparation

As a performance date approaches, do you become more excited or more worried? On stage, do you ever feel overwhelmed by your thoughts or emotions? Thorough mental and emotional preparation arms you to generate clear thoughts and positive feelings under the spotlights.

On the thinking side, when you practice deeply, the ease you create leaves you with abundant mental bandwidth to handle any on-stage to-do. Even so, to make smart spur-of-the-moment decisions during a concert, you have to gain experience doing so in practice performances (p. 199). Otherwise, your thinking capacity on stage may become swamped.

Emotional preparation is fueled by how you ready yourself for a show, but it originates in the reasons that you perform and the degree to which your artistic desires are being met. By minding your emotional needs throughout the preparation process and by getting help if your enthusiasm for preparing abates, you can wholeheartedly commit to a concert and to your role as a performer.

4. Physical preparation

Performing demands strength. If you turn up for a concert fatigued, injured, or famished, you won't have much to give to an audience. Physical preparation entails harmonizing your rest, diet, exercise, and practice schedule similar to the way athletes do. Traveling musicians know how difficult this can be. But even if you perform only on occasion, you still need a plan if you're going to project a commanding presence from the stage.

5. Organizational preparation

To prepare for a concert, you have to put numerous things in order. From scheduling rehearsals to arranging transportation, from printing programs to lining up publicity, you need ways to structure your goals. Your organization starts as soon as an engagement is booked and continues through its completion. If, when you have a performance in your sights, the logistical details tend to slip through your fingers, the coming pages will help you seize control.

The remainder of this chapter explores how the five facets of preparation apply in the hours and minutes before a performance gets under way. As you'll see, the facets overlap, and their distinctive borders blur. One area, however, may stand out in your mind: organization.

Less-experienced musicians, I've found, are often amazed to learn how much planning goes into making performances run smoothly. If you haven't been exposed to the preparatory goings-on of professionals or if you've never been accountable for all of the particulars of a concert, then you might be a bit surprised, too. However, when veteran musicians read the recommendations here, they nod their heads again and again. This is how it is.

Preperformance Routines

Before you play, you must prepare your way—first your violin and next yourself. If I'm doing a concert, I must have a good diet, and I must be in the theatre at least one hour before. I must not be distracted by anything.

—Stéphane Grappelli, violinist

Preperformance routines encompass the things that you do on the day of a show, leading up to your arrival at a concert venue. As Stéphane Grappelli implies, such routines have twin tracks: one that prepares the artist, and another that takes care of equipment, materials, and logis-

> **Preperformance Routines**
>
> • Prepare yourself
> • Prepare equipment, materials, and logistics

tics. Here you'll read about both tracks and find a model preperformance inventory. The ensuing section documents preparatory techniques to use backstage.

Prepare Yourself

When a concert day dawns, you need to coordinate your practice, rest, meals, and activities, as well as straighten out your wardrobe and grooming. Wisely managing each element will minimize stress and prime you for the stage.

1. Practice

On the day of a concert for which you're well prepared, your learning process should be finished. Assuming that's the case and that you aren't putting together an event at the last minute, there's no point in doing any extended practice. But mental rehearsal and strategic review are usually beneficial, more so if any of the music on the program is new to you. Overall, keep any playing or singing on the easygoing end and save your best for the performance. Whatever you do, don't overpractice and invite injury. With ensemble concerts, if your group rehearses in the hours before curtain, pace yourself so that you won't be tired at show time. You might want to "mark" your part at such rehearsals, that is, execute lightly; singers might also drop high passages down an octave.

2. Rest

Many performers take naps prior to evening concerts. Violinist Joshua Bell describes his preperformance routine this way:

> For me, this involves resting for a couple hours in the afternoon so I feel fresh for the concert at 8:00 P.M. I'm just pacing myself, so I'm ready to pop with all my energy when the time comes. Having little or no stimulus before a concert helps me, too. I don't like to talk too much before a concert; I don't like making small talk while I'm being taken to the concert in a car or having music on the radio.[1]

If you don't already rest ahead of concerts, try following Bell's example. When there isn't time for a nap, at least spend 10 minutes in a resting pose (p. 81). Your rest period is also the ideal time to meditate or carry out personal rituals—such as the reading of poetry or prayers—that affirm your commitment to being a performing artist.

3. Meal

A balanced preconcert meal, aptly timed, is crucial. You don't want to perform on a full stomach, nor do you want to be low on fuel. Therefore, your meal should conclude 2–3 hours before curtain—you'll have to experiment to discover the timing that suits you best. Your meal should be on the lighter side, consisting of complex carbohydrates along with some proteins and fats to give you lasting power. Examples include a turkey sandwich on wholegrain bread or a vegetable and tofu stir-fry with brown rice.

Sugary foods should be off your list because they'll lead to a drop in your energy level. Spicy dishes are risky, too, because they can provoke an increase in stomach acid. Concerning beverages, eliminate caffeinated, alcoholic, and acid-laden drinks, and opt for noncarbonated water or herbal tea instead. Be wary of milk if it causes a thickening of phlegm. If you ever have questions about your diet, visit your health center, and consult a nutritionist. General nutrition information is also available online—see www.health.gov/dietary guidelines.

4. Activities

Like Joshua Bell, avoid overly stimulating activities. A mild aerobic workout will be refreshing, as long as you exercise regularly. Even if you seldom exercise, a brisk walk will probably do you good.

Singers: Be smart about using your voice. Cut back on speech, and pass up strenuous use such as shouting, whispering, and loud coughing or throat clearing (see *voice care,* p. 268).

Instrumentalists: Limit hand-intensive tasks, including typing. In the days before an appearance, rough use of the hands should be ruled out—no gardening or auto repair. Skip any sports that put your hands at risk. If you cook, be careful to guard against burns and cuts.

5. Wardrobe and grooming

Sort out your wardrobe and grooming days ahead of time to prevent mixups and to neutralize stresses. Every stitch of your attire should be checked for readiness—it's never fun to find out in your dressing room that you have a rip or only one sock. During foul weather, head to the hall in your street clothes, and carry your stage garb in a garment bag. If you perspire heavily when you perform, bear in mind that your moisturizer, makeup, or hair product might run into your eyes. Choose those that won't burn or look odd when the heat rises. And bring a handkerchief.

6. Socializing

Most performers dodge gregarious socializing before concerts. Sometimes, though, you can't escape doing a bit of mingling, especially when you work with a group. Keep track of your colleagues' preperformance styles; some will be energized by conversation, whereas others will favor quiet. Also be clear about your own needs. Still, stay flexible such that when you interact— whether with coperformers, presenters, the public, or concert hall staff— you're cheerful and composed. Humor helps most people feel at ease.

Prepare Equipment, Materials, and Logistics

In tandem with personal preparation, you also have to organize your music, instrument, gear, transportation, and other particulars. Here are the central issues involved. All of these topics apply on the day of a concert, but some also come into play in the preceding days or weeks.

1. Music

"There's no way that I could forget my music," protested Kevin, a 19-year-old guitarist attending a pretour meeting.

"I'm not suggesting that you or anyone else here is irresponsible," I replied. "Just make sure that all of your things are in order. Trust me. The preconcert details add up, and people often blunder."

He gave a "not me" chuckle, and our meeting concluded.

The next morning, four guitar students and I boarded a van as we set off for the first of five concerts. We arrived at the concert site, and guess what? Kevin had the four-part study score for his quartet pieces but not the separate part that he needed to perform. He always kept the score and the part together, except that on the previous day he had placed the part in an unaccustomed spot. As he assembled his things for the tour, he grabbed his music folder, saw that the score was there, and presumed that his part was, too. Fortunately, I carried duplicate copies of everyone's music, so the tour proceeded without a hitch, but a valuable lesson was learned that day.

Before you depart for a concert, double-check that all parts, scores, song lists, or lyric sheets are where they're supposed to be. If you work with an accompanist, also bring a copy of your accompanist's music.

2. Instruments and gear

Forgetting an instrument may be harder to accomplish than mislaying some music, but promise yourself this: Prior to departing from home, you'll look in your case to be sure that your instrument and its components are there before you close the latch. Many a musician hangs his head as he recalls dashing out the apartment door, case in hand, and getting the shock of his life backstage when he realizes that his instrument, bow, or mouthpiece is back home on the couch. Others relate grim stories of leaving articles in taxis or on trains. Pledge that you'll never be telling such a tale. As you travel to a performance, ensure that necessary items stay with you.

Having your instrument in hand backstage is definitely a good thing; having it in concert-ready condition is even better. Weeks ahead of a performance, scrutinize your instrument's setup, and schedule any needed adjustments. Also, store the extra strings, reeds, mallets, and so forth that you require. Those of you who amplify are going to have quite a bit more gear than acoustic performers—use an inventory to make certain that your mic, cords, flashlight, and so on are set to go.

3. Printed programs

When you print your own concert programs, make the copies days before an event as opposed to procrastinating until the eleventh hour. When your presenter agrees to supply printed programs, you should prepare for the possibility that, when you arrive at the performance venue, the programs will be missing. So, always email yourself a backup copy of your repertoire lineup, and bring a few printouts backstage. In that way, absent programs can often be replaced on the spot.

4. Transportation and logistics

There's nothing like the sound of a frantic musician's voice as he phones in, 30 minutes before a concert, to say that he's lost or that he took Highway 96 instead of 69 and is now 20 miles away. If you abide by the following guidelines, you'll never subject anyone's ears to that sound:

- Obtain addresses for performance sites.
- Verify the addresses online, and print out maps days or weeks before an engagement. If you wait until you're about to leave home, you could be in a fix if the address turns out to be incorrect, your computer freezes up, or your GPS goes kaput.
- Program into your mobile phone an on-location phone number that will be active before your show. In the unlikely event of a transportation breakdown, you can call in.
- Make transportation plans well in advance. If there's any chance that your transportation might be unreliable, orchestrate contingency plans.
- Set a departure time that allows for traffic jams, train stoppages, and other common holdups. Arrive at the concert site early enough to complete your preparations calmly.

If you or any coperformers have concerns about a performance setting, make an appointment to visit it, if possible, long before curtain time to try out the hall and the piano or to do a sound check. At minimum, inquire by phone or email about the facilities and staffing so that you won't be flustered by an atypical situation.

5. Music stand

When you perform from music, if practical, take a stand to your show even if you're sure that one will be on hand. You never know when a venue's music stands might be locked up, missing, or in pieces. Also, if the lighting might be weak, pack a clip-on light and an extension cord.

6. Tools and spare parts

Every performer should carry a sewing kit with needle and thread, safety pins, and extra buttons; it's also prudent to bring standby wardrobe items such as shoelaces or nylon stockings. Instrumentalists should pack things like backup strings, drumsticks, reeds, or a bow. If you depend on a music stand light, grab a second bulb for it. Over the years, things will break, buttons will fly off, and seams will split, but it won't be a problem when you have spare parts and a sewing kit handy.

When you use electronics, tote surplus cords, batteries, fuses for amps, and the like. You don't have to plan for the rare cataclysm, but also bring a screwdriver, wrench, or other tools to remedy plausible equipment malfunctions. When in doubt regarding what to pack, remember the old saying, "Better to have it and not need it than to need it and not have it."

7. Backstage water and snacks

Dehydration is disastrous for singers, and it undermines instrumentalists as well, especially wind and brass players, so bring a bottle of water and sip regularly. For outdoor performances in hot or dry weather, try to keep water at your side on stage.

A balanced preconcert meal will probably preclude your needing a snack, but should a delay occur, you can't afford to let your energy slacken. Ordinarily, take something to nibble on.

8. Timepiece

Many people rely on mobile phones as their timekeepers, but there are pitfalls to depending on a phone before a show. For one, if your phone has to communicate with a tower to display the time, reception may be poor if your dressing room is underground or in the center of a building. Besides, when you travel in rural areas, you never know whether you'll get a signal. Added to that, the battery might fade. To forestall problems, bring a watch.

Figure 8.1 presents a model preperformance inventory. A blank, downloadable version is available from *musiciansway.com*.

Backstage Techniques

> *I don't say that I never feel fear before a performance, but I have learned to channel it.*
>
> —Claudio Arrau, pianist

Let's say that you've arrived at a concert hall, and you have 1–2 hours until your show begins. How will you transition from the street to the stage? Seasoned

Preperformance Inventory			
QUARTET CONCERT 8:00 P.M., Saturday, April 12, 2008 Uptown Recital Hall			
Personal Preparation		**Equipment, Materials, Logistics**	
Practice	*Warm-up, scales, études: 10:00–11:00* *Review excerpts from program: 1:00–1:50*	Music	*Parts and scores in folder*
Rest	*Nap: 3:00–4:00*	Instrument	*Setup confirmed* *Spare items in case*
Meals	*Lunch: 11:30—w/quartet* *Dinner: 5:00—home*	Gear	*Self-recording equipment in gig bag*
Activity	*Gym: 2:00–2:30*	Clothing	*Bagged and ready to go*
Wardrobe	*Cleaned; verified*	Printed programs	*Backup copies in folder*
Socializing	*Lunch with quartet*	Transport	*Depart 6:00; directions printed; car set (gas tank full; parking money in glove box)*
Grooming	*Personal items in gig bag*	Music stand	*In trunk of car*
		Tools/spare parts	*Packed in gig bag*
		Backstage water/snack	*In bag*
		Timepiece	*In instrument case*

Figure 8.1. Model preperformance inventory.

artists create the illusion that the changeover is as simple as starting a car. In reality, there's much to be done before your concert engine will be ready to fire.

Without a plan, though, your stress meter could climb into the red zone, and for many performers, it does: "I hate sitting backstage just before the performance," says pianist Jorge Bolet. "That waiting period is always to me a very disagreeable part of the performance."[2]

This section will help you carry out your final preparations with confidence. By building on what you find here, the time before your entrance can become an art-nourishing part of your concert experience. The following techniques are categorized under the headings from chapter 7: person, task, and situation.

Situational Techniques

Upon entering a performance venue, you need to learn your way around, set up your gear, and more. When you perform solo or function as a group leader, you also have to work closely with any concert hall staff. Here are five ways to take charge of the situation.

Situational Techniques
1. Get your bearings
2. Assume "backstage mode"
3. Clarify staging and procedures
4. Manage the lighting
5. Adapt to the acoustics

1. Get your bearings

Your first order of business is to locate your dressing room or whatever warm-up space you're using and make yourself at home. Then stroll throughout the backstage and on-stage areas to register the layout.

2. Assume "backstage mode"

As you orient yourself to the space, assume backstage mode and maintain it throughout your preparations.

- Uphold an inner smile.
- Move and speak calmly.
- Be mindful of your breath: Emphasize laid-back, abdominal breathing.
- Minimize extraneous speech.
- Foster your desire to perform.

Also take precautions against theft. If you have a costly instrument, for instance, keep it with you or have someone watch it rather than leaving it in an unlocked area.

3. Clarify staging and procedures

  a. *Staging:* If you're collaborating with stagehands, give them printouts of your program that indicate:

   - the approximate durations of your selections

- the equipment needed to perform each piece
- the length of any intermission

Next, work out the setup details. Move the piano, chairs, and music stands; hook up any electronics. If the setup will change repeatedly over the course of a concert, mark everything's position with tape on the floor. When all is to your liking, prepare the stage for your first piece, and leave items you'll need later near the stage door.

b. *Procedures:* Locate the house manager, and communicate your late-seating instructions; at formal concerts, permit late seating solely during applause. Then ask these questions:

- Will there be any announcements or introductions before your entrance?
- Do they customarily begin on time?
- What are their traditions for audience members to meet performers after a show?

4. Manage the lighting

Stage technicians expect you to inform them of your lighting preferences, and, at low-budget sites, you often run the lights yourself. It's your job, therefore, to be knowledgeable about concert lighting. On average, a venue's everyday lighting design will be fine. Nonetheless, you should see how a space will look—for both you and the audience—with the stage lights up and the house lights down.

a. *Stage lights:* If you perform from music, be sure that all of the stands receive plenty of light. Similarly, make certain that each performer's face is brightly lit from the audience's point of view. If, when you're on stage, the spotlights seem to be too strong, you might be able to tweak them, but recognize that, when lighting seems intense to a performer, it probably looks good to an audience, so strike a balance. At many halls, with the stage lights up, performers can't see past the first few rows of seats.

b. *House lights:* Most audiences would rather listen in low light or near darkness. However, if you expect people to read their programs, provide sufficient light.

When you operate the lights, take into account that abrupt changes are unpleasant for an audience, so always dim gradually. What's more, some fixtures hum when dimmed. Listen as you plot the light levels, and compromise between the best look and the least noise. After you figure everything out, review the lighting protocol or write it down so that it won't be a source of stress.

5. Adapt to the acoustics

With the setup and lighting in place, you're ready hear how the hall sounds. This will also be your chance to acclimate to the lighting and any piano. Ideally, you and any group members would have rehearsed on the stage during an earlier visit to the venue. At times, though, you may have 30 minutes or less to try out a hall before a show. If time is short and you're compelled to play or sing cold, use yourself conservatively: Select easy material and moderate tempos.

As you play or sing, gauge the way the space and your tone quality combine. In a reverberant venue, listen to your pitches ricochet, and calibrate your tone colors and timing in response. Halls that lack reverberation—"dry" spaces, as they're known—are suited to amplified music, but they can feel awkward to acoustic performers. If you're performing acoustically and your phrases seem to land with a thud, respond by executing as usual, and don't let the dryness rush you through your breaths. Use extra projection if needed, but resist any tendency to force. Most of all, find pleasure in your sound, and prepare to broadcast that enjoyment to your audience.

Also determine whether noise from heating or cooling systems will intrude. You might want to switch off loud units, but, if that's impractical, remember that listeners typically tune out the interference. Be accepting, and make the best of your acoustical environment.

Finally, use your time on stage to claim the space. Imagine the seats full of people and you and any coperformers in total command. Establish a sense of comfort so that when you step in front of your audience, the on-stage setting will feel welcoming and familiar.

Task-Oriented Techniques

Once you have the situation under control, your next order of business is to get dressed, warm up, and begin embodying the spirit of your program.

1. Get dressed

When you dress up to perform, you become grander, like a judge in a robe. As you change out of your street clothes, transform yourself into an artist who will take control. Whether you don standard concert attire or an extravagant costume complete with stage makeup, make getting dressed a calming ceremony that enhances your stage power.

2. Warm up

Your most decisive preconcert ritual is your warm-up, so allocate ample time to become focused and limber. In general, begin with whole-body movements to clear your mind and get the blood flowing. If you're anxious or tense, additionally employ some of the personal techniques described below. Then, as you play or sing, saturate every sound with emotion, renewing your *habits of excellence* (p. 20). Also oversee your tuning throughout the warm-up process; stay centered on concert pitch so that you avoid the disruption of last-second tuning corrections.

3. Embody the music

When your warm-up is done, begin to embody the spirit of the music that you'll perform. For instance, you and any ensemble partners might review some details of timing, cuing, or execution. Nevertheless, your chief task now is artistic. You have to get into character.

Call up the imagery and feelings that you created in practice; maybe run through a portion of the material, although not so much that you induce fatigue. And take time alone for mental rehearsal: Internally hear the music, mime the playing, vocal, or dramatic actions, and kindle excitement for sharing your program.

Personal Techniques

As you manage the situation and your musical tasks, also nurture your personal preparation by using techniques that meet your physical, mental, and emotional needs.

1. Physical techniques

If your fight-or-flight response sparks, you can act to counter the adrenaline surge. Here are classic methods that steady the breath and ease muscle tension.

  a. *2-to-1 breathing:* Almost any sort of deep breathing helps to neutralize jitters, but this technique is especially effective because it triggers an innate calming response. Perform it in a balanced sitting position with your eyes closed or cast downward.

    i. Empty your lungs, and then, to a moderate mental count, inhale silently through your nose and deeply into your abdomen.

    ii. When your lungs are full, exhale through pursed lips for double the count—that is, twice the duration—of your inhalation.

  Repeat for several cycles or several minutes, but return to normal breathing if you feel lightheaded. To make this exercise invisible to others, exhale through your nose rather than pursed lips.

b. *Muscle contraction and release:* Ideal for freeing the muscles and generating energy, muscle contraction and release is most effective, I find, when combined with breathing. You can contract and release small body areas, perhaps starting at your toes and working your way up, or you might engage large muscle groups. The more muscles you squeeze at once, the more energizing this technique becomes.

    i. Fully inhale through your nose and into your abdomen. When your lungs are full, begin to exhale through your mouth and nose to a moderate mental count—perhaps four ticks of a metronome at 60—and continuously contract your muscles.

    ii. When your lungs are empty, release the muscles you contracted, and inhale through your nose to the same silent count.

Do this exercise twice or more with each muscle group that you contract.

In addition to these techniques, consider adding the following to your arsenal: If your mouth becomes dry, imagine a coin placed beneath your tongue. If your hands feel frigid, putting them in a warm water bath can dilate the blood vessels and promote relaxation. Some musicians also draw on body movements such as those from the yoga or tai chi traditions. Keep in mind that a procedure that works for one person might be fruitless for another, so experiment until you discover approaches that fit your needs. Also, adrenaline, once released, doesn't dissipate right away. When you're hyped up, you may need to employ physical techniques repeatedly.

2. Mental and emotional techniques

Regardless of what mood you're in, when a concert is imminent, you have to gather yourself into a performance-ready state. The seven practices here help bring the mind and heart into creative harmony. At any concert, a musician might use one, two, or all of these techniques.

a. *Mental rehearsal:* In the moments before the stage door opens, mental rehearsal can leave you brimming with music and eager to face a crowd. Here's one worthwhile routine:

    i. Envision walking out, seeing the audience, and, in a recital situation, bowing, setting up, and tuning.

    ii. Prepare to begin: Establish the tempo, cue an upbeat, and mentally perform a few phrases.

    iii. As the music commences in your head, sense the presence of your listeners, and connect to the sound and feel of the music. Move rhythmically, if you feel the urge. Then, keep that musical spirit percolating as you step on stage.

b. *Affirmations:* Self-talk almost inevitably influences your mood. By becoming aware of your self-statements and bringing them in line with your true intentions, you engender constructive thoughts and emotions. Try the affirmations here, or invent some of your own.

- I can handle whatever comes up. I fear nothing.
- This is why I'm here—to create art. I'm grateful for the privilege.
- I'm ready; this is going to be fun.
- The audience is here to have a good time; they'll enjoy my performance whether there are flaws or not.
- I've prepared well. I'm open to whatever the performance brings.
- I'm a student. I'll learn from my performance no matter how it goes. Errors don't threaten me.

c. *Thought stopping:* If negative self-talk arises, thought stopping will work in partnership with your affirmations to thwart destructive effects.

  i. Identify the negative thought.

  ii. Dispute it with a firm "No" or "That's ridiculous."

  iii. Replace it with an affirmation.

For example, if you're prepared for a performance and you hear yourself say something like "I'm a wreck," identify the statement as rubbish, mentally say, "That's ridiculous," and replace it with "I can handle whatever comes up. I fear nothing."

d. *Music therapy:* In *The Mastery of Music* by Barry Green, pianist Jeffrey Kahane recounts how he used the folksong "The Water Is Wide" to gear up for a concert. The tune had nothing to do with his program, but, like a prayer, Kahane summoned it backstage to awaken his musicality. "I would play that piece," he said, "until I found the place inside that I wanted to be in and that I wanted the listener to be in. When I finally reached that place, I knew I could go out there and play."[3] As you experiment with various backstage techniques, think about keeping a beloved melody handy.

e. *Soothing imagery:* Many musicians use soothing mental images to defuse restlessness. Some will recall successful performances that they gave in the past. Others might calm themselves by remembering the face of a loved one or imagining a tranquil afternoon at the beach. Still others evoke the touch of an attractive companion and indulge in a bit of fantasy; then, like magic, their cold fingers warm up. When back-stage pressure puts you off balance, relaxing imagery can prompt a state conducive to sharing your music.

f. *Centering:* If you feel scattered, centering will quiet your mind and stabilize your focus. All of the preceding personal techniques can serve as centering procedures. Also try this breathing exercise recommended by author Thich Nhat Hanh in *Peace Is Every Step:*[4]

In a sitting position, close your eyes, and let your breath pass through your nose and into your abdomen.

    i. Allow your lungs to empty, and then observe as the breath re-enters. Mentally say, "In."

    ii. As the breath exits, mentally say, "Out."

Continue for several cycles or several minutes. Simply observe the breath; refrain from trying to control it. If an exhalation concludes and the breath doesn't reenter immediately, relish the silence.

g. *Venting:* If you're buzzing with energy backstage and you need to vent, psychologist Eric Maisel advocates silent screaming.[5] Close your eyes, open your mouth, and wave your arms back and forth over your head as you let out a soundless, primal yell. Other possibilities for venting include silent laughing, leaping into the air, or mild shadow boxing—all can be combined with affirmations.

Backstage techniques will help make the period before a show truly satisfying. Still, it won't always be easy. Some days there will be instrument malfunctions, cranky accompanists, or chilly dressing rooms to contend with. Be undaunted. As your performance abilities and coping skills grow, your confidence will become unshakable.

Becoming a Performing Artist, II

In this chapter:

- Seven aspects of stage deportment
- Creating a stage presence
- Starting and ending
- Harnessing on-stage energy
- Connecting with an audience

Stage Deportment

When I finally saw how I looked, I realized that I was distracting the audience from the music.

—Alfred Brendel, pianist

Imagine standing backstage before your entrance at either a solo or a small-ensemble concert. As the house lights dim, the audience quiets down. You nod to the stagehand, the stage door opens, and on you go.

Now, everything you do affects your relationship with the audience. From the instant you appear, you can establish a friendly bond or, instead, send clumsy signals that spark disinterest. Your musical skills aren't the only things coming into play. You also need fluent stage deportment and an engaging presence.

Stage deportment encompasses the technical know-how for conducting oneself on the concert platform. Stage *presence*, however, includes artistic dimensions such as showmanship. You won't have much of a presence until you're confident with deportment, so I'll cover deportment issues first and tackle stage presence in the next section.

Here I survey seven topics related to the formal deportment customs used by soloists and

> **Stage Deportment Topics**
>
> 1. Attire
> 2. Entrances and exits
> 3. Bowing
> 4. Setting up and tuning
> 5. Performing
> 6. Handling scores
> 7. Speaking

small groups performing in the classical and jazz traditions. To master these customs, reinforce them in practice performances, and, if possible, video-record yourself and then evaluate your on-stage style in collaboration with a teacher. Even if you've performed for years, it's worth reviewing each item here to verify that your deportment is secure. After that, log on to *musiciansway* *.com* to watch videos of performers modeling both agile and awkward stage deportment.

1. Attire

In all walks of life, attire makes a potent statement. And the grand setting of the stage greatly magnifies the effect of a person's attire. Concert clothing, therefore, usually tilts toward the high end of the fashion scale. Plus, when listeners make the effort to attend a performance, they rightly expect the musicians' wardrobes to harmonize with everyone's musical standards.

Your stage attire is most appropriate when it fits you comfortably and also helps an audience feel receptive. Here are ways to meet both of those benchmarks:

a. Match your clothing to the venue, time of day, and occasion. The stage is a ceremonial locale, so it's better to dress on the classy side than to risk looking indifferent or unprofessional. For evening concerts in ritzy venues, black formalwear is the norm. Women, however, routinely accent with color (as do some men) and for solo appearances may opt for gowns. Daytime performances and those in more casual settings call for less stately apparel: men in the likes of suits or sport coats; women in suits, dresses, or skirts.

b. Try out your concert clothing far ahead of an event. Practice perform-ing in your full get-up, shoes and all, to be sure that the fit is right and that there's no impediment to your playing, singing, or moving.

c. Neatness and quality matter. Under stage lights, wrinkles, blemishes, and lousy tailoring jump out. Everything you wear should go together and be cleaned and pressed. Shoes should be shined, and men's socks pulled up high (think about it: Your feet may be at eye level to many people in the audience). Skip ornate accessories—they can be visually distracting and may rattle.

d. Abide by any ensemble or house conventions. Although you might have your own sense of fashion, it's never a good idea to don an outfit that will alarm your colleagues or presenters. In general, groups look their best when the performers echo their cohesiveness with complemen-tary garb. Ensemble members should also pass up wearing perfumes or colognes because strong scents can annoy other musicians or even trigger their allergies.

e. Page turners and stage hands typically wear black since it's the most understated color they can choose. Page turners should coordinate their attire with that of the performers they assist—when musicians dress up, page turners should do likewise. For example, to aid a pianist wearing black formal attire, a male page turner would put on a dark suit; a female page turner could choose a dark suit or dress.

f. Check with a teacher, group leader, or presenter if you're ever unsure how to dress for a performance.

2. Entrances and exits

When an audience initially sees you, your manner speaks volumes about who you are and why you perform. The combination of your stride, posture, gestures, and attire communicate your personality. Follow these steps to enter and exit smoothly:

a. Move with an energetic stride, more so when traversing sizable amounts of on-stage real estate. Widen your shoulders, lengthen your spine, and carry your head high. Clutch any instrument in an unaffected way.

b. Soloists go before accompanists. Page turners and other assistants enter and exit last.

c. Groups: Enter and exit in the order in which you arrange yourselves on stage. Traditionally, though, women exit first—it's up to you whether to preserve that custom. Regardless, walk at a matching pace. If you have to step out of the way to let someone exit ahead of you, back up and continue facing the audience. Rehearse your entrances and exits before a show to ensure that they'll go according to plan.

d. Direct your gaze to where you're going. If the stage door is to the right or left (and it usually is), don't swivel your head to look at the audience as you walk across the stage. When entering, however, if you have more than a short walk to get to your place, toss a good-natured glance toward your listeners as you pass through the stage door.

e. When men wear coats and they sit to perform, it's customary for them to enter and exit with the coat buttoned and unbutton it to perform.

f. At the end of a concert, if you get a curtain call, walk to center stage, and then bow. When you have an encore prepared, present it on your second or third curtain call, less often on your first.

3. Bowing

Bowing is a courteous response to applause; it's a sign of gratitude and respect. But not all bows are equal. Your bow upon entering can be less deep and held for a shorter duration. At the close of a performance, when applause is enthusiastic, a somewhat deeper bow, held longer, demonstrates your appreciation. Ordinarily, bend no more than 45 degrees—half that much is fine. Instruments are commonly held to the side.

a. For your entrance, walk near to the spot where you'll perform, beside or in front of any chair, and stand facing the audience with your feet together. Broaden your shoulders, breathe normally, and offer a warm facial expression to your listeners. Make eye contact with people in several parts of the audience. If the lighting prevents you from seeing anyone, make imaginary eye contact.

b. To bow, hinge at the hips and not at the waist, back, or neck. Lengthen your spine as you hinge, and let your gaze move downward, that is, don't stare at your listeners as you bow. Pause.

c. Straighten up, and look again at your audience. Pause briefly, and then set up and tune.

d. Use a parallel procedure at the conclusion of a performance. As the audience applauds, stand with feet together, make eye contact, bow, and then straighten up and reconnect visually. Next, either exit or prepare to launch another piece. See page 180 for more about the specific body language used to start and end pieces on stage.

e. To refine your bow, enlist a mirror or video camera in practice.

f. Groups: Designate a leader so that you bow in unison. Practice bowing when rehearsing your entrances and exits.

4. Setting up and tuning

After entering and bowing, many performers feel a feverish urgency. "The audience is waiting," they scold themselves. "Get going and start." But there's no reason to rush. When listeners finish applauding, they need a few moments to settle into a receptive mood.

a. Calmly arrange yourself, your music, and any gear. Confirm your sightlines, and move things as needed. Breathe, stay centered, and support your inner smile.

b. Avoid turning your backside toward an audience unless you're conducting, in which case you might wear a tailcoat. If you have to go upstage—

say, to reposition some chairs—by and large, back up or proceed at an angle.

c. Tuning:

- Complete as much tuning as you can backstage.
- On stage, tune no louder than necessary. Groups should follow a set tuning sequence.
- Be thorough—accuracy takes priority over speed. Your skills should be such, however, that you can tune swiftly under pressure.

d. After tuning, create silence before launching the first phrase (p. 180). Always place the music in a separate sonic universe from the sounds of tuning.

5. Performing

Your body language as you perform can be appealing, neutral, distracting, or negative. By video-recording a practice performance, you'll see where you lie on that continuum. Overall, audiences like it best when your on-stage movements are authentic but graceful.

a. Uphold a balanced posture with your spine vertical and shoulders wide (see chapter 13).

b. Project a composed facial expression. Don't grimace, squint, chew, or otherwise contort your face.

c. Instrumentalists: Move naturally with the music but not to excess— neither rigidity nor wild gyrations look attractive. Above all, maintain an easeful relationship with your instrument.

d. Singers: Be dramatic but not to a degree that you divert the audience or compromise your vocal efficiency.

e. Group members: During rests, remain involved. Look at your colleagues or your score, and transmit your interest via positive body language.

f. Negative gestures have no place on stage. When errors or other surprises occur, keep up a cool exterior and an optimistic interior. Remember that listeners don't focus on mistakes; they engross themselves in the music. If you flinch or make a face at every glitch, however, then errors grab the audience's attention (see *dealing with errors*, p. 190).

6. Handling scores

When scores are handled nimbly, listeners don't really notice them. Cumbersome page turns, on the other hand, can break the musical spell. Most page-turning dilemmas can be forestalled with careful score preparation, for instance, by reducing an image with a photocopier and then cutting and taping (or by using an electronic music display). Still, some music can be vexing to arrange on a stand. When you're confronted with an ungainly edition, confer with a teacher.

a. Prepare scores early, and then complete at least one rehearsal with your music in concert-ready condition so that you accustom yourself to the score configuration. Postponing score preparation can lead to last-minute turmoil, particularly when the copier jams.

b. Before a concert begins, neatly assemble your music in performance order; listeners shouldn't be obliged to wait as you line up jumbled pages on stage.

c. Position your music stand low enough not to obstruct an audience's view of your face. Also, when appropriate, tilt the table somewhat toward the horizontal to streamline its silhouette.

d. Rehearse page turns before a show. Then, turn pages quietly on stage.

e. Singers: When you'll be holding music, position it below and away from your face so that your expressions are visible. In solo performances, make eye contact with listeners as frequently as possible—look at your audience more than you look at the score.

f. When exiting, performers who have been using music stands generally leave their scores behind. Once applause ends, a stagehand or group member retrieves the scores and any other items left on stage.

g. Page-turning assistants: Throughout a performance, maintain an upright posture and keep your eyes on the score. When a performance finishes, stay seated until the performers start to exit, and then trail the last performer off stage. You may transport scores at the discretion of the performer you assist.

7. Speaking

Speaking from the stage can work wonders to enhance audience-performer rapport. If you ever detect an emotional barrier separating you from your listeners, a few well-chosen words can dissolve that disconnection. Besides, speaking may be the only way to communicate program revisions. All musicians, therefore, should be able to address audiences confidently.

a. If you plan to greet listeners upon entering, speak immediately following applause and before you set up and tune.

b. In casual surroundings, welcome your listeners, give an overview of your program, and intersperse succinct commentary throughout your presentation. For example, you might point out evocative features of a composition or relate a brief tale of what a piece means to you. In formal settings, you could speak less or not at all, depending on the circumstances. Consult your teacher or presenter if you're ever uncertain whether speaking might be apropos.

c. To practice your speaking skills, use an audio or a video recorder, and, prior to an appearance, rehearse what you'll say. On stage, though, announce in a way that sounds unscripted.

d. Consciously manage your delivery. Speak with ample volume and clarity, pause slightly between phrases, and shift your gaze among different areas of the audience. Pronounce names, titles, and foreign words crisply, and make your final syllables distinct—untrained speakers tend to mumble at the ends of sentences. If your voice doesn't carry well, rely on amplification.

e. Be congenial but concise. Audiences want to hear music, not monologues.

⁂

If performance customs seem alien to you at first, don't be intimidated. With practice, your musicianship and presentation skills will unite. Then your poise in the concert environment will shore up your confidence, and your on-stage manner, like your smile, will become a genuine expression of who you are.

Shaping Your Stage Presence

I will cast this spell: I know I can open this door and show you something unforgettable and transforming, and I'm determined to take myself there and to take you with me.
—Jeffrey Kahane, pianist

A powerful stage presence begins with expert deportment, but its force emanates from the artist within. To captivate audiences, you need a skill set that ignites your musical spirit and sends it outward. Four vital components of that skill set are preparation, desire, strength, and showmanship.

1. Preparation

Preparation forms the bedrock of stage presence. Audiences can't be bluffed —they see and hear through an underprepared artist. If your practice is superficial, listeners will recognize it in your hazy intonation and lackluster phrasing. Similarly, scant organization saps your poise. If you arrive late, let's say, then you're faced with stresses that are less than conducive to an artistic frame of mind.

But when you thoroughly prepare in all five facets—artistic, technical, mental/emotional, physical, and organizational (p. 154)—your self-assurance is apparent as soon as you step on stage. When you're so prepared that you can fearlessly throw yourself into a piece of music, your imagination runs free, and listeners get swept up in your wake.

2. Desire

Thorough preparation is indispensable, but it's not sufficient to generate a commanding presence. You must also have an acute desire for the music you'll present and for sharing it with others. Jeffrey Kahane's words are bristling with desire. I envision him standing at the stage door, ready to dash out and let loose a barrage of music.

You can fire up comparable passion, but you must begin now because your desire to commune with listeners springs from the reasons that you make music and from how authentically you cultivate the performer's mindset. When you take the stage, if you aren't committed to reaching your listeners— that is, if you aren't happy to see them—then both you and your audience will be affected by your ambivalence. Stage presence takes conviction. If you ever feel a shortage of conviction, talk to your teacher. Your future as an artist depends on overcoming such tentativeness.

In addition, your desire to perform any one title is either fueled or drained by how you practice it. As a piece matures, become more inspired by its content, as opposed to letting the repetition of practice make you stale. When you perform a composition that you've presented numerous times, renew your relationship with it so that, upon meeting your audience, you're infatuated with the music. Singer Tony Bennett put across that sentiment in a 2005 interview. Speaking about his signature song, "I Left My Heart in San Francisco," which he has performed for decades, Bennett said, "That song made me a world citizen. And when I do it, it always feels like the first time."[1]

3. Strength

You're prepared and passionate; what more could you need? Strength, that's what, and lots of it. You need strength to endure the rigors of touring and to stay positive when things don't go right. On top of that, you require the vigor of a leader because to be on stage is to be in charge.

Strength is imparted by your deportment and the sound of your voice or instrument. Nevertheless, your presentation style should also give off the energy that comes from you alone. It's your *inner* strength attracts listeners. Be mindful, therefore, to nurture your sense of purpose in performing and build your self-care skills—manage your nutrition, rest, exercise, and emotional health much like a top athlete. Then, the presence of an audience will refresh you and bring an extra sizzle to each phrase you perform.

4. Showmanship

Showmanship—or show-womanship—doesn't equate with flamboyance; it comes from being who you are, but more so. For instance, take a minute to recall the stage presence of some memorable performers. Don't they seem to be themselves on stage? Don't you get the impression that they're having a great time and that there's nowhere else they'd rather be? That's showmanship. It's rooted in your desire to give an audience a terrific experience, but it flowers when you let your creative self emerge.

Whether your on-stage personality is outgoing or laid back, your presence should broadcast an invitation. The stage and concert hall belong to you, and your listeners are your honored guests. Your demeanor says, "Let's share something magical."

If there's a central tenet of showmanship, it's this: Project; don't reflect. When you perform on a cold, rainy day, and the heat in the dressing rooms isn't working, you convey warmth and enthusiasm from the stage. Then, soon enough, you *are* warm. When you mess up a phrase, you deliver the next one with added joy and conviction. Then, when your performance concludes, you project the same satisfaction as if you had nailed every note. You did your best, recovered from the slip, and performed with devotion. Both you and the audience enjoyed the music no less than if you hadn't slipped at all.

With skillful showmanship, you never transmit anything that's going on within or around you that doesn't serve your artistic aims. You take control of yourself, your material, and the situation, and then listeners place themselves willingly in your hands.

Starting and Ending

You must start well, and you must end well. What is in the middle is not so important because no one is listening then.

—Maurice Chevalier, singer and actor

Chevalier's words always make me chuckle, but they aren't meant as merely a joke. The beginnings and endings of pieces truly are among the most critical parts of any performance. They're the junctures when music passes into and out of existence and also the occasions, akin to dramatic peaks, when your audience listens and watches most intently. Let's get under way with beginnings.

Launching the First Phrase

Suppose that you're about to start your opening selection at either a solo or a small-group concert—you've just walked on stage, bowed, set up, and tuned. The quietness hangs in the air. How do you seize the moment and, out of the expectant silence, breathe the music into being?

In theory, your backstage preparations would have you so in sync with your material that your initial phrase would be as comfortable to perform as any other part of your program. But there's theory, and then there's reality. Beginnings can be precarious because that's when arousal may peak and you feel the most out of sorts. Every musician, therefore, needs a surefire procedure for launching the first phrase. Here's the most effective one I know.

Launching the First Phrase
1. Center
2. Connect
3. Count
4. Begin

1. Center

Centering quiets the body, mind, and spirit. And when you project a centered presence from the stage, your audience becomes attentive and relaxed. A single abdominal breath is your most reliable centering tool. Breathe silently through your nose as follows:

- Lower your gaze, and then inhale into your abdomen as you exude confident body language.

- Exhale with spine long and shoulders wide; release any excess tension. Empty your mind, or repeat an affirmation (p. 169), and go to a place of inner silence.

Like an expanding universe, your performance will unfurl from this center point of stillness.

2. Connect

Continue to breathe smoothly into your abdomen. From your quiet center, mentally connect with the first phrase of your piece: Inwardly hear the music, perceive the tactile sensations to produce it, and conjure up its meaning. Deeply absorb the mood and the tempo; let them permeate every cell in your body.

Take care not to rush this step. Adrenaline can distort your rhythmic sense and cause you to start at a faster tempo than you intend. Employ breathing and mental imaging to set the tempo accurately.

3. Count

Instrumentalists should now bring instruments and hands into playing position; coperformers should make eye contact. As you continue to breathe, prepare to cue the beginning by becoming motionless—use your body language to create a riveting silence.

With the pulse coursing through you, initiate a silent, emotion-rich count ("two, three, *four*..."), cue the entrance, and set the air vibrating with music. When you perform unaccompanied, take an identical route and cue yourself.

4. Begin

As you begin to play or sing, direct your music with soulful awareness. Remain on high alert until you and any group members complete the transition into easeful performance. If a part of you is unstable, take immediate compensatory action. For instance, when your hands are cold from fight-or-flight activation, breathe, release muscle tension, and focus on producing the music. Pianist Anton Kuerti says, "It is only the warmth of the music itself that will thaw out cold fingers."[2]

If you have to put forth extra effort to control the beginning, rather than recoiling in fear, take pleasure in meeting the challenge. Infuse each sound with heart, respond to coperformers, and offset any stiffening with relaxed movement. Then, steadily withdraw effort as your systems line up and naturalness is restored.

Seasoned performers will center, connect, count, and begin in 10–15 seconds. When you're first learning, however, take more time in the centering and connecting phases to counter any tension and to establish the mood and tempo.

To ensure that you have ample capacity to manage your openers, choose music that you can perform well even when you're jittery. Then complete many practice performances to discover the ways that you're affected at the start. Remember that confidence doesn't hinge on eliminating all nervous interference; rather, it results from knowing that you're able to perform well whether you deal with interference or not. As you come to understand your on-stage self, you can have tactical responses ready, and your stage power will grow.

The musicians who have the most trouble starting pieces on stage typically have something in common: In practice, they don't use launching routines consistently. Instead, they plunge haphazardly into their beginnings and don't get their feet under them until at least a measure has passed. When such musicians have to begin pieces in front of the public, their chaotic habits leave them groping for the opening phrases. Anxious thoughts flood their minds, their breathing constricts, and their musical instincts go offline.

To instill the secure habits needed on stage, unfailingly use your launching protocol in practice. When starting any sort of music, center, connect, count, and begin.

Ending Dramatically

As you come within range of the end of a piece, your listeners depend on you to give them closure. You've led them across a dreamscape; now it's time to bring them back to earth. But you must do so without tearing the fabric you've woven. Your endings should satisfy, yet, after the final notes fade, also leave wisps of enchantment hovering in the air.

Ending Dramatically
1. Heighten your focus
2. Place final pitches
3. Craft a profound silence
4. Use clear body language

1. Heighten your focus

Just as you were vigilant at the outset of a piece, closing gestures demand your utmost attention. As the ending nears, verify your link with coperformers— make eye contact if you can—and heighten your focus.

2. Place final pitches

As the music approaches the end, artfully place your closing pitches by adjusting timing, dynamics, tone, and articulation. For extended ritards that stretch your control, mentally count in subdivision. To unify coperformers, add cuing where needed. But watch out: Adrenaline can warp your internal rhythm, so breathe freely, and let go of tension to mold the finish with style.

Then, when you arrive at your last note, drench it with emotion—feel it propel the music toward the certainty of silence.

3. Craft a profound silence

With your last note ringing out, cue a preparatory beat, and then stop the sound with a decisive stroke. Now be still. Listen as the silence forms and the music dissolves into memory. Just as you began with stillness, you return to stillness, and the musical universe you spun into the air contracts to nothingness.

4. Use clear body language

To release the final silence from your grip and prompt the audience to applaud, move out of your motionless state and look warmly toward your listeners. Instrumentalists should take hands and/or instruments out of playing position; if you're seated, rise to your feet. As the applause swells, make eye contact with people in various sections of the audience; then bow in acknowledgment.

In multimovement pieces, when you conclude one movement and you plan to continue without applause, precise body language enables you to trap the intervening silence and hold the audience in suspense.

Transitioning between movements

    i. As you release the closing silence of one movement, keep instruments and bodies toward performance position.

    ii. Create a transitional calm:

- Turn pages quietly.
- Avoid eye contact with listeners (eye contact following a closing silence invites applause).
- Uphold a balanced posture.

    iii. Launch the next movement.

If listeners applaud between movements, signal your appreciation with a nod. "We should welcome applause," says pianist Emanuel Ax, "whenever it comes."[3]

To cultivate failsafe habits for launching and concluding, strategically practice your beginnings and endings. For example, in a quartet rehearsal, you might start or end a piece three times in a row. Similarly, with a four-movement work, you could review the transitions between the movements.

In practice and on stage, take exceptional care with silences. The stillness that falls before, between, and at the end of pieces is integral to your musical communication. Combine your musicianship and stage deportment to frame any piece in eloquent silence.

Harnessing On-Stage Energy

> *It's not about playing well by being comfortable and wiping out nervous energy. It's about finding the right channel for all that energy.*

—Don Greene, psychologist and performance coach

Kim had played the violin since childhood. Although she was a standout in her university orchestra, solo recitals left her baffled. Alone at center stage, her mind would swarm with anxious thoughts, and her control would become tenuous. She had odd sensations, too—her shoes bit into her feet, or the stage would heave upward like a ship riding a wave.

"I'm so embarrassed about all this," she said after telling me her story. "It must sound like I'm nuts."

"You're not nuts," I reassured her. "You're having standard responses to performance stress."

"Adrenaline amplifies sensitivity," I explained. "It's part of the fight-or-flight response that makes people ultraperceptive and wary. Performers often report that their bodies feel foreign or their visual fields warp. The heaving-stage effect could also result from crossing your eyes to look at the fingerboard or from dizziness caused by shallow breathing. Concerning the other issues that arise in solo but not ensemble performance, we'll need to try a few things to get to the bottom of those."

Kim took out her violin and stood to play some Bach. As she brought the instrument into playing position, her knees locked, her shoulders tensed, and the pleasant aura that she had emitted in conversation vanished. She had a big sound, but she didn't vary it much; and although everything was in tune, her phrase ends were much like the middles. In short, she wasn't sculpting the music or using her imagination.

"What does this piece mean to you?" I asked.

"Mean?" she wondered. "It's Bach; it's beautiful."

"For you, though, on a personal level, what emotions does it evoke?"

"I haven't thought of it in those terms," she said. "It's definitely noble."

"I see on the score that you haven't made any markings. Do you ever sketch in expressive ideas?"

"I don't want to wedge myself into anything," she replied evasively. Then, more honestly, she said, "I guess I don't know how to decide what I want."

As our session progressed, the picture became clearer for both of us. Kim felt overwhelmed by the artistic demands of interpreting music. When she played in an orchestra, the conductor provided the interpretation, but on her own, she faltered. She didn't really know where to begin. That same attitude was present in her memorization routine. She was a brilliant sight-reader, yet she hadn't worked out a method for memorizing. She just used mindless repetition, and that fated her to being out of control when the pressure increased.

Regarding the tense playing position, I learned that Kim normally practiced seated. She knew that, when pieces were to be performed standing, she should stand when practicing them, but she got low-back pain from standing, she said. She wasn't aware that her knees locked when she stood, and she didn't realize that her locked knees were probably contributing to her back problem.

Although it took less than an hour to figure all of this out, Kim would need months to turn her habits around. Fortunately, she had access to the help she needed. In addition to continuing our work together, I asked her to make appointments with three other educators. A teacher of the Alexander technique guided her to release muscle tension, stand without back pain, and coordinate her movements. An athletic trainer put her on a workout schedule that corrected the imbalances in her physical strength; the exercises also supplied an outlet for her pent-up frustrations. Third, a therapist enabled her to figure out why she resisted pouring herself into solo music. Kim discovered a long-standing pattern of avoidance that stemmed from fear of criticism and allied self-esteem issues.

As Kim did her inner work, I helped her learn ways to develop interpretations, memorize securely, and manage herself beneath the spotlights. She became more artistically responsible in her practice and started enjoying the challenges of interpreting and memorizing. Gradually she carved channels through which her on-stage energy could flow.

To make use of those channels, during the practice performances that she did in our sessions, I coached her to conceive of upcoming phrases with clarity of sound and execution. In the past, when playing from memory, she had never imaged ahead distinctly. But now that she grasped how to prepare phrases in her mind and body, she could play with minimal effort. The main thing that she needed to remember was to flip her image-ahead switch into the *on* position in the first place and to keep it on.

I also invited Kim to make unrehearsed adjustments to her interpretations so that she could practice being spontaneous. As one success led to another, her confidence grew. She opened up more, and her warm personality came through in her phrasing. After a two-month hiatus from performing solos, she began playing for her classmates, and one appearance proved to be a watershed.

"I was nervous backstage," she told me. "Studio class has always been nerve racking for me. With only violinists in the audience, they hear every mistake. But before I went on, I did some calming breaths, and I mentally rehearsed the opening. I told myself that I was a student and that my goal was to learn; errors wouldn't threaten me.

"Then, as I began to play, my stage power was almost superhuman. For the first time in my life, I wasn't afraid. The bow and strings became my voice, I felt what I wanted each phrase to sound like, and the music came through me without any slips or weird sensations. There was this incredible intensity, but it all seemed easy." She had cried afterward, she said, overcome by the emotional release.

The problems that Kim faced were typical, and the solutions were, too. Like many students, however, she had believed that her troubles were unique to her and that she was either "nuts" or untalented. She soon understood that she had a deficit of knowledge and skill but an abundance of talent. As she filled in the blank spots, she ceased thinking of herself as a musician with inscrutable problems and rightly saw herself as an artist with an unlimited future.

The key to harnessing on-stage energy is to use it for music-making purposes. Your basic strategy for doing so is to breathe, release tension, listen, and image ahead. Still, in any performance, you need to direct your energies in a variety of ways subject to the repertoire you present and how much nervousness you experience.

When you're buzzing with nerves, immerse yourself in the mood of a composition while you also get busy with the self-instructions required to shape the dynamics, mold the articulation, and so forth. All the while, breathe into your abdomen, listen to yourself and any coperformers, and jettison negativity. The more you attend to producing the music and the more aware you are of how to bring it off, the more channels you'll have open to steer performance stress

Harness On-Stage Energy
• Breathe
• Release tension
• Listen
• Image ahead

constructively. Then, assuming that you've prepared thoroughly, your command of the music will help quell your agitation.

When you aren't restless, you won't have to expend so much energy on self-management. Then you can withdraw effort and let the performance situation stimulate your musicality. Nonetheless, whether you're at ease or on edge, you should flexibly maneuver your attention as the performance plays out.

For example, when a slippery passage comes along and control is an issue, open the control channels wide, and consciously pilot your execution. When technical affairs run smoothly, send more energy into inventiveness and coperformer communication. The trick is to have every channel available—that is, to maintain inclusive awareness—so that you never sacrifice artistry for security. Even on the tougher days, when you work hard to prevent your sound from breaking up, you still share something special with your listeners and any ensemble members.

During the early phases of learning performance skills, it may take time at the onset of a show for you to compose yourself. No matter how rough things get, though, stay occupied with the moment. Do what's necessary to perform each phrase the best that you can, irrespective of how previous phrases turned out. And be optimistic. Budding performers often batter themselves with critical self-talk on stage, not realizing that self-ridicule blocks creativity. Keep up an accepting attitude as you play or sing. Whether things go well or not, each performance gives you information that adds to your expertise.

Elite musicians have refined their craft to where they mostly let go in concerts; they function almost entirely in artistic dimensions. Even so, when veteran artists are engrossed in performing without any intrusion from nerves, they still preserve filaments of awareness that connect everything they do. If difficulties pop up, the filaments expand into high-bandwidth channels to bring pitches into tune or an ensemble back into step.

Uninitiated performers often presume that they can achieve comparable freedom by merely emoting on stage and foregoing awareness. They're mistaken. To perform fluently, you must emote and control simultaneously. You have to be able to give yourself over to the emotion of the music while you also lead the music, directing your execution and the emotional flow.

Adept musicians practice such that they can oversee all aspects of performing with the slightest effort. Hence, they execute easily on stage, and their emotions have free rein. For you to become that well versed, you have to acquire the skills needed to prepare for concerts and to direct yourself under pressure. Then you'll have infinite ways to transform the zing of performing into art.

To practice harnessing on-stage energy, opt for accessible music, learn it deeply, and be alert to how you use yourself in rehearsal and in performance.

Play or sing from your heart, but if your muscles stiffen, react with a release. If your mind wanders or noises from an audience distract you, refocus and image ahead. If anxiety or negativity crops up, use breathing and affirmations to help restore your inner balance. To be maximally expressive, however, it's good to open an extra channel—the one that connects you with your listeners.

Connecting with an Audience

I get an audience involved because I'm involved myself. If the song is a lament at the loss of love, I get an ache in my gut. . . . I cry out the loneliness.

—Frank Sinatra, singer

What endows a performance with the power to stir listeners' hearts? At a minimum, a spellbinding concert melds first-rate repertoire, prepared musicians, and a favorable setting. If you peel back those layers, though, I think you'll find a single factor at the core of any gripping performance: relationship. The performers who connect from the stage establish emotional relationships with their audiences. And those relationships are based on one thing: giving. In a concert, performers give and listeners receive, and their mutual interaction lifts them all to a higher plane.

Whenever you give to someone, whether your offering is a song or something surrounded by gift-wrapping, the significance of your gift derives more from the spirit in which it's given than from the item in the wrapping paper. In performance, if you withhold this giving of yourself or if your gift of music isn't heartfelt, then it should come as no surprise when your audience withholds, too. To connect, you have to be eager to share your music with others and also believe in your ability to perform that music meaningfully.

Many musicians, however, find the responsibility of preparing a concert gift overwhelming. Like Kim, they may have unconscious fears or not know how to fashion interpretations. Or they may pick music that's beyond their capacities, and then they can't be secure on stage. The choosing of unattainable music is a form of vanity that corrupts the spirit of giving. Students who want to perform nothing but the hardest pieces are either looking to show off or to live in fantasy worlds. Either way, their selfishness doesn't endear them to listeners. To be openhearted on stage, you must choose material that's within your reach. Then, instead of trying to have the flashiest prize in your gift box, you put forward the most artistic present you can.

Although your generosity begins with the music that you select and continues with thorough preparation, your gift will be appreciated only if you uphold that generous attitude on stage. As you perform, radiate the character of a composition. If a piece is about love, be in love; if it's about joy, emanate joy. And if things get rocky—maybe you drop a few notes, a coperformer misses an entrance, or some listeners start coughing loudly—stay positive and engaged, and give your audience the best possible experience.

What's more, when it comes to connecting from the stage, nothing other than your actual performance beats the clout of the spoken word. Many musicians squirm at the thought of talking to audiences, but I encourage you to connect with listeners verbally, as well as musically. You won't want to speak at every concert. Sometimes you'll prefer to commune on a purely musical level. But when you're able to speak charismatically from the stage, it won't just boost your rapport with your audiences; it can also advance your career.

Speaking skills will charge up your career because, when you start booking performances, you'll appear in situations that range from black-tie concerts to casual encounters. There will probably be more of the casual, low-paying type. The less-formal events are ideal training grounds for you to craft a communication style. In time, if you earn a reputation as a performer who can touch any sort of listener, the demand for your performances will soar.

Over and above the basics of stage deportment covered earlier, develop a verbal delivery where, in appropriate settings, you don't just inform but also entertain. Rehearse the spoken part of a program, record it, and ask your teacher for an evaluation. Make the nonmusical elements of your concerts as lively as the repertoire that you present. Then, wherever you perform, you can make your concert gifts complete.

10

Becoming a Performing Artist, III

In this chapter:

- Responding strategically to errors
- Post-performance routines
- Three ways to practice performing
- Evaluating your progress

Dealing with Errors

It was when I found out I could make mistakes that I knew I was on to something.

—Ornette Coleman, saxophonist and composer

In the discovery phase of practice, all musicians make errors as they try out interpretive and technical ideas. "If you're not prepared to be wrong," says creativity consultant Ken Robinson, "you'll never come up with anything original."[1] Nor are you likely to come up with anything very meaningful either. As you mine the layers of a piece, you experiment freely, hang on to the good stuff, and leave the detritus behind.

Next, in the repetition phase, you polish that good stuff until it gleams. Although discovery can be messy at times—as you test one notion, discard it, and then explore another—the repetition part of practice is meticulously neat. And that neatness is essential to on-stage artistry because, to perform accurately and expressively in front of people, you need accurate and expressive habits of execution.

That may seem simple enough. However, in concert, you strive to be both precise and spontaneous. When you're open to impromptu insights, you're at your most creative, yet you also take more risks because performing in unrehearsed ways makes errors more likely. How do you reconcile the requirements of accuracy with your desire for spontaneity?

First, you have to prepare so thoroughly that the possibility of errors is minimized. No performer can wholly eradicate mistakes, but when you learn your material deeply, your awareness becomes comprehensive. You can then vary timing, inflection, and, for some, improvise without losing security. Even when errors do creep in, you're able to feel around them and maintain the forward flow.

Second, as you'll see below, you must become adept at dealing with errors both musically and psychologically so that, when they occur, they don't threaten your performance or your self-esteem. I'll begin by looking at ways to overcome the fear of errors; then I'll describe strategies to handle on-stage slips.

> **Overcoming the**
> **Fear of Errors**
>
> 1. Errors are not failures
> 2. Errors are not shameful
> 3. Errors are *information*

Overcoming the Fear of Errors

1. Errors are not failures

"I'm scared about Thursday," said Steven, a freshman vocalist who was scheduled for his first performance in his teacher's studio class.

"What's your biggest fear?" I asked.

"That I'll forget words or sing off pitch," he replied.

"Let's say that you stumble," I proposed. "You forget a line, and your high note cracks. What will happen?"

"What will happen," he declared, "is that the other singers will think that I'm a hack and that I don't belong here."

Steven had been at school for a month. His teacher had told him that, at this early phase in his education, the motive for singing in class was to fine-tune his presentation skills and try out ways to counter performance stress. The objective was to grow from the experience. The quality of the performance wasn't a primary concern. Yet even though Steven could articulate what his teacher had in mind, that's not how he saw things.

As we talked, it became evident that it wasn't just the other students' opinions that worried Steven; it was also his self-image that was at risk. In his mind, if he didn't perform to a flawless standard each time he stepped on stage, then he was a failure. His confusion over the difference between errors and failures caused him to see every glitch as a catastrophe. I suggested that, if he didn't act to temper his perfectionism, it would probably undercut his future. He took my advice and talked through his fears with his teacher. His way of thinking is so widespread, however, that it merits further comment here.

There's a profound distinction between errors and failures. Errors are an instructive type of feedback; they tell you that you don't have a firm grasp on something. In answer to an error, you can practice and make corrections.

Failures, in contrast, have lasting consequences. For instance, the drunk driver who is at fault in a fatal car crash has failed as a driver and as a responsible citizen.

In a performance, especially one in studio class, you might commit errors, but you can't fail. If mistakes crop up, you go on with your selection. Later, in the practice room, you tweak your preparation. Then you get back on stage, and the error-and-revision process propels your development. Even in a public show, if you have memory or technical troubles, you give the audience a fine experience nonetheless. An on-stage error can't become a failure unless a musician turns it into one.

2. Errors are not shameful

Coupled with their perfectionism, students like Steven, who confuse errors with failures, often have shameful feelings associated with mistakes. Errors don't just menace their melodies; they also terrorize their self-worth. Needless to say, nobody likes making errors on stage. Still, when a prepared performer has an inadvertent hiccup, that's just human; it shouldn't provoke guilt or shame. On the other hand, if musicians avoid practice and their parts aren't up to par, then it's normal for them to feel guilt when their negligence mars a performance.

The difference between guilt and shame, though, is that you feel guilty when you *do* a bad thing; with shame, you deem that you *are* a bad thing. For example, if someone accidentally backs a friend's car into a pole, that person may suitably feel guilty for having damaged the friend's property. People who also endure shame, however, believe that the collision is proof that they can't do anything right.

When errors trigger shame, every mishap gets magnified out of proportion. After a trivial blip in a performance—say, a single out-of-tune note—rather than going on with enthusiasm, the shame-filled musician feels bleak. "You really stank that up," his internal critic might say. He'll retreat emotionally, and then everything he plays or sings turns lackluster. And all of the self-talk usually rouses shame's roommate, anger. It's hard to get shame involved without anger tagging along, adding italics and exclamations to the internal dialogue: "You *idiot!*"

Entrenched issues of perfectionism, shame, and anger should be worked on with a teacher or therapist. They don't vanish by magic and can elicit a host of destructive behaviors. But on top of the self-improvement work that you do to lessen negativity, here's a technique to douse it with humor.

When you make a juicy mistake, if pessimism follows, think of those angry or shame-ridden thoughts as fleas—ugly critters that you flick away with the back of a mental fingernail. "Hello, anger," you might mentally say with a grin.

"I'm not interested." *Fling!* "Ah, there's shame again: Adiós." *Fling!* Laugh at yourself, and get back to the important work of making art. Errors are inevitable, but suffering as a result of them is optional.

3. Errors are *information*

As you reduce the emotional pain of errors, they'll become less threatening. Once you reach a point where you unconditionally accept yourself, mistakes will cease troubling you much at all. Unfortunately, inflated sensitivity to errors encumbers hordes of student musicians. Working through that sensitivity, it seems, is one of the rites of passage to artistic excellence. Not only are attitudes like Steven's prevalent, often there's also confusion about how differently errors should be treated in performance versus in practice.

In the repetition phase of practice, miscues are dealt with promptly: You stop, fix the problem, and repeat the relevant segment. You work methodically to create a mental map that's devoid of wrong turns. In performance, however, errors should be disregarded. When slips arise, you go on as if nothing unforeseen has happened. You sculpt every phrase as beautifully as you can, and you do your best not to give a mistake a second thought. The day after a show, you evaluate any flaws, and you practice to resolve their causes. While you're on stage, though, you shun error analysis, and you make music.

One way to purge sensitivity to performance errors is to view them as useful information and nothing more. Mistakes don't come with emotional strings attached. They're neutral until a musician combines them with guilt, shame, or anger. If slips upset you, that's a sign that you have some inner work to do, but assigning them neutral emotional weight can strip away many of the barbs.

Keep in mind, too, that, during a concert, listeners mostly ignore errors because they immerse themselves in the spirit of the music. When an anomaly occurs in a well-crafted musical line, the effect is akin to how a passing stutter affects a speech—people listen to the meaning of the words and overlook the stutter. Music audiences do likewise and feel the essence of a phrase as a whole.

Your goal on stage is to create compelling music. Although you can't ensure error-free performances, you can devote yourself to giving artistic ones. In doing so, you put errors in their rightful place.

Responding Strategically to Errors

Having a healthy attitude toward errors is crucial, but you also need techniques to curb their musical effects. The primary strategy for responding to on-stage

The Primary Error Response
• Keep going
• Release tension
• Be positive

mistakes begins with maintaining the pulse and the forward motion of the music. Conversely, if you flub, and instead of forging ahead you backtrack or disrupt the flow, then you've made a second error—and a major one at that. Of all the bloopers that musicians can produce, rhythmic interruptions have the most jarring effect on listeners, so keep going through any gaffe. At the same time, release tension and project a positive air. Display confident body language, come what may.

Here are synopses of the five main types of performance errors along with examples of how you might apply the primary response.

1. Mental lapses

If you let your mind wander while you're on stage, you're courting trouble. Even if no sonic harm ensues, you're like a sleepy driver, nodding off at the wheel, who wakes to find disaster barely averted.

The fundamental skill to help you counter lapses is to be attentive to your inner state so that you recognize any lull and instantly snap back on course. When restoring your attention, be relentlessly nonjudgmental. No matter how

> **The Five Main Types of Errors**
> 1. Mental lapses
> 2. Minor inaccuracies
> 3. Miscalculations
> 4. Technical breakdowns
> 5. Memory slips

often your mind darts away, calmly refocus on the music as you breathe, release tension, and image ahead (mental imaging is defined on page 34).

Students who have frequent lapses in performance typically establish lax mental habits in practice. Be alert in the practice room that your mindful radar never goes on standby. Always direct yourself with broad awareness.

2. Minor inaccuracies

When you blur a couple of notes or drift slightly out of tune, you've committed a minor inaccuracy. These are the most common performance errors, and they usually pass unnoticed by listeners. But they can startle performers. Whatever the cause—often it's a mental lapse—respond by retaining connection to the pulse and the music. Simultaneously, realign any internal setting that may have slid off track: Smooth out your breathing, hear where you're going, and lead yourself onward.

Most of all, while on stage, expunge errors from your mind. Performers who fixate on glitches become mired in mishaps. Instead of preparing the phrases to come, they mentally revisit their flubs, and the distraction causes them to blunder again and again. Whatever the inaccuracy, stay engaged with the music, and let mistakes dissolve into the past. Be like an actor who doesn't break character. Convey buoyant body language, and continue giving your listeners the most magical experience that you can.

3. Miscalculations

Examples of miscalculations include botched entrances and technical misjudgments that result in substantial misses. With a miscalculation, your focus is sharp, your intention clear, but somehow you're no longer riding the same musical train that you boarded at the start.

These errors can deliver a jolting surprise to a performer. Neutralize any shock by resetting your musical and technical guideposts: Mentally count, and image ahead while you let go of tension. In an ensemble, if you lose your place, look and listen to your coperformers for leadership. When you're performing solo, boldly take the lead, and show your accompanist the way.

4. Technical breakdowns

Technical breakdowns consist of things like briefly losing command of your voice or embouchure, skidding off the fingerboard, or dropping a mallet or bow. Your countermeasures may require more effort than lesser mistakes call for, but your emotional response is identical: You remain composed and act purposefully. If you can't immediately return to unhindered execution, mentally sing or count as you adjust. Then reenter the musical context joyfully, sending negativity far out of sight. The more expressively you perform after such a stumble, the more insignificant it becomes.

This doesn't pertain to mechanical breakdowns, however, as when a solo violinist snaps a string. Then you stop performing, explain to the audience, and exit the stage to get the instrument back in working order. Once function is restored, you carry on with your performance. When you don't transmit irritation from mechanical breakdowns, an audience finds them interesting and even amusing. Your showmanship skills will determine how they go over.

5. Memory slips

Among the constellation of errors, memory slips probably strike the most fear. Thorough memorization, covered in chapter 4, will make slips scarce, but no performer is ever immune to the prospect of coming up blank.

When your recall falls short, to preserve the rhythmic flow, you must continue making music by inventing it on the fly. The best choice is to improvise in the style of a piece and work your way to a concrete point where you can pick up the material as rehearsed. Whatever you do, don't stop. If you're a vocalist who can't conjure up the right words, sing an assortment of vowels or syllables. If you're an instrumentalist, play rhythmically in keeping with the profile of the music. Or, when performing unaccompanied, if you aren't a nimble improviser, you might repeat an earlier phrase, jump to a section that's clear, or restart. Failing these, if you still can't get through a piece, gracefully conclude.

Students who lack improvisational agility often cave in when their memories misfire. If you've never rehearsed these sorts of improvisations, you're unlikely to accomplish them on stage. To acquire a fluid response to gaps, integrate improvisation drills into your practice, and periodically simulate memory lapses, obliging yourself to wing it for a few measures. You don't need the know-how of a jazz master to get through slips, but you can cultivate the tools to ad-lib out of trouble.

Expert musicians always have error responses ready. When mistakes occur, they expend little energy setting things straight. For you to become that proficient, you have to practice performing, juggle any goofs, and then review your reactions. Aim to instill a reflex that enables you to engage errors musically while releasing tension and worry.

In closing, there's an old saying that applies to on-stage mistakes and to every other misstep in life: "You don't drown by falling in the water; you drown by staying there." When an error sends you for a dunk, you have a choice: Sink or swim. By practicing your error responses until they're instinctive, you'll learn to swim stylishly out of any predicament.

Postperformance Routines

Our goal is to be able to "experience our experience" fully, without classifying it as either bad or good.

—Barry Green, bassist

When a performance wraps up, how do you cope with postconcert thoughts, feelings, and interactions? A concert may end when the applause fades, but your artistic work and your responsibilities as a performer are far from complete. You might be hyperexcited, yet audience members are coming to meet you. Plus, there's evaluation to be done. You have quite a few things to manage.

Similar to the way that backstage techniques prepare you to perform, postperformance routines bring you smoothly through the aftermath of a show. Here I'll describe a three-part model.

1. Interact and cool down

After your final bow, your feelings backstage can range from elation to remorse. Regardless of how a concert went, though, your foremost tasks afterward are to interact, cool down, and accept your performance.

> **Postperformance Routines**
>
> 1. Interact and cool down
> 2. Assess
> 3. Move ahead

As soon as you exit the stage, congratulate any coperformers. You'll have ample time to reflect on your personal contributions to a concert later on, so while everyone basks in the postconcert glow, tell your colleagues how much you value their involvement.

Next, whether you had a fantastic day or a rough one, acknowledge to yourself that you performed the best that you could at the time. If you're brimming with adrenaline, maybe return to your dressing room and center yourself with some restorative movements (p. 76). Also run through a few gentle scales or lip trills to cool down your music-making muscles.

As you gather up your belongings, privately affirm your commitment to the creative process. If things went well, you know that your skills are developing in the right direction—affirm that. If you performed beneath your expectations, you gained information that will help you progress—vow that you're going to remedy faults and grow as a result. This is not the time, however, for an exhaustive appraisal. But if you have any burning ideas, jot them down or record a memo on your phone. After that, begin to let the performance go. It's already in the past.

When you meet audience members, receive them warmly. Although minutes earlier you were on stage doing the emoting, now things have shifted: It's time for people to share their feelings with you and for you to listen compassionately. Your role resembles that of a host whom guests want to thank for throwing a party. So, just as negativity has no place on stage, it doesn't belong here, either—exhibit no dissatisfaction with any aspect of your performance. Display interest in hearing listeners' thoughts; voice appreciation for their attendance. Before leaving, thank your presenter and any others who facilitated your concert. Then head out to unwind.

2. Assess

Defer your postconcert assessment until the next day at the earliest. Cellist Ross Harbaugh chimes in on this subject and advises groups not to retrace problems right after a performance but to save discussion for a subsequent rehearsal.[2]

To enhance your assessment, there's nothing better than a recording. A video will let you see how your stage deportment came across. A high-quality audio recording, however, is your chief tool to evaluate musicianship.

When reviewing an audio recording, be deliberate. You might first listen to a piece in its entirety to hear the overall impact. Then you could consider smaller sections and home in on diverse elements. You might listen to the opening sixteen bars and gauge your timing; on a second perusal of that same chunk you'd weigh intonation; the third time around, you could focus on tone and dynamics.

Whether you have a recording or not, it's vital that you attribute cause and effect accurately. When the music reached transcendent heights, can you pin down how you achieved the divine outcome? If lapses occurred, do you know what triggered each misstep? Use the best parts as models, and think about how you might learn the thorny segments more deeply, viewing defects as highways to advancement. Clarinetist Anton Weinberg said, "This performance's problems should always be the next performance's insights."[3]

3. Move ahead

With your assessment finished, get busy meeting your practice goals. If your program needs only a few tweaks, practice your revisions, and then line up more performances. If your on-stage skills proved inadequate—say, you were acutely nervous—take a hiatus from high-pressure concerts and build up your confidence via low-stakes practice performances, as depicted in the coming section.

Some artists, however, go through a postconcert fizzle and can't move ahead. For weeks after a big show, they practice little. Should you ever land in such a rut, talk to a teacher or therapist. But you can head off most slumps with the following two-part approach.

First, well before an event, initiate other creative ventures that you can take up afterward. They can be small or large in scope, but the more passion you feel for them, the more positive spirit they'll generate. On the flipside, if you're about to perform a major concert and you have nothing slated for the ensuing weeks, you're setting yourself up for an emotional nosedive.

Second, arrange a vacation. Even if you can get away for only a day, plan a self-reward, preferably right on the heels of a performance. With well-timed vacations, the energy you expend preparing and performing gets recharged. You can then jump back into your work with gusto.

Practicing Performance

People have often said to me, "You're so relaxed when you play." Relaxed, my elbow. It's practice.

—Benny Goodman, clarinetist and bandleader

To become a professional-grade performer, you have to master an array of skills, as you have seen. And the only way that you can gain fluency with those skills is to practice them. This section, therefore, outlines three ways to practice performing.

> **Practice Performing**
>
> 1. Start a performance-development group
> 2. Do private run-throughs
> 3. Arrange public appearances

1. Start a performance-development group

A performance-development group includes two or more soloists or ensembles who agree to perform for each other in a supportive learning environment. Ideally, your group would meet in a recital hall, but any quiet space will do—classrooms and living rooms work well. You might appoint a group leader, hire an accompanist, and convene weekly. Or you could get together intermittently. In any case, the atmosphere you create should be sufficiently like a concert to enable you to ascertain how to harness on-stage energy and determine whether your memory holds up. It should give you chances to buff up your stage presence, hone error responses, test interpretations, and so on.

Such a group is a necessary supplement to a teacher's studio class because students require many more performance opportunities than teachers can provide. For example, if there's time in your class for you to perform once a month and on one occasion you have trouble with nervousness or memory slips, you need more chances to perform, and you need them soon. With a group available to hear you, you can practice for a few days and perform again. Correspondingly, when preparing for an audition, you'll want to run your program repeatedly, and your group will be there to hear you.

Psychologists Paul Salmon and Robert Meyer wrote, "Musicians who become enthusiastic and competent performers generally do so through systematic analyses of their strengths and limitations, along with continuous experimentation with and exposure to performance opportunities."[4] Your group is a laboratory where you can analyze and experiment without fear. You and your peers serve as allies in your pursuit of excellence. You supply each other with a lower-stakes situation than a public concert but a much higher-stakes one than a jam session. However, your group will be an effective training ground only if you adopt a formal protocol. If you share feedback, too, you'll benefit from faster improvement in your performance skills.

Adopt a formal protocol

To make your performances as concertlike as possible, implement the same stage deportment that you use in public. Whether you present solo or ensemble repertoire, walk on to applause, bow, announce the titles of your selections, and then perform whole pieces. When you conclude, look to your audience for applause, and bow again. Also, position a video or an audio recorder in front of you so that your assessments will be on target.

When planning your performances, set developmental goals, and devise strategies to attain them. To triumph over jitters, let's say, you could present a pair of elementary solos at moderate tempos. Your aims would be to release tension, image ahead, and shape the music expressively. At your next gathering, you'd perform the same titles once more, thereby reinforcing secure performance habits. Such regular, measured presentations are central to reversing a history of performance anxiety.

Share feedback

After performing for your group, your evaluation begins at once, unlike at a public show, where you cool down first. It's useful, therefore, to hear feedback from your listeners. When your group is newly formed, though, stick with specific, positive comments:

- "Your entrance and bow looked natural; you seemed happy to be performing."
- "You're timing at the end was exquisite."

Once you've built up trust, you may also want to offer constructive criticisms. As a rule, start with a positive remark, and use "I" statements to convey critiques (p. 118):

- "Your tempo and rhythm were solid, but I wonder whether the final ritard could have been more prolonged."
- "Your sound was rich and full. I would also have enjoyed hearing the quieter end of your range, maybe on one of the repeats."

As you share feedback, be encouraging. Every aspiring performer has challenges to overcome. So whatever difficulties you face individually, help each other do the groundwork necessary to master performance skills.

2. Do private run-throughs

In a private run-through, you practice performing—either solo or in an ensemble—but without listeners present. Schedule your run-throughs at fixed times so that, as with an actual show, you carry out your backstage rituals and gear up to perform irrespective of your mood that day. Whether your run-through takes place in a practice room or a recital hall, switch on your recorder, and envision being under the gaze of a rapt audience.

Launch each piece with a conscious procedure (p. 180), and then perform complete compositions. Project poised body language, treat errors as in a public event, and play or sing your heart out. If you're a soloist performing without your accompanist, mentally hear the accompaniment, and softly vocalize it during your rests.

As you perform, rehearse the techniques that will keep you centered in a real concert: Image ahead, release tension, breathe into your abdomen, listen to any coperformers, and manage your self-talk. If your mind drifts, return to full engagement with your music. Only through steady practice of on-stage skills will you garner proficiency using those skills.

The worth of any practice performance depends on how candidly you appraise it and what corrective actions you take. So, after running a brief selection, listen to your recording, take notes, and practice your revisions right then. Following a long set, hold off practicing for several hours or more to rest your body and clear your mind. Later on, when you're fresh, review your recording, and then use your observations to structure your practice.

3. Arrange public appearances

Private run-throughs and performances for peers are indispensable, but they aren't the same as public concerts. "Public performance is a potent truth serum," writes pianist William Westney.[5] If you believe that you're prepared to perform under pressure but, in fact, you aren't, you'll get a wake-up call when you step in front of a crowd.

To bridge the gap between practice performances and the highest-stake shows that you'll ever put on, when you're ready, it's wise to arrange public appearances at community venues such as churches and synagogues. Additionally, you and members of your performance-development group could organize salon concerts in various homes. When you have a major event on the horizon, plan several such performances so that you can elevate both your music making and your confidence to the highest possible levels.

Evaluating Your Progress

The single most important goal for performing artists is to see how they are doing.

—Itzhak Perlman, violinist

The route to becoming an accomplished musician is seldom smooth and trouble free. Some skills you'll pick up with ease; others will challenge you to the core. Throughout the learning process, however, one aptitude surpasses all others in importance: self-evaluation. Astute self-evaluation equips you to work from your strengths and correct any weaknesses. Without the ability to "see how you're doing," you won't identify problems, and, consequently, you'll reinforce useless habits and languish on a treadmill.

This section presents two self-evaluations that measure performance development. Use table 10.1 to size up a particular performance (figure 10.1 provides an example of how a student used it to do a verbal evaluation after playing a solo in her teacher's studio class). Employ table 10.2 (p. 204) to gauge your overall knowledge, skills, and attitudes.

When assessing your evolution as a performer, perceive things as objectively as you can and regard errors as valuable information. For example, if you had recurring slip-ups during a show, refuse to feel glum about them. Consider the probable causes, get help if needed, and commit to practicing differently. Objective evaluation lifts the fog of distorted thinking. It empowers you to pinpoint shortcomings and formulate action plans.

Table 10.1 **Performance-Evaluation Tool**

1. Note three or more aspects of your performance that went well.
2. Note three or more things that you'd like to improve before your next performance.
3. Determine the reasons for your successes.
4. Specify action plans to achieve improvements.

Sample Performance Evaluation

1. *Three or more aspects of your performance that went well*
   a. Before going on, I felt confident and connected to the music.
   b. On stage, I was tense for the first minute, but I was still able to control things; then I settled in comfortably.
   c. My beginnings and endings went exactly as I wanted; my timing wasn't distorted like last week.
   d. The second movement went beautifully; I pulled off expressive things that I had never thought of before.

2. *Three or more things you'd like to improve before your next performance*
   a. I'd like to be less tense in the shoulders.
   b. I felt disappointed at the beginning when things didn't line up immediately. I want to be more accepting and let go of negativity.
   c. I want to be more technically solid in the fourth movement.

3. *Reasons for the successes*
   a. Backstage, I warmed up gradually. Just before my entrance, I mentally rehearsed the opening.
   b. At the start, I was consciously hearing ahead while breathing and releasing. I had the adrenaline buzz, but I kept shaping every phrase.
   c. I practiced my launching routines all week, and I verified my tempos backstage with a metronome. On stage, I was mindful of how I was transitioning between movements.
   d. The slow tempo of the second movement allowed me to feel ahead easily. Also, when I practice that piece, I'm always experimenting with new expressive ideas.

4. *Action plans to achieve improvements*
   a. In my private run-throughs, I'm going to remember to move my body more at the beginning and let my shoulders widen.
   b. Backstage, I need to remember my inner smile and remind myself that my purpose in performing is to share music; it's not about me.
   c. I'll practice the fourth movement daily at a slower tempo and in sections, targeting the areas that aren't stable. Then I'll do a couple of practice performances for friends to make certain that I've learned it thoroughly.

Figure 10.1. Sample performance evaluation.

The next self-evaluation compiles 25 true/false statements derived from topics covered in this and the previous three chapters. Read each statement, and then circle your response. Any statement that you can't respond to in the affirmative points to an area that needs your attention. To address deficiencies, study this book, confer with your teacher, and then return to the evaluation to monitor your progress.

Table 10.2 **General Evaluation of Performance Development**

1. I'm building my understanding of how performance stress affects me before, during, and after a concert. T or F
2. I feel less threatened by performance stress. T or F
3. I'm more aware of the personal, task-related, and situational causes of performance anxiety in general and with me in particular. T or F
4. When I have trouble on stage, I always know how to practice to bring about improvements in my next performance. T or F
5. Of the five facets of preparation (artistic, technical, physical, mental/emotional, organizational), I know the areas in which I'm most capable and those in which I need to make more progress. T or F
6. In the areas of preparation in which I'm weakest, I have plans for how to advance. T or F
7. On the day of a concert, I know how to prepare myself and my things to minimize stress. T or F
8. Upon arrival at a venue, I'm capable of managing the backstage environment, supervising stage setup, and working with any staff. T or F
9. When I'm restless backstage, I use specific techniques to ease my discomfort and awaken my creativity. T or F
10. I feel secure walking on stage, bowing, and carrying out all of the other aspects of stage deportment. T or F
11. I can project a stage presence that contributes to an audience's enjoyment of my performance. T or F
12. I'm able to start and end pieces with consistent control. T or F
13. During a performance, I know how to employ tactics—such as deep breathing, mental focus, and positive self-talk—that lessen the unwanted effects of arousal. T or F
14. Even if I'm nervous, when performing accessible material, I can still be sufficiently accurate and expressive. T or F
15. Performing often stimulates me in constructive ways and helps me be creative. T or F
16. When performing, I'm committed to giving my listeners the best possible experience; I don't give in to self-conscious worries. T or F
17. I can speak to an audience in a personable way. T or F
18. I can handle on-stage errors to curtail their musical impact. T or F
19. While performing, I let errors go and seldom become distressed. T or F
20. After a concert, I'm able to accept my performance and not berate myself for slip-ups. T or F
21. Following a performance, I'm supportive of my colleagues and courteous to my listeners. T or F

Table 10.2 (*Continued*)

22. I deliberately evaluate my performances.	T or F
23. I regularly practice performance skills by doing private run-throughs and performing for peers.	T or F
24. I know where to find expert help for performance problems that I can't solve on my own.	T or F
25. I'm confident that my performance skills are improving.	T or F

As you work to heighten your facility as a performer, don't hesitate to seek aid for problems. A reputable music teacher is your primary source for advice to boost your skills. In addition, if at least one of the following four statements applies to you, then you should also seek the guidance of a therapist to help you discern the hidden, personal reasons for performance-related difficulties. Therapists can be found at most campus health centers; physicians can make referrals as well.

Signs that you should consult a therapist

- Even though you and your teacher are making your best efforts, you aren't seeing improvement in your on-stage security.

- Your performance anxiety can be so severe that sometimes you have to leave the stage without finishing a piece.

- You have persistent anxious feelings or troubling thoughts about performing that interfere with your sleeping or other aspects of your life.

- You often feel overwhelmed by the demands of performance preparation and are unable to practice consistently or effectively.

An honest analysis of your performance ability may expose a number of areas that need work, but don't let weaknesses deter you. The dilemmas that you tackle today will make you a better musician tomorrow. Cellist Jacqueline du Pré spoke to that very point: "Music making is a never-ceasing process of change and progress," she said. "One never arrives at the perfect performance but nevertheless draws increasing knowledge and insight and enthusiasm from every moment."[6]

Performing like a Pro

Performing like a Pro

> *It cannot be like a race. It is about beauty and feeling.*
>
> —Long Yu, conductor

When you perform outside of educational settings, you're expected to display the know-how of a professional. Not only will musicianship and performance skills be required, but it will also be assumed that you're adept at organizing concert programs. Your grasp of the music business will have to be substantial, too, so that you're self-assured in the world of commerce. Plus, you'll need to know the fine points of performing in diverse venues.

Still, professional expertise alone won't suffice. As your bookings multiply, personal challenges will mount as well. If you're not prepared to balance the demands of working as a performer against your needs as a person, then you might not endure in the music profession. To succeed, you have to cultivate self-care skills, pace yourself, and lower any internal barriers—such as perfectionism and fear—that prevent you from working productively. As you strive, you must also retain your connection to the beauty in music so that your artistry isn't trampled in a feverish race.

This chapter and the ones to follow in part III will help you flourish in professional, educational, and personal spheres. To begin, I'd like to clear up a bit of confusion about the nature of high-level performance and, in the process, flatten a common obstacle to artistic excellence.

The Peak-Performance Myth

When I play, I make love—it is the same thing.

—Arthur Rubinstein, pianist

If you've read much about performing, then you've probably run into the terms "peak performance," "flow," and "being in the zone." Those synonymous labels refer to a zone of optimal functioning, an ideal inner state in which a performer achieves maximum fluency with minimum effort. When you're having a peak experience with your music, your creativity seems boundless, and, technically speaking, you feel as though you can't miss.

Discussions of peak performance now appear widely, and all of the talk has spawned a problematic myth. The premise of the myth is that all high-level performances are peak performances and that, therefore, unless a musician attains a peak inner state on stage, the performance falls short. Nothing could be further from reality.

Musicians deliver inspired performances when they're in all sorts of inner states. Sometimes things flow easily, sometimes they don't, and a performer works harder to execute with artistry and precision. Being in the zone is pleasant, but it's beside the point. *Art* is the point, emotion-laden, penetrating art, irrespective of whether the musician is in the zone.

To put it another way, when you perform, the music and the audience are what count. Whether you're cruising effortlessly or working through every phrase isn't relevant to the music's impact or the audience's experience. An analogous example would be the athlete who scores a winning goal. The team is victorious, and no one cares whether the scorer was in the zone or whether she wrestled with a throbbing headache and a loosely tied shoe. Correspondingly, when an audience is transported by beautifully presented music, it's unimportant whether the musician performed with ease or had to contend with distracting thoughts and a stubborn itch. Of course, every performer wants to be as free as possible on stage. But if you can't perform well unless you're in a peak state, then you can't function as a professional musician.

To reach professional standards in your music making, you have to be able to prepare such that you don't require ideal circumstances to play or sing expertly. You need the flexibility to adapt to varied internal and external situations and then perform without a fuss. The musicians who lack preparatory skills fall apart when things aren't just so. After going bust on stage, they often claim that in an earlier practice session they were in the zone and performed flawlessly. Actually, their fragile learning creates only an illusion of control. Because of their belief in the peak-performance myth, however, rather than improving their preparation skills, such musicians look for extraneous ways to induce a zone-like state in which their flimsy foundations might somehow hold up.

To counter the peak-performance myth, I propose the *thorough-preparation principle:* When you prepare thoroughly, you don't need to be in the zone to excel in performance, yet your security provides you with the most direct route into the zone (not that being in the zone matters). For example, if you're a thoroughly prepared string player performing in a cold church and your fingers feel stiff, you don't despair. You breathe and lead yourself through the music. Your fingers may be icy, but your spirit catches fire, and the music soars. Were you in the zone? Nobody cares, including you.

The peak-performance myth infects countless budding artists with a self-defeating attitude toward public performance. First, musicians may wrongly believe that getting into the zone is essential to performing. Second, instead of celebrating concerts as unique events, they rate them as peak or not peak and, by default, as either acceptable or unacceptable. It's perfectionism by another name.

To make the most of a performance, the key is to be open to your experience and to discover new things in both the music and yourself. Author Jack Kornfield wrote, "This capacity to be open to the new in each moment without seeking a false sense of security is the true source of strength and freedom in life."[1] It's also the true source of artistry on stage.

That brings me back to the quotation that begins this section. For Arthur Rubinstein, performing and lovemaking were of the same stuff. What did he mean by that? For one thing, I think he was conveying the sense of immersion that an artistic performer enjoys on stage. That is, when you hold someone closely, you don't judge; you hug and let your emotions take over. As you perform, adopt an equally accepting attitude. Prepare thoroughly, and then embrace the music, audience, and performance situation, whatever they bring. Your listeners will thank you for it.

Designing Concert Programs

> *There are different programs for different places.*
> —André-Michel Schub, pianist

Memorable concerts have three indispensable ingredients: prepared performers, suitable settings, and the focus of this section: terrific music. In many ways, concert programs resemble lavish meals. A full-length recital, for instance, typically begins with an appetizer—something bite size or easily digestible—and then centers on main courses: longer, more emotionally intense music. Finally, for dessert, performers often serve up encores. A shorter program might follow a comparable pattern but consist of briefer selections. Whatever the length, when you assemble a concert menu, your listeners expect you to leave them satisfied. So here I've compiled seven concepts to boost the likelihood that your programs will hit the spot.

Designing Concert Programs
1. Know your audience
2. Choose music you can handle
3. Begin with welcoming music
4. Vary the energy
5. Indulge and surprise
6. End strongly
7. Evaluate

1. Know your audience

Audiences differ as much as individuals do. It's crucial, therefore, that you match your repertoire choices to each concert situation. When programming for less-experienced listeners, sensibly limit the duration of a performance, and pick material that leans toward the approachable end of your repertoire. For instance, a jazz combo with an affinity for avant-garde styles would be wise to mix in straight-ahead numbers when appearing outside the circle of jazz aficionados.

When performing for connoisseurs, you can liberally program cutting-edge or extended compositions. But be careful not to overestimate the adventurousness of your audiences. At the outset of your career, it's prudent to offer distinctive elements in your programs, such as premieres of new pieces, while also including mainstream styles. In that way, you establish an identity through your programming, yet your interpretive voice can also be weighed against other artists in your genre.

You can further entice listeners by organizing programs around titles or themes. When coming up with titles, avoid those that read like dissertation topics: "Keyboard Music from Eighteenth-century France." Instead, spark your audience's imagination: "Seduction at the Keyboard." And, in this case, add a clarifying caption: "Ravishing Music from the Royal Courts of France." Many concertgoers wouldn't know that eighteenth-century French music is rich with innuendo, but upon reading a title like that, they'll get the picture, and their curiosity will be piqued.

Whether you favor titles or not, think about including program notes. You might pepper your presentations with engaging words and add written commentary to any printed programs. Bear in mind that, when listeners aren't conversant with your style, they depend on you to trigger emotional connections. Well-crafted program notes help captivate audiences.

2. Choose music you can handle

During your apprenticeship, your programs include many freshly learned compositions. Veteran soloists, in contrast, mostly perform titles that they've known for years. Take heed not to overextend your capacity by packing every program with challenging new material. Collaborate with your teacher to choose music that's within your capacity and chart realistic preparation timelines.

3. Begin with welcoming music

Your opening selection is like a plate of hors d'oeuvres before a banquet. By beginning with straightforward, succinct, or lighter music, you introduce listeners to your sound and whet their musical appetites. You can commence in a gentle mood or with explosive force, but save your longest, densest, loudest, or most exotic titles for later.

Also be sure that your initial piece fits your needs as a performer. If you require time to settle in to being on stage, get under way with material that's easy for you to execute, even when you're buzzing with adrenaline. Your listeners will pick up on your confidence, and they'll quickly become receptive.

4. Vary the energy

Unlike a recording, which may be designed to deliver a consistent feel, concerts need contrast—and lots of it. As a general rule, when a program has two parts with an intermission, increase the musical energy up to the interval, and then escalate to greater heights in the second half. Create variety from piece to piece and also from one half to the next. Then, in the final quarter of your program, beware of letting the energy slacken; that's seldom the place for your slowest tempos or thinnest sonorities. And plan for your second half to be somewhat shorter than the first, or make the halves roughly equal. It's better to leave listeners wanting more than yawning.

With programs that lack intermissions, you'll often want to build momentum from start to finish. Another strategy is to intensify toward a midpoint, return to more intimate material, and then crescendo to a powerful closer.

5. Indulge and surprise

When people attend performances, they bring with them a host of expectations. Meeting their central expectations is vital to your success. If an audience expects to dance, you must supply dance tunes; if they come to hear a traditional piano recital, classical piano music has to be in the offing. But that's only the start. Memorable concerts don't merely deliver what's expected; they also take audiences beyond what they can envision.

It's up to you to concoct programs that indulge expectations while you also surprise listeners, at least to some degree, with your creativity. If you're clever at devising surprises, you might even gain a reputation for championing certain genres or composers. So, when drawing together well-known titles, try to include something unanticipated, as the American Chamber Trio did in the first model program ahead (p. 213). If you're partial to avant-garde or ethnic styles, integrate them into your concerts, but don't overdo it unless you're performing for a themed event as in the second model program below. Your most effective programs will both proclaim your personality and also fall within what your audiences can accept.

6. End strongly

Whatever the shape of your program, leave your audience with a strong impact. Usually, performers step up energy toward the finish and put the loudest and liveliest music last, but other designs can work, too. A standard orchestral program, for instance, might culminate with Beethoven's Symphony no. 5 (fast and loud). To commemorate a solemn occasion, however, a director might wrap up with Barber's *Adagio for Strings* (slow and soulful). Both closers are high-voltage, albeit in different moods.

Nevertheless, concerts don't always conclude with the final piece on the roster. After hearing a commanding performance, an audience often wants more, and I hope that you receive many such requests from your listeners. So have encores ready to go, but construct programs that satisfy without anything tacked on.

Keep your encore pieces brief, and contrast them with what came right before. For example, when your program ends in a fierce mood, try something serene or lighthearted as your first encore. Then, fire off a flashy showpiece for your second.

7. Evaluate

If you end a concert and your listeners rise to their feet, you know that your programming is on target. But when the reaction is so-so, how do you decide what to change? You can query your teacher, presenter, and listeners; still, you're the one who's accountable. Therefore, after every performance, appraise the outcome with questions such as these:

- Was the audience as you predicted, or did you misjudge their interests and concert experience?
- Were your selections within your performance capacity?

- Did the audience remain absorbed throughout, or did they become restless at times? When did their engagement peak? If their interest waned, when did they seem to drift off?

- Was the first piece welcoming enough and the final one conclusive enough?

- Was there sufficient variety in your program to both meet and exceed the audience's expectations?

- Did the sequence of pieces lead listeners across contrasting emotional and sonic terrain?

- Did your program notes and stage manner draw the audience in?

When a program doesn't succeed, sometimes a simple adjustment to the order of your selections will do the trick. At other times, major alterations will be needed, including the replacement of pieces or the revision of an underlying concept. Regardless, if your programming ideas aren't working, don't blame your audiences; instead, reevaluate your repertoire, rethink your presentation style, and seek advice from teachers and colleagues.

Three Model Programs

Programs are a little bit like prix-fixe menus in a restaurant: We can't serve music à la carte ... so our menu has to be quite diverse and—tasty.

—Eckart Preu, conductor

To demonstrate how programming concepts play out, this section features three model concert programs along with commentary on their designs (figures 11.1–11.3). To clarify the program structures, I've indicated the approximate durations of pieces, together with the dates of composition.

In model program no. 1, the American Chamber Trio chose time-honored works that New York classical music fans would enjoy, yet they also blended in a set of newer compositions by a local composer. Beginning with the melodic Shostakovich piece, the program increases energy in the first half and culminates with the *Finale* of the Brahms. In the second half, the extended soulfulness of the Mendelssohn contrasts with Ryden's ragtime-style music. The program indulges, but the Ryden surprises, and the ending makes for a witty dessert. In a sense, the encore is built in.

Model program no. 2 is taken from a Sunday afternoon chamber music series at the Brooklyn Museum that reflects on connections between music and visual art. The program shown on page 214 was tied to the museum's

Model Program 1

(A traditional chamber music concert with a twist)

THE AMERICAN CHAMBER TRIO

Eric Larsen, piano • Daniel Morganstern, cello • June DeForest, violin

Saturday, June 9, 2007, 8:30 P.M.
Weill Recital Hall at Carnegie Hall, New York City

Trio no. 1 in C Minor, op. 8 (1923)	*Dmitri Shostakovich (13 min.)*
Andante–Molto più mosso	*(1906–1975)*
Trio no. 2 in C Major, op. 87 (1880–1882)	*Johannes Brahms (29 min.)*
Allegro	*(1833–1897)*
Andante con moto	
Scherzo: Presto	
Finale: Allegro giocoso	

— INTERMISSION —

Trio no. 1 in D Minor, op. 49 (1839)	*Felix Mendelssohn (27 min.)*
Molto allegro ed agitato	*(1809–1847)*
Andante con moto tranquillo	
Scherzo: Leggiero e vivace	
Finale: Allegro assai appassionato	
Three Rags for Piano Trio	*William Ryden (14 min.)*
Irish Stew (1989)	*(b. 1939)*
Lisa's Spell (1992)	
You're a Grand Old Rag (2000)	

Figure 11.1. Model program no. 1.

permanent exhibit, American Identities. Its press release explained, "The concert explores the twin impulses of American art: proudly unschooled individualism versus European-trained internationalism."[2]

The concert opened with the individualistic atonal counterpoint of Carl Ruggles, the only composition on the program for solo instrument. Then, Thomson's Violin Sonata—tonal, lyrical, and built on the four-movement European model—represented internationalism. In a striking departure from

---

Model Program 2

(An innovative program organized around a themed event)

The Brooklyn Philharmonic presents
MUSIC OFF THE WALLS
"AMERICAN IDENTITIES"
Sunday, April 29, 2007, at 3:00 P.M.
Iris B. Cantor Auditorium, Brooklyn Museum, Brooklyn, New York
Paul Garment, clarinet • Katherine Hannauer, violin • Peter Vinograde, piano
Chris Nappi, percussion • Guillermo Cardenas, solo percussion
Jerome Kitzke, vocalist and composer

Evocations: Four Chants for Piano (1937–1954)   *Carl Ruggles (10 min.)*
    Largo   *(1876–1971)*
    Andante con fantasia
    Moderato appassionato
    Adagio sostenuto

Violin Sonata (1930)   *Virgil Thomson (13 min.)*
    Allegro   *(1896–1989)*
    Andante nobile
    Tempo di valzer
    Andante–Doppio movimento

A, B, C Identity Songs (2007) *World Premiere*   *Cristian Amigo (13 min.)*
    (violin, clarinet, piano, percussion)   *(b. 1963)*

Haunted America (2002)   *Jerome Kitzke (18 min.)*
    (violin/vocals, clarinet/vocals,   *(b. 1955)*
    piano/vocals, percussion/vocals)

Figure 11.2. Model program no. 2.

custom, the performers interspersed the movements of the work by Ruggles with those of the Thomson piece: After the first movement of Ruggles came the Thomson *Allegro*, then the second movement of Ruggles, and so on. Next, the program moved on to more recent individual expressions. The Amigo piece was commissioned for the event; the Kitzke was composed in the aftermath of 9/11 and combines instruments and speech.

Like many Sunday afternoon programs, this one was shorter than an evening concert and had no intermission. A host provided spoken program

---

Model Program 3

Lance's Senior Violin Recital

"247 STRINGS"

Campus Recital Hall

As Night Falls on Barjeantane (2001)   *Richard Danielpour (10 min.)*
                                            (b. 1956)

Music for 247 Strings (1981)   *Judith Weir (10 min.)*
                                            (b. 1954)

Sonata no. 2 in D Major, op. 94a (1942–1943)   *Sergei Prokofiev (23 min.)*
    Moderato   *(1891–1953)*
    Presto
    Andante
    Allegro con brio

— INTERMISSION —

Violin Concerto (1993)   *John Adams (33 min.)*
    Quarter note = 78   *(b. 1947)*
    Chaconne
    Toccare

Figure 11.3. Model program no. 3.

notes, and, during the performance, images from the museum's collection were projected behind the musicians.

The program includes avant-garde elements that surprise, yet it also features traditionalist music, the Thomson. It varies the energy, introduces a new work, and ends strongly. Also, the projected images and the use of a host make the concert interesting to a crossover audience. Note that the opening piece isn't the most straightforward in compositional style but is the lightest in sonority. Then, from the beginning on, the program builds drama.

Lance's recital (p. 215) began with the Debussy-like shimmer of the Danielpour piece and then progressed to the articulate musings of the Weir composition, which inspired the title for his program. The number 247 refers to the total number of strings on the violin and the piano. Given that the entire concert was performed on those two instruments, it struck Lance as an evocative header. After the Weir, the first half came to a bravura climax with the Prokofiev.

Although the second half presented a single piece, the Adams concerto carried the audience across an undulating topography, and the virtuosic third movement powerfully completed the recital. The program reflected Lance's fondness for newer music but also balanced indulgence with surprise by incorporating the more conservative Prokofiev piece and by drawing on both accessible and adventurous contemporary works that stood out against one another. Lance earned a standing ovation that night and then finished off with the poignant *Adagio* from the Sonata no. 1 in G Minor for unaccompanied violin by J. S. Bach.

The possibilities for programming are vast, and there's always room for innovation, so don't wait to start designing programs. Open a computer file, and periodically document themes around which to organize concerts. In a separate file, keep a running list of titles that you might like to perform in both the near and distant future. Look into composing and commissioning music, too, so that you contribute to the repertoire in your genre. Your imagination with programming can make the difference between your becoming either a busy performer with an eager audience or one who performs little.

Creating a Preparation Timeline

I find my greatest pleasure, and so my reward, in the work that precedes what the world calls success.

—Thomas Edison, inventor

Suppose that your concert program is set. In the preceding weeks and months, how do you ensure that all of your plans run smoothly? With big events, the artistic and logistic details can reach nerve-racking proportions, so it's wise to employ written timelines that itemize what and when things are going to get done.

I recommend a clear-cut format with two rows: one artistic; the other practical (p. 218). The artistic side lists your musical goals. It sets down which pieces should be ready when. With your artistic timeline set, you can work out individual and group practice schedules. The practical side of a timeline spells out the logistics. It specifies when to book your travel arrangements, submit programs, send promotional materials, and the like.

Lance assembled the timeline in figure 11.4 in preparation for his senior recital. It covers a 12-week period, over which Lance spread out his preparations, allowing him to be in shape for his concert and also meet his other commitments. You can download a timeline document from *musiciansway .com.*

Preparation timelines are useful not only for full-length recitals but also for all performances that involve complex planning, including the sorts examined in the next section: auditions and competitions.

Auditions and Competitions

> *When you are a student, the true value of participating in competitions comes from the educational opportunity.*
> —Rachel Barton Pine, violinist

In the life of almost every aspiring musician, auditions and competitions are crucial to career advancement. Yet in spite of their necessity, such performances rank among musicians' least favorite and most stressful appearances. The ideas here will equip you to understand why auditions and competitions arouse distaste and help you take on these types of performances with enthusiasm.

First, let's agree that no matter whether you perform at a closed hearing or in a public concert, the fundamental goal remains the same: to play or sing beautifully and securely. Aside from that, auditions and competitions have little in common with conventional performances.

Distinctive features of auditions and competitions

- An applauding audience is normally absent.
- Pieces are frequently presented incomplete.
- Performers may be interrupted.
- Musicians often get critiqued, sometimes harshly.
- The performance and backstage environments may be atypical.
- Performers are usually surrounded by peers who hold parallel aspirations.
- Awards may be won or lost, and expenses can be steep.

Lance's Preparation Timeline

Senior Violin Recital

Date	Artistic Timeline	Practical Timeline
Week 12	*Finish memorization of Danielpour. Finish determining fingerings/bowings for Adams.*	*Submit accompanist request form. Submit catering request for post-concert reception.*
Week 11	*All Prokofiev movements should be at or near their final tempos.*	*Submit recording services request form. Submit form to play Danielpour and Prokofiev at schoolwide performance hour.*
Week 10	*Play first two movements of Adams in lesson. Determine fingerings/bowings for Weir.*	*Stow backup photocopies of all music. Drop off music for accompanist. Schedule all rehearsals with accompanist.*
Week 9	*Play third movement of Adams in lesson at half speed. Finish memorization of first movement of Adams.*	*Write news release and public service announcement (PSA).*
Week 8	*Finish memorization of second movement of Adams. Play Weir in lesson.*	*Submit news release and PSA to campus public relations office.*
Week 7	*Third movement of Adams near final tempo.*	*Line up volunteer ushers. Begin writing program notes.*
Week 6	*Perform Danielpour and Prokofiev in studio class.*	*Email invitations for concert and reception.*
Week 5	*Finish memorization of third movement of Adams.*	*Drop off bow to be rehaired. Check for violin setup flaws.*
Week 4	*Weir at final tempo*	*Submit program to Music Office for printing. Pick up bow; buy extra strings; replace strings.*
Week 3	*Perform Weir and Adams in studio class.*	*Buy new tuxedo shirt, bowtie, and shoes. Buy thank-you gift for accompanist. Create and post promotional flyers.*
Week 2	*Play Danielpour and Prokofiev at schoolwide performance hour.*	*Verify schedule with recording engineer, ushers, and caterer; send email reminder to invitees.*
Week 1	*Confirm memory through daily mental practice.*	*Take tux to cleaners; get haircut. Pick up programs.*

Figure 11.4. Model preparation timeline.

Auditions and contests are concert-like in many ways, but they're also loaded with idiosyncrasies. To do well in the audition/competition setting, you have to amass a suite of personal, situational, and task-oriented skills to supplement those that you use with other performances. Here's a septet of strategies for developing those skills.

Audition/Competition Strategies
1. Select appropriate engagements
2. Choose material wisely
3. Practice and plan
4. Perform passionately
5. Exemplify professionalism
6. Capitalize on opportunities
7. Accept the results

1. Select appropriate engagements

Consult with your teacher on which engagements you should pursue and when—students are unlikely to succeed in the audition/competition arena without a teacher's guidance. Nonetheless, prowl the Internet on your own for promising events that fit your level. If you're going to audition for college or graduate programs, identify several viable ones so that your educational future won't be riding on one or two tryouts.

Also mull over financial and personal issues. Given the cost and effort involved, along with the probability that few entrants will prevail, if you apply for an audition or a contest, you should be prepared to absorb the expenses and walk away without winning a prize, landing a position, or being admitted to a given school. Therefore, adopt an expansive set of goals rather than an all-or-nothing mindset. The knowledge, contacts, and experience you collect may surpass the benefits of any one-time award.

2. Choose material wisely

Auditions and competitions often have strict repertoire requirements, so be sure to scrutinize any published rules. When you have some freedom in the choice of material, the music you perform should be within your capacity and display three qualities: drama, lyricism, and virtuosity. The dramatic impact should be powerful, spanning a range of emotions. Lyrical ingredients should show your knack for sculpting expressive lines. Virtuosic content should exhibit your instrumental or vocal command, especially at competitions.

To highlight those three qualities within the limited time that you'll be allotted to perform, choose contrasting pieces that demonstrate your flair for programming. Be wary, however, of committing to free-choice pieces that you haven't yet mastered; opt instead for titles from your core repertoire. Also, leave out original compositions except when the guidelines encourage them.

3. Practice and plan

Although you prepare thoroughly for all of your performances, for an audition or contest, you have to be particularly geared up. Create a preparation timeline, and then draw on the principles of artful practice and fearless performance described in the previous chapters. Then, because you may not be at liberty to pick the order in which you present your pieces, arrange practice performances where you line up your selections in various ways. Also put together a mock hearing: Recruit a teacher or colleague to play the role of a judge who requests pieces in random sequence and stops you intermittently.

Above all, plot a healthy practice schedule. Prior to weighty performances, some musicians intensify their rehearsing to an extent that they incur injuries. Don't make that same mistake. Pace your learning of material, rely on mental rehearsal, and, if you need to increase your physical practice, step up no more than 10–20% per week (p. 12).

As far as planning goes, tackle the logistics early on: Submit your application, hire an accompanist, organize travel, and so on. Plan, too, for how you'll handle things on-site to avoid being undermined by an atypical situation. Inquire about the facilities, but expect that warm-up rooms may be scarce. Be willing, therefore, to limber up in a hallway, a stairwell, or even a bathroom. With major appearances, arrive a day or more ahead to tour the location and rehearse. When you arrive at a venue for your performance, if you hear other competitors rehearsing, don't eavesdrop. Use your backstage routines, and stay focused on your primary goal: the presentation of a gripping concert.

4. Perform passionately

Upon entering the performance space, convey with your body language that you're happy to be there, and then dive wholeheartedly into your music. Whether you perform in a small room, a near-empty concert hall, or behind a screen, play or sing as dramatically as if you were presenting to a packed auditorium.

Also, dispel any concern for the outcome. Sports psychologist Harvey Dorfman says, "Dwell on external results, and pressure will build. Focus on execution, and pressure will lighten."[3] So treat errors as you would in a public show, and let go of any thoughts as to whether the judges like your performance or whether they'll interrupt. If you're halted and asked to begin something else, forget about the preceding music, stay centered, and launch your next piece. If you're cut short and informed that your audition is over, graciously exit.

5. Exemplify professionalism

Everything you do at a contest or an audition should support your image as a rising professional. Your attire should complement the performance situation; your conduct should be impeccably courteous. If, on the other hand, you come across as sloppy or brash, then it's likely that another musician will rise to the top. Check with a teacher if you're ever unsure about protocol.

6. Capitalize on opportunities

To maximize what you learn from auditions and competitions, seek feedback as appropriate. Let's say that you perform a favorite piece at a school audition, and then a faculty member declares, "I'm not sure that repertoire suits you." Although you might be taken aback, don't clam up; ask what pieces would make a better fit and why. Later you can revisit the pointers you gathered and decide how to use them, but while you have access to authorities, glean all the insights that you can.

If any networking opportunities arise, such as at a postcontest reception, strike up conversations with fellow musicians, and ask to exchange contact information. The connections you make with peers could evolve into lasting professional relationships.

7. Accept the results

Whenever you audition or compete, you offer yourself up for criticism. That criticism may be overt, as when judges provide comments, or it may be implied, as when a performer is passed over for a prize or a seat in an orchestra. If the thought of getting critiqued or of not winning a position makes you cringe, then your qualms about criticism and rejection will feed your performance anxiety. To make good in such situations, you have to welcome the judgment that comes with the turf (see *appreciating criticism*, p. 296).

Inevitably, when capable performers vie for the same prize, the spontaneous side of music performance combines with the subjective nature of evaluation to cook up a stew of unpredictability. Sometimes it's obvious who deserves an award; other times judges agonize to select a winner from a pool of comparable finalists. Pledge to accept the results of any audition or contest, whether you think they're apt or odd. And approach an event with a broad-based career plan and a solid sense of self so that the stakes don't assume inflated importance.

In sum, you can control your performance but not the result of an audition or a competition. If you prepare thoroughly and perform as well as you can, you have succeeded. If you underperform because some feature of your preparation was inadequate, you also benefit because competing teaches you things that you aren't able to learn otherwise. Either way, your participation fuels your growth.

᭦

Even after you become adept at performing at auditions and competitions, they may continue to feel more stressful to you than other performances. Still, you can learn to manage that stress. Auditions and contests may be among your most significant career-building performances. Why not enjoy them, quirks and all? I'm not saying that they're rip-roaring fun, but by respecting their demands, you can take pleasure in meeting those demands head-on.

Finally, for college music students, one particular audition is inevitable: the jury. Once a semester, each student performs individually before a panel of faculty members. Professors furnish written comments and may assign grades; the purpose is to document a student's progress.

The jury is a wellspring of criticism that calls for many of the same preparatory steps listed here. Prepared students profit from juries because the feedback they receive contributes to their growth. Juries also groom students for real-world auditions. If juries make you shudder, though, talk to your teacher. As you hone your coping strategies, all of your performances will improve.

The Recording Studio

If artists cannot produce themselves, what's the point?

—Branford Marsalis, saxophonist and bandleader

Just as you need special preparation to compete or audition successfully, performing in a recording studio involves a specific skill set. For example, from an artistic angle, compared to how you play or sing on stage, in the studio, your tone may need to be more refined and your expression less exaggerated—you aren't projecting to the back rows of an auditorium but molding music to be captured through a mic. There are also personal and

> **Recording Topics**
> 1. Practicing for a recording session
> 2. Organizing for the studio
> 3. Setting up and recording
> 4. Self-producing
> 5. The final steps

situational adaptations to make. That is, many musicians perform freely in front of people but become self-conscious when recording.

This section covers fundamental actions that soloists and small groups can take to excel at self-produced recording sessions. I don't address the technicalities of sound engineering. Instead, the goal here is to outline five topics that will help you perform artistically in the studio and create the best recorded product that you can.

1. Practicing for a recording session

When practicing for a recording session, your chief goals are to elevate your artistry and control while preparing for the studio situation. Here are the top things to keep in mind:

a. Spruce up your style. Purify your tone and attack, ripen your interpretation, and mitigate extraneous sounds such as shifting feet and loud breaths.

b. Maintain a stable position. When recording, the sound source and the microphones have to be in a steady relationship. Keyboardists aren't troubled by this issue, but for many others, steady positioning can be tiring. During practice, accustom yourself to any positioning constraints, and you'll be more at home in the studio.

c. Manage your beginnings and endings. Use longer silent counts to begin and extend your closing silences to frame each take in stillness.

d. Solidify tempos. Jot down metronome settings on your music, and be a stickler for consistency of tempo in practice. For editing purposes, all takes of a piece should be at identical tempos.

e. Plan the length of takes. If you're dividing pieces into smaller sections that you'll record individually, practice starting and ending each chunk.

f. Polish intonation. Regularly refer to a keyboard or a tuner to guarantee that your intonation is reliable.

g. Practice performing. Enlist a personal recorder, and employ the same protocol to be used in the studio: Announce titles and take numbers ("Prelude, first section, take one"), create ample silence, and maintain a stable position.

h. Ensure quality. Engineers can edit your takes together, but they can't turn a mediocre performance into a superior one. Schedule a session only after your performance reaches the benchmark of excellence.

2. Organizing for the studio

For complex sessions, preparation timelines (p. 218) and preperformance inventories (p. 163) will simplify your organization. The following are six additional considerations:

a. If possible, visit the recording site in advance, and get to know the layout.

b. Pick out comfortable clothes, and skip jewelry or accessories that could rattle.

c. Coordinate instrument adjustments. If you're replacing strings, drumheads, or parts, do so early enough that everything is broken in.

d. Schedule intelligently. At each session, plan to record a few selections superbly rather than plowing through numerous titles without rigorous quality control. Quality trumps quantity every time. Also rule out strenuous, marathon sessions—schedule multiple shorter appointments so that you'll perform at your best and you won't invite injury.

e. Budget sensibly. When funds are tight, don't try to produce a full-length album; just record a handful of pieces to use as a demo or to post on your website.

f. If you intend to record copyrighted titles, you must obtain mechanical licenses. Such licenses can often be purchased online.

3. Setting up and recording

At your first session at a professional studio, it might take longer than you expect to set up and find the best recorded sound, so ask your engineer to give you a time estimate beforehand. For soloists and small groups who perform acoustically, 2–3 hours is a good bet, depending on your instrumentation and the staffing at the studio. If you use electronic instruments, that may extend your setup time. Regardless, throughout the setup process, preserve your creative mindset with backstage techniques (p. 162).

When the setup is finalized, document it so that you can get a matching sound at every session: Mark the placement of mic stands and equipment with tape on the floor; maybe snap some photos with your phone. Also note the settings for the mixer and other electronic gear.

Here are a few things to remember before and during your takes:

a. Remove jangling keys from pockets, and turn off unneeded portable electronics.

b. Announce the title and number of a take, and then add silence at the start and the finish.

c. Deal with errors as in a live performance. For the most part, execute complete takes, even when things bet bumpy midway. If you repeatedly trip on the same spot, record that portion separately.

d. Tune often—uniformity of pitch is essential to joining the various takes. Also keep tabs on your tempos by frequently checking them with a metronome.

e. Pause for breaks. Yes, the studio meter continues to run, but breaks will keep you fresh and help protect against exhaustion. On balance, your total studio time will probably be less than if you were to push on through fatigue.

f. Play or sing from your heart. Even though recording is hard work, have fun. That spirit of enjoyment will be heard in the final product.

4. Self-producing

With high-budget pop recordings, producers work out the instrumentation, musical arrangements, and other features that lift recordings to their artistic peaks. When you're an up-and-coming musician, however, and making low-budget recordings, your task as self-producer becomes vastly simpler. Your main job in the studio, besides directing the setup, is to be in charge of quality control and log the details about each take. You're responsible for ensuring that all of the material needed for editing winds up in the can. So listen attentively to your live performance and periodically to some playback to be certain that everything is up to par. Position a notebook at your side to facilitate logging.

When a session concludes, bring your notes and the audio files home with you to verify that you have what you need or to plan for retakes. Then, after your last session winds up, you'll be supervising the editing, mixing, and mastering processes. If you're creating CDs, you'll also be overseeing the artwork and the manufacture.

5. The final steps

I'd like to make one suggestion here: If you're doing the editing and mixing yourself, unless you're a whiz in the studio, it's worth hiring a mastering engineer to put a final polish on your product. You might do some initial mastering on your own, but an expert can correct undesirable elements that you may not be hearing (at this stage of the project, you've lost your objectivity). Given all the work that you've done to create your recording, avoid rushing to the end. Take the time to show the world your best.

Before the twentieth century, musicians could share music with audiences only via live performances. Now, in the twenty-first century, artists and listeners commune in cyberspace, and you can circulate your music globally. No serious musician can afford to be ignorant of the basics of sound recording. If you deem yourself deficient in the area of music technology, enroll in a course. The knowledge you acquire will enable you to reach audiences on a scale that musicians in past generations could not have imagined.

Part III

Lifelong Creativity

12

Injury Prevention, I

In this chapter:

- Causes of injury
- Warning signs and responses
- Injury-prevention basics
- Recovering from injury

Lifelong Creativity

When we are in touch with the refreshing, peaceful, and healing elements within ourselves and around us, we learn how to cherish and protect these things and make them grow.

—Thich Nhat Hahn, author and peace activist

Some musicians continue creating throughout their lives. Others, though, succumb to burnout, frustration, or injury. What do the lifelong creators know that the others do not?

Besides being adept at practice and performance skills, the musicians who carry on creating take active roles in caring for themselves. They respect their physical limits; they renew their passion for music; they embrace rather than retreat from the challenges of music careers. They're connected to "the refreshing, peaceful, and healing elements within."

Part III of *The Musician's Way* explains how you can attain comparable inner awareness. Chapters 12 and 13 explore the physical aspects of self-care —they sort through the injuries that undercut musicians and catalog the habits that hold injuries at bay. Chapter 14, *Succeeding as a Student,* confronts the trials that aspiring musicians face both in and out of music schools. In all, these chapters spell out self-care tactics that can equip you to make music for life.

Musicians and Injuries

*People take such wonderful care of their $40,000 violin or $10,000
flute—they need to take care of their bodies the same way.*
                                    —Richard Norris, physician and flutist

Most people know that musicians work hard to develop and maintain their
abilities. But few seem to realize that practicing, performing, and teaching
music can trigger life-changing injury. Even musicians themselves aren't well
informed about their occupational health risks. For instance, researchers have
found that approximately two-thirds of professional orchestral musicians
incur playing-related injuries such as tendonitis. The mildest of these mal-
adies might stop artists from performing for several days; the more serious
may result in extended disability. Similarly, singers and teachers suffer
damage to their voices, and hearing loss plagues performers and educators
in almost every musical genre.[1] Among student musicians at a Midwestern
university, 79% of incoming freshmen admitted to having experienced pain
linked to playing or singing.[2]

Still, there is good news: Nearly all of these musicians' injuries are preventable. What blocks musicians from adopting healthier habits? Lack of
information, apparently. Most music students receive scant instruction in
occupational health, and workplaces often expose performers and teachers
to long hours and extreme sound levels. Even when musicians recognize that
music making can have adverse effects, many either feel powerless to take
corrective action or are unaware of what to do.

In response to the high rates of health problems among musicians, this
chapter and the next examine ways that you can pursue your musical dreams
without injury setting you back. They tackle this intricate subject by drawing
on current research, but they don't go overboard on the particulars of anatomy
and physiology. Nevertheless, scientific data and anatomical images are
available via resources listed in the bibliography and at *musiciansway.com*.

I'll begin by investigating three topics as they pertain to instrumental musicians: causes of injury, warning signs and responses, and prevention strategies. Together, these themes represent a knowledge base that no performer
can afford to overlook. To conclude this chapter, I'll also describe a protocol
for recovering from injury. Matters of vocal health and hearing protection
are deferred until chapter 13 to make the content here more streamlined.
Vocalists who don't play instruments may be tempted to skip ahead. If you're
a singer, however, I invite you to read on because the following principles
will help you collaborate with instrumentalists; what's more, parallel concepts
apply to the voice.

Causes of Injury

I continued to play with a sore arm with the rationalization that I could play through the pain and that the discomfort would just miraculously go away as I got into better shape as a cellist. But the pain didn't go away. It got worse.

—Janet Horvath, cellist

The injuries that instrumentalists incur stem, by and large, from five causes: overuse, misuse, accidents, anatomical differences, and individual sensitivities. All five are summarized here.

Causes of Injury
1. Overuse
2. Misuse
3. Accidents
4. Anatomical differences
5. Individual sensitivities

1. Overuse

Bodies have limits. When musicians exceed their physical limits by overplaying, vulnerable tissues may tear, and then injury results. Veteran performers possess the expertise to work within their capacities. Less-experienced musicians might not appreciate the fact that things like sudden increases in playing time or a lack of breaks can wear them down and bring on injury. With an understanding of how overuse leads to trouble, you can boost the likelihood that you'll stay within safe margins. First, you need insight into how overuse affects muscles, tendons, and nerves.

a. Muscles

Muscles can do only a finite amount of work before they have to rest. When muscles are overused—say, from incessant or vigorous playing—microscopic ripping can occur. Slight damage may heal overnight, but when an injury goes beyond what the body can repair quickly and the musician continues to use the strained muscle, added trauma usually takes place. Then pain appears. If the musician doesn't back off and allow the muscle to heal, significant impairment may follow and even require protracted rehabilitation before the musician will be free of pain. Generally, the longer a musician plays despite fatigue and pain, the worse an injury becomes, and the more prolonged the recovery period will be.

Such overuse injuries can be caused not only by playing instruments but also by any repetitive or hard-hitting movement. Instrumentalists should be mindful of all hand-intensive tasks and balance their daily hand usage. For instance, to compensate for an increase in playing time or intensity, a perceptive string player will restrict computer use accordingly.

b. Tendons

Muscles initiate movement, but they don't attach directly to bones; nonelastic tendons tie bone to muscle. Tendons, like muscles, are made of living cells that have limits. Furthermore, where tendons pass near joints, they're typically surrounded by protective sheaths. As you wiggle your fingers, for example, tendons glide through sheaths in the wrist, and a lubricating fluid ensures that there's no friction.

Overuse can harm both tendons and their sheaths. Physician Emil Pascarelli explains that the fluid that lubricates tendons is used up by movement and restored during rest.[3] When musicians play without taking breaks, the fluid can become depleted, and friction then arises between tendon and sheath. This chafing damages cells, and pain and swelling ensue. If a musician continually overuses tendons and sheaths, chronic pain can develop. Also, the sites where tendons bind to bone or muscle are especially at risk of injury— tennis elbow is a familiar manifestation.

Physicians classify the inflammation of tendons as tendonitis and the swelling of tendon sheaths as tenosynovitis. Musicians, however, often use the label "tendonitis" as a catchall to refer to painful conditions that affect the inclusive muscle-tendon unit.

c. Nerves

Nerves form the body's electrical system. They transmit motor impulses from the brain to the muscles and conduct sensory information back to the brain. The most prevalent nerve problems among musicians come about when nerves are impacted by the swelling of neighboring tissues. In the slender confines of the wrist, for instance, inflammation of tendon sheaths can compress a nerve, thereby inciting pain, tingling, and weakness in the hand. If symptoms crop up, it's vital that swelling be reduced to thwart nerve damage. Nerve compression happens in locations other than the wrist as well, such as at the elbow, but because the wrist area is termed "carpal" and the pathway through which the abovementioned nerve and tendons pass resembles a tunnel, nerve compression at the wrist is known as carpal tunnel syndrome.

❀

In addition to muscles, tendons, and nerves, overuse also affects musicians' lips, skin, and joints. Brass and wind players who practice relentlessly can exhaust their chops and be temporarily handicapped by pain and swelling. Those who persist despite such discomfort risk lasting disability. String players who flout their limits might play their fingertips raw; violinists and violists can also irritate the skin on their neck. And those musicians who overload their joints, perhaps by holding up heavy instruments, can suffer crippling pain.

Women are stricken by overuse injuries significantly more than men, although the reasons aren't entirely clear.[4] Researchers suggest that women may be more susceptible due to their smaller stature and hand size, greater joint flexibility (explained later in this chapter), and the fact that they tend to have less muscle bulk. On the whole, though, the strategies for preventing overuse injuries are identical for both men and women. They include finding a good fit between player and instrument, stepping up playing time gradually, limiting repetition, taking regular breathers, and maintaining overall health. Musicians can also fend off overuse through managing stress—when preperformance anxiety rages, musicians frequently overpractice to the point of injury.

2. Misuse

Misuse occurs when musicians employ movements or postures that are contrary to the body's nature. It causes strain that can break down tissues and spark injuries akin to those instigated by overuse. For example, when musicians slouch while playing, their misaligned posture can precipitate pain in the back and the neck.

In contrast, "good use" entails moving and playing in efficient ways. Musicians who practice "good use" cultivate awareness of their movement habits— they take up balanced postures and avoid excess muscular tension. Hence, their playing appears effortless. By comparison, those who misuse themselves seem awkward at their instruments. Their clenched muscles and twisted joints undermine both their well-being and their effectiveness as performers.

When the strain of misuse mixes with the repetitive techniques of music making, musicians often develop repetitive strain injuries. Such injuries affect people in all occupations that require repetitive movements. Hands, arms, backs, and necks are commonly involved. To dodge such troubles, musicians have to move proficiently when playing and when doing other hand-intensive tasks such as typing. Chapter 13 offers guidelines for achieving good use.

3. Accidents

Like everyone else, musicians are subject to accidents. From sports injuries to car crashes to stumbles, cuts, and burns, performers can be felled by a multitude of mishaps. Most musicians have heard ample counsel regarding safety in daily life, so I won't itemize injuries that aren't related to music making or enumerate the myriad strategies for preventing them. Suffice it to say that performers should buckle up in the car, wear protective equipment when playing sports or operating machinery, and think twice before handling sharp tools. Physician and bassoonist William J. Dawson also recommends that wind and brass players hire dentists to make molds of their upper and lower teeth to aid dental reconstruction in the event of a traumatic injury.[5]

Let's look at two classes of accidental injuries associated with music making: those caused by hauling gear and those indirectly provoked by performance stress.

a. Hauling gear

When I ask professional musicians to recount their run-ins with accidents, many of them tell stories about hurting themselves transporting instruments and gear. A cellist injured his arm lifting a suitcase from the trunk of a car; a flutist harmed her shoulder raising a bag into an airplane's overhead bin; a guitarist fractured his wrist when he tripped while moving an amp. Others recall agonizing back spasms set off by carrying instruments.

To sidestep such injuries, when you haul equipment, remember that injury is possible, and then make safety your top priority. First, because hurrying makes accidents more likely, allow plenty of transport time. Then, when lifting, squat rather than bending at the waist, and use wheeled carts to shift weighty objects. If you play a bulky instrument or you ever have to carry an instrument for some distance, ask your teacher for pointers on how to transport it without strain—tips can also be accessed at *musiciansway.com.*

b. Performance stress

When a concert date nears, certain players become prone to misfortunes such as getting their fingers crushed in car doors. It's as though mental preoccupation short-circuits their safety practices.

As you get ready for a show, exercise care in all of your activities. Slow down when driving; walk cautiously on slick winter terrain. If you're affected by intense preperformance anxiety, study part II of this book to acquire coping strategies, and then consult a therapist if problems remain. Stressed people are predisposed to all sorts of afflictions, so stress management should be at the forefront of your self-care plans.

4. Anatomical differences

The natural differences in human anatomy not only give each person a unique appearance and voice quality but also enable some musicians to adapt easily to the demands of playing instruments while causing difficulties for others. Here I consider two categories of anatomical differences that influence one's risk of injury: body size and body structure.

a. Body size

Although people vary greatly in their proportions, musicians don't always play instruments that fit their bodies. When a mismatch occurs between player and instrument, misuse becomes more likely, and so does injury. In fact, researchers observe that as instrument size increases, injury rates rise, too.

Ideally, all performers would be matched with instruments that complement their stature. Among preteen violinists, fitting for size is traditional. Instruments come in assorted dimensions, and ergonomic devices such as shoulder rests are widely employed. Other performers are benefiting from more recent innovations, such as narrower piano keyboards. Actually, ergonomic adaptations exist for most instruments. They can accommodate disparities in hand span, for instance, and also lessen the load on the body when supporting an instrument. For example, clarinetists can reduce the weight on their right thumbs by wearing neck straps; bassoonists can sport harnesses or shoulder straps. English horn players, bass clarinetists, and other instrumentalists can enlist endpins, which transfer much of an instrument's mass to the floor. See *musiciansway.com* for an inventory of tricks.

Unfortunately, ergonomic strategies don't necessarily receive widespread acceptance. When musicians need accommodations for their size but are unaware of available fixes, they might strain when they could otherwise be comfortable. Keep in mind that world-class musicians come in a variety of shapes and sizes, so physical attributes don't inevitably confer career-changing advantages or disadvantages. Finding the right fit between musician and instrument and adopting habits of good use are what count most.

b. Body structure

Here I'm referring to structural differences apart from those that affect size. One such difference concerns a joint's range of motion. Minimal range of motion in a finger joint will curb a musician's reach, so he might struggle or be unable to execute fingerings that others play easily. Conversely, extreme flexibility in a joint, found among musicians who might be called "double jointed," can also be troublesome because, in attempting to stabilize a floppy knuckle, a musician might misuse or overuse certain muscles. Physician William J. Dawson writes that hypermobility is seen in 5–8% of people.[6] However, hypermobility has been found in the finger joints of a disproportionately large number of musicians with hand and arm pain, so it's a noteworthy risk factor for injury.[7]

Can a joint's range of motion be altered? For healthy adults, the range of motion is typically set, although past injuries or exceedingly tense or weak muscles may present limitations that can be improved upon. Regardless, prudent musicians pass up trying to amend a joint's range of motion on their own—rashly chosen exercises could induce injury rather than gain. To avoid problems, students who suspect that they may have either taut or hyper-mobile joints should seek the help of physicians, physical therapists, or hand therapists. Concurrently, they should work with their teachers to choose repertoire, instruments, and techniques suited to their anatomies. They may also want to modify their instruments, perhaps by putting extensions on wood-wind keys. For the most part, the solution to range-of-movement issues lies in harnessing appropriate therapies, working intelligently with the range that one has, and never forcing beyond one's physical boundaries.

Another structural variation affects finger independence. When anom-alous tissues in the forearms or hands link the finger tendons, the autonomy of the digits is restricted.[8] As an example, a guitarist with a type of linkage between the left ring and little finger tendons will struggle to place the ring finger on the bass string while the little finger depresses the first string. Yet players with standard anatomies will do so effortlessly. When independence is hampered by anatomy, musicians are liable to strain and injure themselves unless they adapt their fingerings, instruments, and movement habits. Can independence be acquired? With respect to muscular coordination, yes. Anatomically speaking, the die is cast except for conditions that need reha-bilitation.

Just as one size doesn't fit all when choosing instruments, differences in body structure also mean that one manner of playing is unlikely to suit every instrumentalist. If musicians feel discomfort with conventional techniques, instruments that are right for their stature, and reasonably good use, they should consult medical experts to determine whether they're dealing with structural matters that require accommodation.

5. Individual sensitivities

Human diversity encompasses more than anatomical disparities—there are also genetic and other factors that provoke playing-related woes. For instance, similar to the way numerous people are allergic to pollen, some musicians develop skin reactions from contact with their instruments. The metals in mouthpieces or strings are among the substances that can produce rashes or inflammation. Fortunately, alternative materials are available. Many per-formers also contend with chronic diseases such as arthritis, which make aches and inflammation more likely. Musicians with such sensitivities should collaborate with their physicians and teachers to head off setbacks.

Another kind of sensitivity appears in the nervous system of certain per-formers such that, over time, they lose control of their playing motions. Termed *focal dystonia,* musicians who are afflicted with this condition find that muscles contract uncontrollably during playing yet function normally in other activities. For example, a brass player's top lip might pull upward when she plays in a particular register; a pianist with focal dystonia might experience involuntary curling of the right fourth and fifth fingers when he plays passages on a keyboard.

Needless to say, dystonia is debilitating and, at present, isn't wholly curable. With treatment and retraining, though, some players can continue performing. Physician and researcher Eckart Altenmüller writes that about 1% of musicians will be affected by dystonia, although the condition turns up more in male than female performers and is diagnosed most often among musicians in their thirties.[9] Scientists haven't yet pinned down its causes, but several insights have emerged. Dystonia isn't the most pervasive malady, but, given its devastating effect, musicians ought to know of its existence and take steps toward prevention.

Focal dystonia results from changes in the motor area of the brain. For some musicians, the changes arise with no traceable origin other than repetitive movement—it seems that they're genetically predisposed. For others, dystonia evolves subsequent to a surge in playing or a modification of technique or after they become engrossed in a new hand-intensive task. That is, learning a new technique or task or pushing through fatigue and overuse compels the brain to concoct a novel motor program. In the process of creating that fresh program, the established one used for playing becomes corrupted.

Because of such findings, neurologist Michael Charness advises musicians to "Begin slowly and increase gradually any unaccustomed use of the hands."[10] Therefore, in addition to regulating playing time, when musicians make major technical adjustments, whether involving their hands or embouchure, they should introduce new movements in stages. If they take up unfamiliar instruments (for instance, if a saxophonist starts playing the flute), performers would be wise to step up usage little by little.

Warning Signs and Responses

Injuries often develop at the least convenient times—for example, while preparing for important auditions or concerts—and musicians typically "tough it out." While a musician delays seeking help, his or her injury tends to get worse.

—Angela Myles Beeching, music career counselor

When your body comes under stress, it will almost always let you know, sometimes softly and sometimes with a jolt. But if you don't recognize the signals you receive, you won't respond constructively. When you do detect an alert, you also have to know how to react so that you promote healing and ward off serious injury.

In reality, spotting signals and taking action aren't as easy as you might think. Many musicians misinterpret symptoms or become anxious about what to do and then pay a steep price when they defer getting aid. Such was the case with violinist Christine Harrison, whose injury sidelined her for years: "I ignored all my body's warning signals in the name of 'dedication' to what I was doing," she wrote. "I had absolutely no idea that this little problem would in fact threaten my career."[11]

This section lists the principal warning signs of injury and describes healthy ways to respond when they show up. As mentioned earlier, the following won't include issues of voice care and hearing protection; they'll be covered in the next chapter.

Warning Signs

When you push your body past its limits, the most common signals are fatigue, pain, or odd sensations such as tingling.

1. Fatigue

Both physical and mental fatigue ought to start your caution light blinking. On the physical side, tired muscles are more prone to injury, as are tendons, lips, and skin that have reached their thresholds. Mental fatigue doesn't cause injuries directly, but as attentiveness wanes, performers may unconsciously tense up as they grapple to hold things together. Simply put, mental fatigue leads to misuse.

2. Pain

Pain can surface in various guises, but whether it shoots, throbs, or twinges, unrelenting pain means trouble. Many musicians, however, don't acknowledge the implications of pain. Physician Alan Lockwood found that 79% of a group of teen music students believed that pain was acceptable if they were overcoming technical hurdles.[12] Don't subscribe to any such misconceptions about the meaning of pain. Although temporary achiness may follow intense muscle use, it shouldn't hurt to play. Persistent pain is a signal that something's wrong.

3. Odd sensations

The body is made up of differentiated cells that perform distinct functions and, metaphorically speaking, communicate in diverse languages. For example, stressed nerves may produce tingling, weakness, or numbness without signaling any pain. Other tissues indicate their irritation by causing joint stiffness, a decrease in your facility, or a reduction in your stamina. Be on guard. Painless warning signs are easy to brush aside, but all symptoms call for urgent action.

Responding to Symptoms

When a warning sign appears, whether it screams or whispers, your unfailing response should be to stop what you're doing, rest, and, when the symptom is more than ordinary fatigue, get help.

1. Stop

Whether you're making music or engaging in some other task, a warning sign is a message to stop. Even if you're rehearsing with a group or typing a report that's due in an hour, when you notice symptoms, you must halt what you're doing or you risk turning a mild problem into a severe one.

How can you stop playing midway through a rehearsal or postpone submitting a time-sensitive report? You don't take such actions lightly, but when your well-being is jeopardized, you have to find a way to put on the brakes and deal with the consequences. No consequence is worse than injury, so compassionate teachers, colleagues, and employers will work with you to find solutions. Even so, the social issues that surround the handling of symptoms can be thorny, so I'll spotlight that topic in the coming paragraphs.

2. Rest

Along with stopping, it's essential that you rest so that tissues can heal. If you feel fatigue, pain, or odd sensations in your arm, you must back off repetitive or strenuous use of that arm. How long should you rest? A skilled helper will tell you. In general, when symptoms are treated promptly, only a brief period of total rest is required. Then a phase of relative rest takes place, leading up to a return to normal activity.

3. Get help

When a warning sign stops you in your tracks—something beyond run-of-the-mill fatigue—consult both your teacher and a medical professional. If you're unsure whether your symptoms are significant enough to warrant calling a doctor, go by the advice of physician and arts medicine specialist Alice Brandfonbrener: "Symptoms that persist more than a few days or progress should be evaluated by a physician."[13]

Many students turn solely to their teachers when symptoms arise, but I urge you to see a medical professional, too. Informed teachers will help you correct technical faults that might have caused your symptoms, and they can facilitate aspects of your recovery. But music educators rarely have medical training, so they're unlikely to know all of the ins and outs of warning signs and the range of available therapies. Furthermore, it's in your best interest to protect the confidentiality of your medical history within the confines of the healthcare system.

If you need specialized care, either your teacher or health provider can make referrals. There are clinics in the United States, Europe, and around the world that treat musicians, and you can track down many of them at *musiciansway.com.*

◆◆

Although these symptoms and responses may seem clear cut, hordes of knowledgeable music students still don't respond appropriately to warning signs, and I've noticed three main reasons for this: dysfunctional student-teacher relationships, anxiety, and misinformation about consequences and accommodations.

Obstacles to Healthy Responses

- Dysfunctional relationships
- Anxiety
- Misinformation

Chapter 14 probes various features of student-teacher relationships, but in the context of how to handle warning signs, I assume that all music educators want their students to stay well. Nonetheless, when a student who is to play a vital role in an upcoming performance reports an injury symptom, some teachers might exhibit anger upon learning that the student is obliged to rest rather than perform. Of course, injured students can predict how a teacher might react to their news. When students fear a teacher's reaction, they may hide their symptoms and plow ahead, sometimes with tragic results.

If you have a distressing pang before a performance, don't vacillate. If you're practicing alone, you notice a warning sign, and you foresee an unsympathetic reaction from your teacher, obtain a medical evaluation first—it's confidential—and ask for advice on communicating with a teacher and on the subject of possible accommodations. In the event that a signal pops up in the middle of an ensemble rehearsal, stop playing, ask to speak privately with the director, and request guidance. No director, no matter how hot headed, wants a musician to make light of discomfort; directors know that ignoring symptoms hastens injury. I hope that, after studying this book, you'll be armed to avoid exceeding your limits and you won't be struck by pain during a rehearsal. Still, unexpected things happen, so you need to be prepared.

Also, the emotional burden of getting a symptom often kindles anxiety, guilt, or distorted thinking. For example, a student who is in pain might incorrectly imagine that an ensemble concert will be canceled if she doesn't take part. In her angst, she'll think that she has no choice but to grit her teeth and perform, when the director could readily recruit a substitute. Or, if her symptom is caught early, neither cancellation nor substitution might be necessary—it's conceivable that she can receive treatment and go on with a minor accommodation such as curtailing solo practice.

Granted, you don't want to inconvenience anyone by pulling out of a show. But if you respond at the first hint of trouble and your doctor or teacher advises you not to play, you'll probably miss just one concert. If you defy your body's messages, though, and wind up with a major injury, then the impact on your career—and on your ensemble partners—will be much more substantial. Therefore, don't make exceptions. When a warning sign emerges, stop, rest, and get help.

Finally, some musicians fear that they'll be penalized if they rest on account of symptoms. They worry about losing their placement in an orchestra or being thought of as weak or unreliable. Such overblown consequences may have occurred in decades past, but with the mounting awareness of musicians' health, harsh reprisals are unlikely today. If you call off or modify an appearance due to a warning sign, your proactive stance will foster healing and preclude further cancellations. Your status won't diminish; rather, you'll be known as a responsible performer with the long view in mind.

Injury-Prevention Basics

Three qualities are essential in a professional musician ... the first is good health and the other two are the same.
— Mark Hambourg, pianist

This section records ten practices that encourage wellness and protect against playing-related injury. If the details of injury prevention are new to you, periodically review the information here until self-care becomes second nature.

1. Increase playing time gradually

Injury rates peak at the beginnings of school years, during summer festivals, and before recitals, juries, auditions, and contests since, on those occasions, musicians may abruptly increase their playing until overuse cuts them down. Don't fall into that same trap.

- Pace your practice by upholding a consistent schedule and learning material well in advance of performance dates. When you need to master music in a hurry, rely on mental practice (p. 34) to conserve your physical resources.

Injury-Prevention Basics

1. Increase playing time gradually
2. Limit repetition
3. Regulate hand-intensive tasks
4. Manage your workload
5. Warm up and cool down
6. Minimize tension
7. Take breaks
8. Heed warning signs
9. Take charge of anxiety
10. Keep fit and healthy

- Before the start of a festival or school year, build up your playing time incrementally, increasing no more than 10–20% per week (p. 12). If a school or festival program subjects you to an upsurge in playing, ask for help in planning a favorable agenda.

- When a high-stakes performance is on the horizon, prepare thoroughly, and then cut back somewhat on your physical practice in the final days before the event. In that way, you'll be rested and strong when your big moment arrives.

- After a vacation or other hiatus, plot a return-to-playing routine whereby you initially restrict how much you play and then step up in stages. A layoff lessens your playing fitness, so your physical capacity after the break is markedly diminished.

- Another period of high risk occurs when musicians buy new instruments or make technical revisions. Then, enthusiasm may whip up overplaying, or a shift in movement habits could exhaust muscles that are unaccustomed to new patterns of use. In such circumstances, reduce your total playing, and increase judiciously.

2. Limit repetition

Overuse can spring not only from an escalation in the quantity of playing but also from too much repetition. For instance, the thrill of exploring a novel technique might cause a musician to overrehearse a fingering or bowing. Similarly, infatuation with fresh repertoire can bring on the excessive playing of a single piece. Always rotate material in practice; you'll enhance both safety and learning.

Concerning repetition in group settings, ensemble directors should organize rehearsals to prevent any one section of players from having to repeat passages unduly. If one of your ensembles is working on music in which you play at length, time your solo practice such that you come to rehearsals prepared but unfatigued.

3. Regulate hand-intensive tasks

How you use your hands in everyday life will influence your chances of overuse, misuse, and accidental injury. To stave off overuse, strike a balance between the amount that you play and how much you use your hands in other tasks—an increase in one calls for a decrease in the other. If you enroll in a class or start a job that requires many hours of typing, arrange a transition phase where you bump up your computer use bit by bit. And don't put off writing assignments. All-night binges of typing cause countless students to develop hand and arm pain.

Defend against misuse injuries by implementing positive habits in any hand-intensive activity: Be attentive to your posture, minimize tension, and take breaks. If you write extensively by hand, use a light touch and a thicker, more ergonomic pen.

To sidestep mishaps in the kitchen, when using a knife, angle the blade away from you, and, as you grip an item to be sliced, curl the tips of your gripping fingers so that they can't intersect the path of the blade. Be equally careful to avoid burns. Outside of the house, if you participate in sports or do any rigorous labor, set realistic caps. You aren't obliged to pamper your hands; just be sensitive to how you use them.

4. Manage your workload

As your musical abilities advance, more performance opportunities will come your way, and your workload will grow in complexity. Then you'll need to be extra vigilant to stay within your limits. Many up-and-coming musicians can't resist performance offers; they take every concert or gig they can get and then become hobbled by overuse. Don't be one of them.

If you're enticed by performance prospects that could swamp your capacity, seek your teacher's advice before making any promises. When you decline a performance request, tactfully explain that physical limits dictate your decision.

5. Warm up and cool down

Warming up readies the body, mind, and emotions for making music. From a physical standpoint, an effective warm-up heightens blood flow to working muscles and stimulates lubrication in the joints—it makes metabolism more efficient and tissue strain less likely. Mentally and emotionally speaking, warming up generates the integrated attention that's crucial to easeful execution and transcendent expression.

Warm-up procedures are described on page 37. In a few words, before playing, loosen up and center yourself with some whole-body movements.

Play moderately at first, increasing speed and volume by degrees. Aim to finish your warm-up in 10–15 minutes; overly long warm-ups can cause premature fatigue during concerts and rehearsals.

To conclude a playing session, treat yourself with the same care as an athlete after a workout. Thwart muscle stiffness and cramping by cooling down with the likes of gentle scales or lip trills, and then do some restorative movements (p. 76). Five or 10 minutes of cooling down should suffice. Then, curb hand-intensive tasks to give your muscles a chance to recover.

6. Minimize tension

When you minimize tension while playing, you cultivate good use and prevent repetitive strain injuries. The following six avenues promote strain-free artistry; all of them are expanded on in chapter 13:

- Employ balanced posture (p. 250).
- Get a good fit between you and your instrument. Match your instrument to your size, position it for utmost advantage, and exploit ergonomic aids to accommodate special needs.
- Play with your wrists primarily in their midranges of motion (p. 263).
- Reduce mental and physical effort. Choose suitable material, learn it thoroughly, and never exert excess force with hands or embouchure.
- Use agile breathing habits. Efficient respiration, especially when playing brass and wind instruments, demands the coordination of numerous muscles. Whatever your instrument, regularly ask your teacher to evaluate your breathing; clumsy breathing greatly contributes to tension and misuse.
- Sign up for lessons in movement awareness—the Alexander technique and the Feldenkrais method are two approaches espoused by musicians worldwide. Resources to locate teachers are posted at *musiciansway .com*.

7. Take breaks

Nonstop playing is a prescription for overuse injury. Skilled musicians shrewdly blend playing with rest to deflect fatigue and preserve an artistic edge. Overall, rest about 10 minutes of each hour that you spend in the practice room. In your solo practice, you might take 5-minute breathers every 25 minutes, or you could slot in breaks of 2–3 minutes every 15. At large-group rehearsals, when playing straightforward material, your entire ensemble might pause for 10 minutes after working for 50; high-intensity playing, though, merits more frequent timeouts.

During your breaks, steer clear of hand-intensive tasks. Instead, do things that contrast with your playing actions—stretching or lying down can be eminently restorative (see *taking breaks*, p. 75). In large ensembles, when you have a protracted pause but you can't leave your place, subtly move rather than remaining in a static position. If you ever play with a group that foregoes breathers, speak up.

8. Heed warning signs

Revisit the preceding section so that you're primed to stop, rest, and get help if symptoms loom. Musicians who ignore warning signs risk grave injury.

9. Take charge of anxiety

Although this chapter highlights physical injuries, psychological pressures often drive the behaviors that trigger those injuries. Stress and anxiety, for instance, push some musicians to overpractice, play aggressively, or discount warning signs. Given that performers frequently work under stressful conditions, all musicians need skills to help them cope with anxiety.

Chapter 7 unravels the performance-related anxieties that saddle musicians. Review that text, and be on the lookout for self-limiting thoughts and behaviors. Psychologist Anthony Kemp, author of *The Musical Temperament*, warns that musicians may be at greater risk for anxiety and depression than people who don't work in creative fields.[14] If you experience inordinate nervousness or a loss of motivation or you feel that you aren't living up to your potential, visit a therapist. Seek assistance for psychological pain with the same zeal that you get aid for physical symptoms.

10. Keep fit and healthy

Physician Richard Norris recommends that musicians take up exercise programs that include a trio of components: cardiovascular fitness, flexibility maintenance, and strength training.[15] To accomplish all three, you might swim and do bit of stretching. Alternatively, many performers enjoy assorted activities such as jogging, yoga, tai chi, exercise classes, tennis, or low-resistance weight lifting.

Fitness brings profuse benefits. In terms of injury prevention, when you boost the strength of the muscles in your back, shoulders, abdomen, and arms, those muscles become more capable of postural support and of doing the work of playing. Conversely, performers with feeble or poorly toned muscles are more likely to be injured by playing and carrying instruments. Exercise also provides an emotional outlet and stabilizes one's mood. Psychologist David Holmes declares, "I have never run across any stress-relief method as strong as aerobic fitness."[16]

Before starting an exercise regimen, get a medical checkup to rule out the existence of a hidden infirmity that could make exercising dangerous for you. If you'll be lifting weights, enlist an athletic trainer to teach you safe practices.

On top of exercising, shore up your fitness by embracing a healthy lifestyle. Get plenty of sleep, adopt sensible habits of nutrition, and plan regular medical, dental, vision, and hearing exams. At the same time, avoid tobacco, illicit drugs, and heavy drinking.

Also take precautions against catching colds. Most days, your hands contact surfaces that sick people have touched, and germs are thereby transferred onto your fingers. When you enter a public building, for instance, untold numbers of people have already touched the entry doors or elevator buttons. Many colds originate after people with contaminated hands reach for their eyes, nose, or mouth—or handle food—and the germs then infect the cells that line the throat, sinuses, and nose. Therefore, routinely wash your hands, or use a waterless hand sanitizer in a pinch, and refrain from touching your face. When you attend a reception where people shake hands, skip eating finger food; use utensils or don't eat. You can further deter colds and oral infections by never sharing mouthpieces, beverage containers, or straws. And when you're ill, be careful not to expose others.

Added guidelines for healthy living can be found on the website of the Centers for Disease Control (www.cdc.gov) and through links on *musiciansway .com*.

When it comes to the injuries rooted in overuse and misuse, it falls on each musician to compile the know-how to forestall trouble. We can't preempt every illness; we can't obstruct every accident. But in the words of trumpeter and researcher Kris Chesky, codirector of the University of North Texas Center for Music and Medicine, "The problems we can prevent are the ones we create."[17]

Recovering from Injury

The earlier the symptoms are recognized and treated, the sooner and more completely recovery occurs.

—Richard Norris, physician and flutist

Whether you incur a mild or harsh injury, a well-managed recovery will incorporate the four components below. When you skillfully carry out each component, you ensure the swiftest possible return to unhindered playing.

1. Obtain expert advice

As discussed previously, if you develop an injury symptom, you should seek the advice of both a knowledgeable teacher and a responsive physician. Reputable teachers are found at conservatories and university music departments—they can scrutinize your playing habits and help

Recovering from Injury
1. Obtain expert advice
2. Follow a treatment and rehab schedule
3. Transform playing habits
4. Modify activities of daily living

you renovate habits of overuse or misuse. To select a physician and make the most of an appointment, here are a few suggestions.

Selecting a physician

You can access medical care at a campus health center or at the office of your family physician. From there, needed referrals can be made. If you live in a large city, you'll probably find a performing arts medicine specialist working locally (see *musiciansway.com* for listings). If you're drawn to alternative therapies, begin with a medical doctor, and then coordinate treatments through your physician so that you preclude overtreatment and hazardous drug interactions.

Making the most of an appointment

When you're dealing with a playing-related injury as opposed to an accident, try to bring your instrument to the medical evaluation. Then you can demonstrate the movements that provoke the troublesome symptoms, and the physician can evaluate your playing motions. Percussionists might tote just drumsticks or mallets and a practice pad. Pianists may be able to demonstrate on a tabletop, although, at the request of your doctor, a friend could bring a portable keyboard (some specialized clinics, however, have pianos). Also carry an audio recorder or a phone with voice memo capability. Doctor visits can be upsetting, and some patients mix up their doctor's instructions. With a recorder handy, you can guarantee that none of the advice you receive is forgotten.

At your appointment, a physician will inquire about the history of your complaint and perform a physical examination. To expedite that assessment, before your meeting, review how your symptoms arose—document it if the story is complex—and assemble relevant health records, as well as an inventory of any medications or dietary supplements you're taking. A doctor will work to pinpoint causes and may order diagnostic tests. Once a diagnosis is made, you'll then receive recommendations for treatment and rehabilitation. If your physician concludes that you must significantly rein in your playing or computer use, ask for a written statement that you can show to your teachers, employer, or ensemble directors.

2. Follow a treatment and rehab schedule

Treatment and rehabilitation may consist of rest, physical therapy, medication, counseling, and retraining (only a tiny fraction of playing-related injuries require surgical intervention). For injuries that arise from misuse, retraining is essential in order to reverse the destructive habits. An injured musician could well benefit from a rehab team, which might include the following professionals:

- a physical therapist, hand therapist, massage therapist, or an athletic trainer to promote healing, enhance flexibility, and foster strength in weak muscles
- a music teacher and a movement educator to correct faulty technical habits and suggest beneficial ones
- a counselor or psychotherapist to guide the overworked musician on an inner journey toward whole living

With regard to resting, music medicine specialists ordinarily prescribe a brief period of total rest followed by relative rest. For example, your doctor or physical therapist might design a return-to-playing calendar where, after a few days off, you'd intersperse short episodes of playing with extended breaks. Then, you'd gradually step up the duration of each playing session.

Occasionally physicians advocate the use of splints or movement-limiting bandages. Don't strap on such devices, however, except when so directed by a healthcare professional. If you take it upon yourself to immobilize a joint, you could unwittingly stiffen the joint, weaken the muscles, and make matters worse. Your treatment may also involve the use of heat and ice. Physician Emil Pascarelli states that heat should never be applied to an acute injury— it can actually exacerbate swelling and tissue damage—while the main function of cold therapy is to reduce pain and inflammation.[18] If you ever suffer a trauma such as a fractured bone, slap on ice immediately and get medical care. When treating playing-related injuries, to make certain that you employ therapeutic heat and cold correctly, abide by the specific guidance of your physician or physical therapist.

I've observed that injured students often botch their recoveries. Many musicians, it seems, fail to realize that inadequate rehabilitation of one injury multiplies the likelihood of another, so they prematurely start playing full time, unintentionally hurting themselves again and again. Stick with your recovery plan even if symptoms abate sooner than expected; imperceptible healing may continue for weeks. Additionally, if your symptoms don't improve, go back to your physician. A lack of progress will reveal important things about your condition and enable treatment to be optimized.

3. Transform playing habits

If your injury stems from overuse or misuse, some of your playing habits will need revamping. For misuse problems, a skilled music educator will help you zero in on technical defects and recalibrate your relationship with your instrument. If overuse is the culprit, a teacher will coach you to configure a healthy playing schedule and navigate the social labyrinth that surrounds trimming your workload.

Aside from music lessons, injured performers also profit from movement training—the Alexander technique and the Feldenkrais method are the most chosen avenues. Through such instruction, musicians can learn to sit, stand, breathe, and move with ease; as a result, their playing becomes more easeful as well.

4. Modify activities of daily living

Strenuous or repetitive activities of daily living can sabotage the healing process. Ask your physician or physical therapist to inform you of the sorts of activities that might be problematic for your case. Depending on the injury, typing and driving habits may require attention, sports could be off limits, and backpacks will probably need lightening. With intricate cases, occupational therapists can assist with devising adaptations. Be alert for everyday sources of overuse or misuse, and get help with certain tasks, like heavy lifting, that would put your recovery at risk.

As you supervise the physical side of healing, nourish your spirit, too. Depression and other psychological difficulties are more likely to occur when a musician's lifestyle is upended by injury. If you're unable to do much playing for a while, practice mentally, listen to music, read, and enjoy life. By maintaining a positive attitude throughout your recovery, you keep your creativity alive and support your healing. But if you can't shake a morose mood, see a counselor.

In the long run, a temporary respite from full-time playing is unlikely to have any negative effect on your musical development. The time you take off may even inspire personal growth. So use any rest interval to stoke your love of music. Go forward in the knowledge that an encounter with injury, albeit unfortunate, will educate you to sidestep future setbacks.

$$\equiv 13 \equiv$$

Injury Prevention, II

In this chapter:

- Guidelines for sitting and standing
- Meeting your instrument
- Voice care
- Hearing conservation

Balanced Sitting and Standing

I see so many young musicians don't even stand properly, don't know how to breathe. My power comes from breathing properly, from using my chest and abdomen.

—Cootie Williams, trumpeter

Unless you appear in some unusual venues, I expect that, when you practice and perform, you normally sit or stand. And your habits of arranging yourself in a chair or on your feet will impact your breathing, your sound, and your risk of injury. In fact, awkward postures lie at the root of many physical problems because they trigger strain. This section, therefore, outlines ideas for rethinking your posture and learning optimal ways to sit and stand.

Rethinking Posture

In his book *On Piano Playing,* Gyorgy Sandor points out that beneficial postures have two main features: stability and mobility—they support the weight of the body and any instrument while allowing for unconstrained movement.[1] Both stability and mobility maximize physical ease because they enable larger muscles to do more of the work of music making, thereby taking the load off of the smallest, most vulnerable body structures. For example, a favorable posture at the piano permits a player to generate power using the muscles in the arms, shoulders, and back. A less-desirable position would delegate excessive work to the fingers.

Mobility also staves off fatigue because it frees up the muscles to be used in a variety of ways. Conversely, when muscles contract relentlessly, the blood flow becomes restricted, and waste products accumulate; then exhaustion and cramping won't be far behind. Imagine, for instance, lifting a suitcase by the handle and holding it a few inches off the floor—soon your hand and arm will tire and stiffen if you don't let go. Similarly, when sitting or standing in a rigid manner, static muscle contraction in the back can bring on spasm and pain.

Advantageous postures have an active quality; they're always subtly in motion. As a result, there is no single "correct" position for sitting or standing since both involve movement. However, there are *principles* of body alignment and balance that bring about postural ease. The following is a summary of those principles.

Balanced Sitting

The concepts and images here will help you sit effortlessly. To begin, you need an armless chair or a piano bench of average height and with a level seat. If possible, set up a mirror or video camera at your side.

Balanced Sitting
1. Balance on your sitting bones
2. Position your hips higher than your knees
3. Release your shoulders
4. Align and lengthen your spine

1. Balance on your sitting bones

Musicians achieve balanced sitting postures in a number of ways. Some instrumentalists, such as cellists, are obliged to sit toward the front of a seat; others have more options for positioning. But irrespective of your musical specialty, with an understanding of how to balance on your sitting bones and align your body, you can acquire the know-how to adapt to most chairs and to the technical requirements of your instrument.

- For starters, sit on the front edge of a chair or bench with only your pelvis contacting the seat.
- Put your feet flat on the floor so that the centers of your feet line up beneath the front of your knees.
- Position your knees anywhere from hip-width to shoulder-width apart.

With your pelvis, feet, and knees in place, rock your pelvis forward and back to feel your two sitting bones—the protrusions at the base of the pelvis. Then, balance on the tips of those bones so that your spine is neither slumped nor overarched (see figures 13.1–13.3). To confirm your alignment, check your side view in a mirror or video monitor. Also, distribute your weight equally on both sides of your pelvis, and avoid leaning to one side.

After you find balance, if you like, back up from the chair edge, and share the weight with the undersides of your thighs. Many musicians sit toward the backs of their chairs; some employ lumbar supports for added stability. And although lumbar support is a prudent choice for many performers, you'll enjoy the greatest mobility when you balance on your sitting bones near the edge of a chair or bench. To balance easefully, though, you must have adequate muscle strength and coordination in your abdomen and back. If you readily become fatigued when sitting, see a physical therapist or an athletic trainer to obtain a strength assessment and to learn some exercises.

2. Position your hips higher than your knees

If a chair fits your stature, when you sit toward the front with your feet flat on the floor, your hips will be somewhat higher than your knees. Flutist and physician Richard Norris explains that this arrangement unburdens the lower back muscles and facilitates breathing.[2] Therefore, you should outfit your practice space at home with a chair or bench that suits your physique. In the real world, however, you'll commonly be in performance or rehearsal situations where the seating isn't ideal, so you need to be skilled at sitting in chairs of varying heights.

If a nonadjustable chair is too low for you—and for tall musicians, rehearsal and practice-room chairs often aren't high enough—one remedy is to pad the seat with a phonebook or cushion (many musicians prefer cushions with a forward slope; see *musiciansway.com*). When you're compelled to sit on a low chair and you don't have a cushion or phonebook handy, you might tuck your feet under your thighs to lower your knees. In the opposite circumstance, if you're stuck with a chair that's too high, elevate your feet on a block or a portable footrest.

3. Release your shoulders

Release your shoulders down and away from each other so that your arms will be mobile and powerful. Look in a mirror or video monitor to verify that, from the front view, your shoulders are symmetrical and, from the side, they aren't raised, slumped, or jutting forward or back. To ease any muscle tension in the shoulder area, roll your shoulders a few times.

4. Align and lengthen your spine

From your tailbone to your head, let your spine lengthen toward a vertical alignment, and allow your head to rise as if it were a helium-filled balloon.

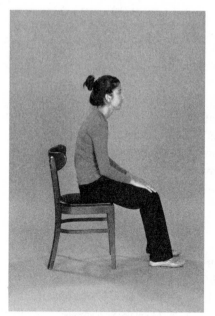

Figure 13.1. Slumped sitting.

Figure 13.2. Tense sitting.

Figure 13.3. Balanced sitting.

The stability provided by your sitting bones and feet should make your upper body seem light and nimble. When you face forward with an aligned spine, your ears will be above your shoulders and hips.

In figures 13.1–13.3, notice how different the model's spine appears when she slumps, tenses, and balances.

As you review the image of balanced sitting in figure 13.3, take into account that photographs are static, but sitting is dynamic. Whether you sit toward the front or back of a chair, incorporate subtle movements into your sitting posture. Then, whenever you take a seat, rather than plopping down mindlessly, find balance anew so that your postural awareness energizes your creativity.

Balanced Standing

To achieve stability and mobility on your feet, it's ideal to be adept at standing in two ways: with feet more or less parallel, as well as with feet offset. Both options are explored below. Try these postures wearing relatively flat shoes. A mirror or video monitor aids learning.

Balanced Standing
1. Place your feet hip-width apart
2. Maintain pliable knees
3. Release your shoulders
4. Align and lengthen your spine

1a. Place your feet hip-width apart and more or less parallel

Stand with your feet hip-width apart such that your ankles line up under your hips and your weight is shared equally by each leg (figures 13.4–13.5). Either point your feet straight ahead or aim them slightly outward, whichever feels more comfortable. To discover your natural foot placement, briefly march in place.

1b. Point one foot forward; place the other behind and at about a 45° angle

Stand with your feet parallel, and then bring your right foot back approximately 6 inches (15 cm) so that the left toes point forward and the right foot angles outward at 45 degrees or less (figure 13.6). Again, march in place to release any tension and find your natural foot placement. As with the parallel stance, arrange your feet hip-width apart, and distribute your weight equally on both legs. The feet may also be reversed so that the right points forward. Offset feet permit ample mobility and, for women who are wearing heels, can provide extra stability.

Figure 13.4. Balanced standing.

Figure 13.5. Balanced standing.

Figure 13.6. Balanced standing, offset feet.

2. Maintain pliable knees

Whichever stance you use, maintain pliable, unlocked knees. To help free up your knees, try this:

a. Stand with your feet hip-width apart and roughly parallel.

b. Vigorously contract your leg muscles, locking your knees. Hold 3–5 seconds.

c. Release your leg muscles, notice the microbend in your knees, and sense your weight distributed broadly across the soles of your feet.

d. Bounce a little, and enjoy your stability and mobility.

3. Release your shoulders

As with sitting, let your shoulders release down and away from each other. Use a mirror or video monitor to verify that, from the front view, your shoulders are at equal height and, from the side view, they don't slump. Roll your shoulders to help release any tension.

4. Align and lengthen your spine

Allow your spine to lengthen toward a vertical alignment, and let your head "float" freely. The stability and mobility of your stance should make your upper body feel agile, as though it were riding on your legs. When you face ahead, your standard alignment will have your ears above your shoulders, hips, and ankles.

If you're accustomed to standing with a floppy posture, you'll also need to pay attention to your abdominal muscles and gently contract them to lengthen your lower back. If, instead, you let the abdominals slacken, your pelvis will rock to the rear. Then, the shortening of the low back muscles could provoke a backache. If it strikes you as odd to deliberately contract your muscles to attain balance, remember that sitting and standing are dynamic activities— they require the use of your muscles. Easeful postures, therefore, aren't limp; they entail well-coordinated action.

Here's an exercise that highlights how the pelvis and the back are affected by the abdominal muscles:

a. Position a mirror at your side.

b. Stand with your feet parallel.

c. Alternately contract and then slacken the abdominal muscles, watching your reflection as the pelvis swivels and the low back shortens and lengthens (to contract the abdominals, suck in your stomach area).

Ample strength in the abdominal muscles is crucial to standing. Musicians with weak abdominals should see athletic trainers or physical therapists to learn strengthening exercises.

Experiment with both parallel and offset foot placements so that you can adapt your stance to a given situation. When you'll be standing for an extended period, vary your stance somewhat to engage your muscles in different patterns of use.

If you have ingrained habits of postural imbalance (and many people do), then your perception of how you sit and stand may be distorted. In that case, these guidelines can serve as landmarks, but they won't suffice in your quest to arrange yourself as comfortably as possible. You'll need further assistance to reset your self-perceptions.

Ask your teacher to comment on your postural habits. If you have work to do, sign up for customized instruction with a movement educator. Many music schools offer movement lessons from teachers of either the Alexander technique or the Feldenkrais method; you can also locate instructors near you via links on *musiciansway.com*. Such specialists can awaken your innate sense of movement so that, instead of being an unconscious victim of your postures, you'll be able to sit and stand in ways that support fluent music making.

Meeting Your Instrument

The better you use yourself, the better you will play.
—Pedro de Alcantara, cellist and Alexander technique teacher

To perform at a high level, you have to attain a kind of unity with your instrument. Then nothing will stand in the way of your translating musical thoughts into sound. From a physical standpoint, the preceding postural concepts form the foundation for playing with unfettered ease. Here, allied principles will help you move fluidly at your instrument.

As chapter 12 explains, musicians often incur playing-related injuries due

> **Meeting Your Instrument**
>
> 1. Align and lengthen your spine
> 2. Balance your head
> 3. Release your shoulders
> 4. Use wrists in their midranges of motion
> 5. Arc finger joints in the same direction

to the strenuous movement habits termed "misuse." In contrast, "good use" involves moving and playing with optimal efficiency and minimal effort. But good use supplies more than physical benefits; as effort is reduced, barriers to musical excellence fall away.

The following principles and images demonstrate universal ways to achieve good use. To best implement these ideas in your practice, enlist a mirror or video camera. Visit *musiciansway.com* for instrument-specific tips.

1. Align and lengthen your spine

Whether you sit or stand when you play, aligning and lengthening your spine will free the larger muscles to do more of the work of playing and thereby set you up to move gracefully. Two key strategies are:

- Adopt a balanced posture.
- Bring your instrument to you, using ergonomic devices if needed, rather than reaching or leaning toward your instrument.

Figures 13.7–13.13 show musicians employing both favorable and unfavorable spinal alignment. The guitarists in figures 13.12–13.13 are using ergonomic adaptations developed by Aaron Shearer. In figure 13.12, the guitarist employs both an instrument support and a footstool; in figure 13.13, the guitarist foregoes the footstool and attaches a strap by means of suction cups.

2. Balance your head

When your head balances unconstrained on your neck, the neck muscles are liberated and can move the head freely. Many performers, however, tense their neck muscles in response to anxiety, technical faults, or gawky music stand placement. Hence, neck pain is a common complaint among hurting performers.

Concerning music stands, in *The Musician's Body*, authors Rosset and Odam write, "The eye works most comfortably when scores are placed around 15° below the horizontal plane."[3] They further advise situating a score 24–28 inches (60–70 cm) from your body. When you need to use a lower stand position (perhaps to give an audience an unobstructed view of your face), continue lengthening you spine, look downward a bit with your eyes, and subtly hinge at the base of your head, as exemplified by the percussionist in figure 13.8.

Figures 13.14–13.17 show musicians playing with both clumsy and agile habits of head alignment.

Figure 13.7. Misaligned spine.

Figure 13.8. Aligned spine.

Figure 13.9. Misaligned spine.

Figure 13.10. Aligned spine.

Figure 13.11. Misaligned spine.

Figure 13.12. Aligned spine.

Figure 13.13. Aligned spine.

Figure 13.14. Misaligned head and neck.

Figure 13.15. Aligned head and neck.

Figure 13.16. Misaligned head and neck.

Figure 13.17. Aligned head and neck.

3. Release your shoulders

Released shoulders permit unrestricted use of the arms. Even so, when many musicians draw their hands into playing position, their arm movements lack refinement, and so their shoulders stiffen. For instance, a violinist bringing the bow to the strings might unnecessarily lift the right shoulder. If the shoulder then remains clenched, movement becomes hampered, tone suffers, and muscles may spasm painfully. Take note of your own patterns of shoulder use at your instrument, and ask your teacher to critique your movement habits.

Figure 13.18. Elevated left shoulder.

Figure 13.19. Elevated right shoulder.

Figure 13.20. Released shoulders.

Figure 13.21. Elevated shoulders.   **Figure 13.22.** Released shoulders.

Figures 13.18–13.22 illustrate how the shoulders look when used awkwardly versus when allowed to release.

4. Use wrists in their midranges of motion

The muscles that primarily power the finger movements used in playing instruments are located in the forearms, and those muscles connect to the fingers via tendons that pass through the wrists. When wrists are in the middle of their range of motion—that is, in neutral positions—tendons can slide unencumbered, and fingers have maximum strength and mobility. When the wrists are crooked out of alignment toward their limits of movement, the tendons are bent around a corner, reducing finger agility and provoking strain.

To experience the difference between effortless hand use with an aligned wrist and strenuous use with a crooked wrist, try this:

a. Grasp an imaginary tennis ball with one hand, and notice how your wrist naturally aligns and your fingers move easily.

b. Crook your wrist in any direction and, maintaining that crooked position, attempt to grasp the imaginary ball. Sense the awkwardness and strain.

Figure 13.23. Misaligned wrist.

Figure 13.24. Aligned wrist.

Just as you wouldn't grasp an object with a crooked wrist, you shouldn't habitually play with a wrist out of alignment. Figures 13.23–13.35 depict wrists favorably and unfavorably aligned. They show how the wrists appear when playing instruments and when doing another hand-intensive task that affects musicians: typing.

Wrist alignment at the piano and computer keyboards (p. 267) partially depends on bench or chair height. When you play piano or type, modify the height of your seat so that, when your fingers touch the keys, your forearms are parallel to the floor.

As you explore wrist alignment at your instrument and your computer, don't freeze your wrists in fixed positions. Instead, let them move in supple ways as dictated by the music you play or the characters you type. If a musical passage obliges you to bend a wrist beyond its midrange, minimize tension, and return to a midrange alignment when possible. Also, avoid overrepetition of phrases that compel a wrist to be markedly bent.

Figure 13.25. Misaligned wrist.

Figure 13.26. Misaligned wrist.

Figure 13.27. Aligned wrist.

Figure 13.28. Misaligned wrists.

Figure 13.29. Aligned wrists.

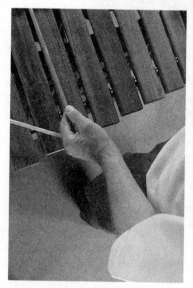 

Figure 13.30. Misaligned wrist.   **Figure 13.31.** Aligned wrist.

Figure 13.32. Misaligned wrist.

Figure 13.33. Aligned wrist.

Figure 13.34. Aligned wrists.

Figure 13.35. Aligned wrist.

If you're unable to align one or both wrists when playing, consult a teacher. You may need a different-sized instrument, a new way to position it, a fresh technical approach, or your instrument might require ergonomic tweaking.

5. Arc finger joints in the same direction

With your wrists aligned and your hands free of tension, your finger and thumb joints naturally arc in the same direction. For example, grasp another imaginary tennis ball, and observe how the joints of all five fingers curve in unison. Also notice the archlike shape of your hand and the power afforded to your fingers. Aim to arrange your body and instrument to encourage this arching.

Keep in mind, though, that the execution of some techniques will necessitate the temporary unarching of a finger joint, as when a cellist shifts the left ring finger far up the neck. When that happens, resume an arched position when feasible. Remember that there is no single "correct" posture for finger joints or any other body part because playing instruments calls for ongoing physical adjustment.

Figures 13.36–13.40 show aligned versus misaligned finger joints.

Proficiency with movement and posture, like any technical skill, doesn't develop overnight. However, by patiently learning to direct your playing actions according to healthy movement principles, your chances of injury will shrink, and your playing skills will be able to expand unimpeded.

Voice Care

Resting becomes a discipline in itself.

—Plácido Domingo, tenor

The human voice is perhaps the most sublime of instruments, capable of heart-wrenching music and world-changing speech. Yet its power is generated from the most delicate of tissues: the vocal folds in the larynx. Professional vocalists are attuned to this interplay of grandeur and vulnerability, and so they acquire consummate voice-care skills. But singers aren't

Voice Care Basics
1. Drink plenty of water
2. Humidify dry environments
3. Employ healthy vocal habits
4. Avoid strenuous vocal use
5. Adopt a voice-friendly lifestyle
6. Treat allergies and prevent colds
7. Heed warning signs

Figure 13.36. Misaligned finger joints.   **Figure 13.37.** Aligned finger joints.

Figure 13.38. Misaligned thumb joints.

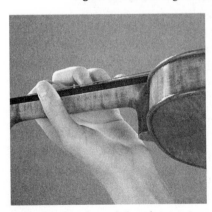

Figure 13.39. Aligned thumb joints.   **Figure 13.40.** Aligned thumb joints.

the only ones who profit from knowledge of vocal health; anyone who can speak has much to gain. Therefore, although this section is tailored to students of singing, the seven practices here apply to anyone interested in vocal fitness.

1. Drink plenty of water

Hydration is vital to healthy vocal use. According to the website of the Texas Voice Center, "The vocal folds need to be lubricated with a thin layer of mucus in order to vibrate efficiently. The best lubrication can be achieved by drinking plenty of water."[4] Bear in mind that, when you drink water, your throat is moistened, but the liquid doesn't contact the vocal folds. If it did, you'd gag. The water you drink has to be processed by the digestive system for the lubrication to be produced. If you become even minimally dehydrated—and by the time you register thirst, dehydration has begun—the lubricating mucus is likely to thicken and lead to inferior sound. When dehydration worsens, vigorous vocal use can irritate the folds and bring on injury. Here are ways to ensure that you get ample water:

a. Keep a half-liter bottle of noncarbonated water handy, and steadily sip so that you go through the equivalent of about four bottles a day (64 ounces). Consume extra water in sweltering conditions, if you're highly active, at the onset of a cold, and in arid environments like you find on commercial jets. If you have any health issues, however, such as impaired kidney function, ask your physician how much you should drink. You also get water from other sources, among them soups and juices, so you may not need to swig two liters of water daily if you have alternative sources in your diet. Still, it's better to err on the side of slight overhydration than under.

b. Restrict caffeinated and alcoholic beverages—they draw water from your system. Partake of them in moderation, or abstain, and increase hydration in step: Drink an extra cup of water for every cup of coffee. Also consider diluting regular coffee with decaf. Limit, too, your intake of high-acid soft drinks. Not only are many soft drinks spiked with caffeine, but the phosphoric acid in some of them is corrosive enough to dissolve a nail. What do you suppose that a steady bath of that acid would do to your throat?

c. Watch out for two signs of dehydration:
   • Often needing to clear your throat (as mucus thickens due to dehydration, it can accumulate in globs). If boosting your water consumption doesn't yield improvement, see a laryngologist—a physician who specializes in voice care.

- Dark urine. Your urine should be pale yellow or colorless, with the possible exception of when you first rise in the morning or because of coloration from vitamins.

2. Humidify dry environments

When you breathe arid air, it dries your throat and vocal folds. Use a room humidifier as needed to maintain a 40–50% relative humidity level. Without humidification, in cold climates, indoor heating can drop humidity levels to below 10%. Also, clean your humidifier often to thwart the growth of mold.

To monitor changes in humidity where you live and practice, purchase a hygrometer. You can find hygrometers at stores that stocks thermometers. Humidification is so crucial that many professional vocalists travel with humidifiers, and some hotels and opera companies supply guest singers with humidifiers.

3. Employ healthy vocal habits

The vocal mechanism comprises three basic parts: the sound source (that is, the vocal folds), the respiratory system, and the structures that create articulation and resonance, including the throat, tongue, lips, and jaw. How you use each part affects the health and quality of your voice. Here are ten guidelines:

   a. *Invest in individualized instruction.* The skills needed to sing beautifully and with ease arise little by little. Just as you wouldn't expect to become a competitive athlete without extensive training and preparation, excellence in singing results from a long-term commitment to developing technique and artistry. So take lessons from a reputable teacher, if you aren't doing so already. You can track down teachers via the website of the National Organization of Teachers of Singing: www.nats.org. For help with speech, you may also want to confer with a drama coach or speech therapist.

   b. *Practice regularly and increase gradually.* The physicians at the British Association for Performing Arts Medicine caution that "The biggest risk factor for a breakdown in your vocal health is a sudden increase in the quantity or quality of practice, for instance, in the run-up to a concert or audition."[5] Collaborate with your teacher to pace your learning and to establish a healthy pattern of practice and performance. After an illness, however, or other vocal layoff, reduce your customary practice time, and then step it up incrementally.

   c. *Choose appropriate material, and prepare it thoroughly.* Work with repertoire and vocal exercises that fit your range and level of ability. Then draw on the principles of preparation catalogued in parts I and II of this book to craft secure performances and avert anxiety.

d. *Limit singing at the extremes of your range.* Vary material in practice, and avoid excess repetition so that you don't overuse any one feature of your voice. Always emphasize unforced singing.

e. *Use agile breathing habits.* To inhale and exhale efficiently when singing calls for fine muscular coordination. In *Solutions for Singers,* Richard Miller states, "Breath-management requirements for artistic singing far surpass those of speech."[6] He explains that, in normal speech, a respiratory cycle rarely lasts more than 5 or 6 seconds, but singers produce phrases that may continue for 15 seconds. A discussion of breathing is beyond the scope of this text, so ask your teacher to evaluate your breathing habits. Also review the posture guidelines in the opening section of this chapter—balanced sitting and standing postures are key to fluent respiration.

f. *Minimize tension.* Physician and voice expert Robert Sataloff says that one of the most prevalent technical errors among singers is "excessive muscle tension in the tongue, neck, and larynx."[7] He points out that the tongue should remain relaxed while singing a scale; it should neither pull back from the lower teeth nor elevate in the rear. He also says, "The larynx should remain in a relatively constant position throughout a scale."[8] In contrast, pulling the larynx down in low registers or up in high registers is contrary to healthy vocal use. If you believe that unneeded tension creeps into your singing, talk to your teacher.

g. *Speak in your natural voice.* As with singing, speak with a relaxed, open-throated feel. Also manage your airflow: Breathe easefully, and speak in comfortable phrases that don't use up all of your air. Insist on moderate volume, and don't converse in an artificially low or high pitch. The Texas Voice Center recommends speaking in "the same range where you say, 'Umm-hmm?' "[9]

h. *Amplify when speaking to groups.* A good-quality amplification system lets you project your voice effortlessly in a large room and facilitates listener comprehension. Amplification is especially useful when you direct ensembles. If you conduct without voice amplification, though, stop your group before you speak. Never shout.

i. *Reduce vocal use before and after concerts.* When you have a performance in the evening, limit both speech and singing during the day. Postconcert, speak gently and sparingly.

j. *Warm up, take breaks, and cool down.*
   - Warm-ups focus the mind, awaken coordination, and heighten blood flow to muscles (see *warming up,* p. 37). You might begin a

warm-up with whole-body movements, lip trills, and silent laughing and continue with pitch glides across a narrow range. Then you could broaden your range and add articulation by degrees. Ask your teacher to suggest warm-up procedures customized to your voice; sample routines are indexed at *musiciansway.com*.

- Take frequent breaks (p. 75). Aim to rest five minutes for every 20–25 minutes of steady singing, and sip water during your timeouts. Such pauses are fundamental to vocal health because both the muscles involved in singing and the vocal folds can grow fatigued. And pushing through fatigue is a fast track to injury. Soprano Birgit Nilsson exhorts vocalists to "sing less and think more."[10] Therefore, use mental practice and score study to complement your actual singing.
- Cool down. Doctors urge singers to cool down after prolonged singing for the same reasons that athletes walk and stretch after running: to prevent cramping, swelling, and blood pooling in muscles. Singer and speech pathologist Deirdre Michael counsels that "easy talking" can serve as a cool-down, as can 5–10 minutes of other gentle voice use, such as soft sighs, humming, and pitch glides, followed by rest.[11] It's also restorative to do some whole-body movements (p. 76).

4. Avoid strenuous vocal use

Many everyday habits can put your voice at peril. Below is an octet of strategies to halt vocal misuse:

a. *Give up loud throat clearing and coughing.* If you noisily cough or clear your throat, you slam the vocal folds together with enough force to cause trauma. When you need to remove surplus mucus, swallow, sip water, or use the near-silent coughing action espoused by the Texas Voice Center: Take a deep breath, hold it momentarily, and then sharply expel air with a soft "H" sound.[12]

b. *Sneeze or yawn without vocalizing.* Strident sneezing can be as hazardous to the vocal folds as coughing. Never stifle a sneeze, however.

c. *Eschew grunting during exertion.* Rest your voice during exercise or any other energetic activity.

d. *Don't whisper.* Whispering strains the vocal folds, particularly when you have a cold or laryngitis. When you must speak quietly, use a soft, natural voice.

e. *Shun singing or speaking at excessive volumes.* People who habitually push their voices may develop, among other problems, callouslike nodules on their vocal folds, which cause voice quality to decline steeply. Stay within your volume limitations, amplify when appropriate, and use sufficient monitoring. If you consistently perform amplified gigs, invest in some in-ear monitors (p. 291). Also pass up cheerleading, and encourage your team instead with clapping, banners, and minimal vocal use. Yelling, like violent coughing, can cause severe damage such as hemorrhage of the blood vessels in the folds.

f. *Curtail vocal use in noisy, dry, or smoky environments.* Rein in conversation in cars, planes, cafeterias, and dance clubs, as well as on raucous city streets. Such loud or arid settings can induce vocal strain and overuse. Also cut back on vocal use in smoky or dusty venues, and limit your exposure to the artificial fogs used in some theatrical shows. In the days leading up to a performance, dodge all unhealthy atmospheres. If you're ever obliged to sing in a smoky club, plan many breaks away from the smoke, and drink extra water.

g. *Eliminate unnecessary and forceful speech.* Besides talking less in noisy surroundings, moderate the amount of time you spend talking on the phone, and use a natural voice when you do. The absence of visual cues in phone conversations causes many people to overdrive their voices.

h. *Ration vocal use when you're not at your best.* Colds, allergies, and other conditions can cause the vocal folds to swell, making you hoarse and the folds more susceptible to injury. If it hurts to swallow, for example, don't sing unless your laryngologist gives you the go-ahead. Refrain from whistling, too—like whispering, it can stress the folds.

5. Adopt a voice-friendly lifestyle

Your lifestyle can either contribute to vocal health or multiply the likelihood of problems. The following six practices will help keep your voice in prime shape:

a. *Don't smoke.* Smoking is one of the worst things that you can do for your voice and your health.

b. *Curb eating before sleep.* Consuming food, alcohol, caffeine, or carbonated beverages soon before bed raises the possibility that stomach acids might be spilled onto the larynx while you snooze, a malady commonly known as *reflux.* Doctors recommend that evening meals conclude no later than 2–3 hours before you retire for the night. If you do eat late, do so moderately, and choose a sleeping posture that places your head and neck above the level of your stomach. Also maintain a healthy weight so that no undue pressure is placed on the stomach as you recline.

c. *Eat wisely before performances.* On the day of a concert, beware of dairy products—they may trigger a thickening of mucus. Also steer clear of foods and beverages that boost stomach acid, such as those that contain chocolate, alcohol, caffeine, and fiery spices. Say no, as well, to foods that are highly salted or are easy to aspirate; examples include nuts, chips, popcorn, and raw carrots. See *preperformance routines,* page 157, for more pointers.

d. *Exercise, rest, and eat well.* Voice quality reflects overall health. Physicians warn that singers are unlikely to perform their best or have enduring careers unless they practice disciplined habits of self-care. Adequate sleep, for instance, is central to vocal excellence.

e. *Take charge of anxiety.* The voice is intimately connected with the emotions. Worried singers not only underperform but are also prone to vocal misuse. Go over the anxiety-management suggestions in part II of this book, and visit a therapist if you ever feel that anxiety or depression is impairing your quality of life.

f. *Consult your doctor before taking medications or dietary supplements.* Many over-the-counter potions can undermine vocal health. Physicians caution singers not to take antihistamines or mentholated lozenges because of the drying effect. They also advise vocalists with sore throats to refuse drops or sprays that numb—numbing can disguise symptoms and prompt inappropriate vocal use. Concerns have also been raised about the use of aspirin and ibuprofen because those types of drugs can make bleeding more likely in the vocal folds. See *musiciansway.com* for links to websites that detail how medications affect the voice.

6. Treat allergies and prevent colds

Allergic reactions occur when the body launches its defenses against an agent that isn't harmful. If you inhale pollen that you're allergic to, let's say, your body responds as if it were being invaded by a cold virus. It marshals its resources to attack and destroy, complete with profuse mucus and swelling.

When symptoms arise, how can you know whether you're dealing with a cold, an allergy, or some other problem? Only a physician can make a conclusive determination, but the color of your mucus will give a clue. Yellow to green secretions usually mean that infection is present; clear ones might lack the dead cells that indicate infection, implying that an allergy or some other condition could be the culprit.

In *Keep Your Voice Healthy,* physician Friedrich Brodnitz writes, "Treatment of an allergy is part of vocal hygiene."[13] He states that, when people who depend on the voice suspect an allergy, they should see an allergist—a medical doctor who focuses on treating allergies. Brodnitz further says that, when allergies are confirmed, "They can be dealt with in three ways: by eliminating the offending agents, by building up resistance through so-called desensitization, or by the use of drugs."[14] Your allergist can adapt those three approaches to meet your needs.

To help prevent colds and oral infections, never share beverage containers, straws, or eating utensils. Also, wash your hands frequently, or use a waterless sanitizer in a pinch, and, to keep from spreading germs that could infect your throat, sinuses, or nose, don't touch your face with unclean hands. Correspondingly, if you attend a reception, pass up the finger food. And when you're ill, be vigilant not to expose others: Stay home if you can, skip shaking hands, and restrict vocal use in public so that you don't spray germ-laden saliva into the air.

7. Heed warning signs

When you detect a cold coming on, drink extra water, rest, and regulate vocal use. If you need treatment, go to a health center, and inform your care provider that you're a singer. Don't self-medicate with drugs or herbs unless you're well versed in those that aren't suitable for vocalists.

During and immediately after a cold you're at greater risk of incurring a voice disorder, so use your voice with restraint. Then gradually increase vocal use in the aftermath of an illness—at a rehearsal, for example, you might "mark" your part, that is, sing lightly and drop high passages down an octave.

If you're not sick and any of the symptoms from the following list appear, rest your voice and see a laryngologist. Vocalists who disregard these warning signs risk grave injury. Links to prominent voice clinics are posted at *musiciansway.com*. At any large medical center you can also locate voice specialists, who may be listed in directories under the category of "ear, nose, and throat" (ENT) or "otolaryngology." It's likely, however, that your teacher will be able to make a referral.

Warning signs of vocal trouble

    i. breathy, raspy, or hoarse tone

    ii. uncontrollable vocal trembling or quivering

    iii. constricted range or ongoing inability to sing softly at the upper end of your range

    iv. pitches break up

    v. unexpected problems singing on pitch

    vi. hoarseness after singing ("If you are hoarse after singing, something is very wrong," says physician Clark Rosen.[15])

vii. loss of your voice that lasts for more than 2–3 days

viii. pain in the larynx

ix. unrelenting coughing, throat clearing, or postnasal drip

x. reduction in voice quality along with either a persistent "lump in the throat" or, in spite of excellent oral hygiene, an unshakable bitter or bad taste in your mouth, notably in the morning (such symptoms may indicate reflux)

In addition, follow this policy from the University of Pittsburgh Voice Center: "If your voice feels less than perfect for more than two to four weeks (including time spent with a cold), seek care immediately."[16]

For singers, voice care is a 24/7 operation. If the specifics of vocal health are new to you, revisit this section often. Soon enough, nurturing your voice will become routine. Soprano Cecilia Bartoli puts it this way: "The voice will guide you—will tell you what to do. In order to do that, you must be quite sensitive with the instrument and accept this daily conversation with your voice."[17]

Hearing Conservation

The real reason that I haven't performed live for a long time is that I have very severe hearing damage. It's manifested itself as tinnitus—ringing in the ears at the frequencies that I play the guitar.

—Pete Townshend, singer-songwriter

Pete Townshend isn't alone in having incurred hearing damage from overexposure to loud music. According to trumpeter and researcher Kris Chesky, codirector of the University of North Texas Center for Music and Medicine, "Experts agree that 30–50% of musicians have problems with hearing loss."[18] You might guess that rock musicians make up the majority of sufferers, but researchers have found higher rates of music-induced hearing loss among classical artists than rockers. Audiologist and clarinetist Marshall Chasin explains: "Classical musicians rehearse, perform, and teach more hours each week than typical rock musicians. And classical musicians tend to be clustered closer together than rock musicians. So even though the peak sound levels in a rock band may be higher than in an orchestra, the total weekly dosage of a classical musician is greater."[19]

Whatever the style of music, lengthy exposure to intense sound is a recipe for disaster because, once a person develops hearing loss due to music or noise, the damage is permanent. The effects may include reduced sensitivity, tinnitus, and, in some cases, pitch distortion —that is, not hearing pitches accurately. Many musicians, like Townshend, endure a cruel disability.

> **Hearing Conservation Guidelines**
> 1. Appreciate healthy hearing
> 2. Schedule regular hearing exams
> 3. Recognize dangers
> 4. Heed warning signs
> 5. Protect your hearing

Nonetheless, sound-induced hearing loss is 100% preventable. It seems that musicians either aren't aware of the risks or, if they are, don't protect themselves. After studying the guidelines here, you'll know better.

1. Appreciate healthy hearing

If you're fortunate enough to have healthy hearing, it's likely that you take your ability for granted. Yet your wondrous sense of hearing, aside from being primary to making music, is interwoven with almost every aspect of how you interact with the world. You hear where you cannot see, for example, behind you, around corners, and through solid objects. When it's quiet, you perceive silence, unlike those who are burdened with tinnitus, for whom the ringing never ceases. At the beach, you absorb the relaxing sounds of the waves. In the city, you listen for cars as you cross a street. And if your hearing were to diminish, not only would your capacity to enjoy music and sound be compromised, but you also wouldn't easily understand speech. By safeguarding your hearing, therefore, you don't just look after your music career; you preserve your quality of life.

2. Schedule regular hearing exams

A decisive step in taking responsibility for your hearing is to have it evaluated by an audiologist. Many universities operate audiology clinics. You can also locate audiologists via the website of the American Academy of Audiology: www.audiology.org. Preferably, select an audiologist with experience working with musicians. Also, be sure to obtain a comprehensive workup; a cursory screening won't do.

Scheduling a hearing exam is important for two reasons. First, you'll be checked for any existing problems—modern tests can spot the preliminary stages of hearing loss long before deficits become noticeable to musicians themselves. If your test were to reveal an anomaly, you could then act to ward off further damage. Second, a test will provide you with a record of your current hearing status that you can use to track changes over the years.

How often should you arrange hearing tests? For people routinely exposed to loud music or noise, audiologists recommend annual exams. However, as discussed below, if you ever have difficulties with your hearing, you should see an audiologist without delay.

3. Recognize dangers

Your ears are exquisite sense organs, but their capacity to detect sound comes at a price in that they can be injured by too much sound. More specifically, the hairlike cells in the inner ear can get overwhelmed, like grass that's been trampled, and then they become unable to convert sound waves into signals that the brain can interpret (see *musiciansway.com* for images of healthy and sound-damaged inner ears). To prevent problems, you have to know where the boundaries lie between safety and danger, but that's no easy task.

Except in the presence of exceedingly loud sounds, you can't always perceive when your hearing is being stressed. Often, it's only after harm has been done that hearing overload becomes discernible. Worse still, music-induced hearing loss, by and large, comes on gradually, so musicians who don't schedule hearing tests seldom realize that something's amiss until it's too late. The following illustrates how exposure to intense sound leads to trouble and will help you identify unsafe situations.

Sound intensity is measured in decibels, abbreviated as dB. The quietest sound that healthy ears can hear is quantified as 0 dB. Intensity then doubles for every 3 dB increase. The dial tone on a landline telephone held to your ear averages around 80 dB—sounds measuring 80 dB or less are unlikely to cause damage. Normal conversation runs 60–70 dB. Violin playing spans a range of approximately 84–103 dB.

As the intensity of a sound climbs, safe exposure time decreases. The standards established by the National Institute for Occupational Safety and Health (NIOSH) state that human ears can tolerate 85 dB for up to eight hours a day without risking injury. Above 85 dB, for each 3 dB rise, the doubling of intensity means that safe exposure time is cut in half (table 13.1).[20]

Although a 3 dB rise represents a doubling of intensity, you won't perceive it as a twofold increase in sound. Human ears are attuned to minuscule variations in pitch, but they don't have an equally fine ability to gauge volume. It takes about a 10 dB surge before most people sense that volume has doubled. And that perceptual inaccuracy is one reason that many musicians don't use hearing protection—dangerous sound levels don't seem as threatening as they actually are. Even so, the 3 dB rule is constantly in force. For example, if you compare sounds at 115 dB and 85 dB—perhaps a loud trumpet versus a quiet violin—the 30 dB difference signifies that the 115 dB sound is a thousand times more intense than one that measures 85 dB. Hence, you find a huge

Table 13.1 **Sound Levels and Safe Exposure Time**

Continuous sound level	Safe exposure time
85 dB	8 hours
88 dB	4 hours
91 dB	2 hours
94 dB	1 hour
97 dB	30 minutes
100 dB	15 minutes
103 dB	7.5 minutes
106 dB	Less than 4 minutes
109 dB	Less than 2 minutes
112 dB	About 1 minute
115 dB	30 seconds

From the National Institute for Occupational Safety and Health, 1998

disparity in table 13.1 between the durations of safe exposure (30 seconds compared to eight hours).

When sound levels reach 120 dB (the intensity of a nearby thunderclap), almost no exposure is safe. At 125 dB, you'll feel pain. With sounds approaching 140 dB, say, a gunshot, jet engine, or explosion, the dangers are acute. If you think that you'll never be around such deafening sounds, think again. Rock concerts can escalate to those levels; fireworks and theatrical pyrotechnics hit 140 dB. Many performers have had their hearing suddenly impaired on the job, including actor William Shatner, who acquired life-changing tinnitus from an explosion on the set of Star Trek in the 1960s.[21] Table 13.2 lists the intensities of some musical and nonmusical sounds.[22]

Using tables 13.1 and 13.2, you can see that the sound level in a dance club (110 dB) is safe for less than two minutes. Even if the level were to drop to 100 dB, the maximum safe exposure would be 15 minutes. Of course, club patrons usually hang out for longer than that, so you might suppose that in ordinary conversations they would often say, "What?" In fact, that's the case. According to Hearnet.com, "a study in Great Britain found that 62% of regular clubbers have hearing loss."[23]

Personal stereos also bathe the ears in risky levels of sound. At half volume, such devices, if they generate 94 dB (many produce higher levels), are safe to listen to for one hour a day at most, if the listener has no other exposure to loud sounds. At full volume (120 dB), their use is perilous. "Many kids who are using this type of technology are plugging virtual rock concerts into their ears,"

Table 13.2 **Typical Sound Levels**

Sound source	Approximate level in decibels
Violin	84–103
Cello	82–92
Oboe	90–94
Flute	85–110
Piccolo	95–112
Clarinet	92–103
Moderately loud piano playing	92–95
French horn	90–106
Trombone	85–114
Timpani/bass drum rolls	106
Personal stereo at 50% volume	94
Symphonic music peak	120–137
Rock concert	110–150
Dance club	110
Power mower or saw	107–110
Jet engine at 100 ft.	140

From www.hearnet.com, 2007

warns audiologist Pam Mason.[24] Not surprisingly, hearing loss is being discovered among users of personal stereos. In response to consumer complaints, some devices have downloadable software that restricts a machine's volume.

Other than personal stereos, common sources of unsafe sound levels include home and car audio systems, sporting events, power tools, and movie theaters. So where does that leave music students?

Assuming that college-level instrumentalists practice alone in small rooms for two or more hours a day and that they also play in rehearsals with large ensembles, most are getting overdosed with sound. If they additionally listen to personal stereos or car hi-fis or they frequent dance clubs, their exposure may be extreme. As a case in point, audiologist Susan Phillips has found that about half of the students at a university music school had some degree of sound-induced hearing loss.[25] When researchers Vanessa Miller, Michael Stewart, and Mark Lehman measured the sound exposure of 27 college music students who rehearsed and performed in pep bands, they discovered that *all* of the students were being overdosed with sound—most of them recorded exposure levels more than 40 times the NIOSH one-day safety limits. They conclude that "university student musicians appear to be at high risk of permanent noise-induced hearing loss." They go on to say, "These results support the need for ongoing hearing conservation programs to educate student musicians about the dangers of excessive exposure to loud music."[26]

Here's an illustration of how music students' daily sound exposures add up. Consider that woodwind, brass, and percussion players may produce an average of 90–95 dB during solitary practice.[27] That equates to 48 minutes to 2.5 hours of safe exposure. But after practicing alone for at least a couple of hours, students often participate in one- to two-hour ensemble rehearsals with orchestras, wind ensembles, and jazz or other bands, where sound levels may hover in the region of 94 dB. At 94 dB, safe exposure would total one hour if the musicians had no other doses of intense sound that day. Many ensembles, though, produce average levels that exceed 100 dB. It's a grim scenario, but, as discussed in the coming pages, protective measures abound.

It might seem that vocalists would be better off than instrumentalists, but unamplified voices can be as loud as instruments. A publication from the Canadian organization known as SHAPE (Safety and Health in Arts Production and Entertainment) asserts, "Many sopranos can generate levels of 105–110 dB, and some can reach peak levels over 115 dB."[28] Singers won't attain those volumes often. But when you add the time that vocalists spend practicing in small rooms—both alone and with pianists—to the hours that they rehearse in choirs, their sound exposure can be comparable to that of instrumentalists. If singers also perform with amplified groups, listen to personal stereos, or go to clubs or sporting events, then they're likely to be awash in injurious sound levels.

Given all the overdosing that's going on, it's no wonder that researchers are finding prevalent hearing loss among musicians. If you're amazed that not all performers have a hearing impairment, the reason is that people's ears don't have identical tolerances. Some individuals can withstand higher doses of sound than others, yet there's no way to know what any one person's exact threshold of safety might be. Therefore, everyone should go by the exposure guidelines in table 13.1. To ignore those limits is folly.

Besides the dangers of sound, hearing can also be compromised by aging, diseases, a genetic predisposition to hearing problems, and medications. Large doses of aspirin, for instance, can cause temporary hearing loss or tinnitus. What's more, dehydration and cigarette smoking may make sound-induced hearing damage more likely, as can exposure to the chemical solvents in paint. Audiologist Susan Phillips warns that, on a day when you use paints, you should be extra vigilant in caring for your ears.[29] Log on to *musiciansway.com* for more facts concerning general hearing health.

4. Heed warning signs

In light of this information, it's reasonable to conclude that you'll encounter unsafe sound levels both when making music and in everyday life. But how

Table 13.3 **Warning Signs of Hearing Damage**

1. You notice ringing, buzzing, or whooshing in the ears.
2. You find that sounds seem muffled or garbled.
3. You have difficulty understanding speech, especially in the presence of background noise.
4. You adjust the TV louder than others in your household.
5. One ear hears better on the telephone.
6. You often ask people to repeat themselves.
7. You're frequently told that you play, sing, or speak too loudly.
8. Pitches seem different in one ear than in the other.
9. You've become hypersensitive to sound such that you feel discomfort or pain when others do not.

can you tell whether a sound is too loud? One way is to use a sound level meter such as those catalogued at *musiciansway.com.* In addition, the National Institute for Occupational Safety and Health puts forward two recommendations: "First, if you have to raise your voice to talk to someone who is an arm's length away, then the noise [or music] is likely to be hazardous. Second, if your ears are ringing or sounds seem dull after leaving a noisy place, then you probably were exposed to hazardous noise."[30]

If you notice ringing or a loss of sensitivity after exposure to music or noise, audiologist Marshall Chasin recommends that you avoid intense sounds for at least 16 hours; the problem is likely temporary.[31] That is, the cells in the inner ear are traumatized, but, if the exposure wasn't too great, they'll recover with a day's rest. However, repeated episodes of temporary ringing or impairment characteristically lead to permanent injury, so it's vital that you learn to apply the protective strategies outlined ahead. Furthermore, many musicians never experience ringing when they overload their ears, so you need to protect yourself and have an annual hearing exam regardless of whether you notice symptoms.

Table 13.3 lists nine warning signs of hearing damage.[32] If any of the listed symptoms persist, see an audiologist.

5. Protect your hearing

Like visual artists who learn to work safely with toxic paints and chemicals, musicians need the expertise to handle high-intensity sounds. The ability to manage sound levels is as much a part of a musician's creative process as is the knowledge of how to organize a practice schedule, collaborate, sight-read, or interpret a composition. Musicians who don't control their sound exposure lack understanding of their medium. Their obliviousness then undermines both their musicianship and their hearing.

When you anticipate being around sound levels above 80 dB, there are three fundamental ways to protect your hearing:

a. Modify acoustic environments.

b. Reduce and manage exposure.

c. Wear earplugs.

a. Modify acoustic environments

It might appear that you can't do much to change an acoustic environment, but you can actually make a number of modifications to temper the volume in concert halls, rehearsal spaces, and practice rooms. Because a 3 dB reduction in sound intensity doubles your safe exposure time, modest fixes, such as the following eight strategies, add up. To determine whether adaptations are needed in the places where you rehearse and perform, your best bet is to use a sound level meter to measure sound intensities (*musiciansway.com* contains information about such meters). Then, after making improvements, a meter will equip you to appraise the effectiveness of your efforts.

i. *Install sound-absorbing materials.* When sound bounces off hard surfaces and returns to your ears, you get dosed with both the original sound and its reflection. Reducing reflections, therefore, diminishes sound intensity. If you practice in a room with bare windows, floors, or walls, hang some thick drapes, buy a rug, and attach foam or sound-dampening panels to the ceiling and walls. If you conduct an ensemble, don't stand in front of reflective walls or blackboards; alternatively, cover such surfaces with drapes or panels.

ii. *Rehearse in larger spaces.* In more spacious surroundings, reflected sound will have less energy when it returns to your ears.

iii. *Place trumpets strategically.* High-frequency pitches emanate from trumpet bells like laser beams. In an ensemble, if the trumpeters are seated in the back of a group and at the same level as the other players—and if they point their bells forward—their high notes will shoot directly into the heads of the musicians sitting in front of them. Then the downwind musicians get blasted, and the trumpeters have to play harder since some of their sound gets absorbed. But when trumpeters are seated on risers and play with bells aiming forward, their sound travels over the heads of their colleagues, and they can play more lightly. In *Hear the Music: Hearing Loss Prevention for Musicians,* Marshall Chasin writes that, with reference to downwind players, "a 5–7 dB high-frequency decrease in sound energy was achieved when the trumpet section was placed on risers."[33] If risers aren't available or if the trumpet players in a group angle their bells downward, try seating them to the side or in the front of an ensemble so that the other musicians aren't in the line of fire.

iv. *Position an ensemble back from the edge of a stage.* A stage surface makes an excellent acoustic mirror. By keeping some of the downstage area bare, high-frequency sounds can bounce off the flooring and fill a concert hall, thereby allowing both performers and listeners to hear more clearly. For musicians, clearer sound translates into less playing force. Chasin recommends vacating a space of at least two meters between the front of an ensemble and the edge of the stage.[34]

v. *Avoid seating violinists and violists beneath the overhang of an orchestra pit.* Chasin writes that, when the overhang of an orchestra pit is within about two meters of the players' heads, high-frequency pitches are absorbed, and that makes it harder for the musicians to hear themselves and each other.[35] As a result, they tend to overplay, augmenting their sound exposure and stressing their bodies as well. If possible, seat violinists and violists forward in the pit, in the open-ceiling area beyond the ledge of the stage.

vi. *Experiment with sound shields.* Usually made of transparent materials, sound shields work in two ways. First, placed around or behind a musician's head, they can reduce the intensity of directional, high-frequency sound waves coming from other players; they don't affect frequencies below about 250 Hz. Sound shields are effective, however, only when they're within seven inches (18 cm) of a musician's ears.[36] If you need protection from players sitting behind you, with the shields that mount on seat backs, be sure to adjust the shield or your seating to bring your head near the panel. Shields should also be angled to deflect sound away from upwind players.

Shields also protect by impeding sounds at their source. Chasin proposes that a shield next to a cymbal or drum can lessen the intensity of sound hitting the musicians performing alongside. Such shields shouldn't reach the height of a drummer's ear, though, or they could sling the sound back toward the drummer.[37]

Nevertheless, shields can be problematic to use, especially in tightly clustered ensembles. Upwind players can get hit by reflected sound, plus some of their own sound may be absorbed, and then they have to increase their volume to compensate. Shield technology may continue to advance, but, for now, shields should be employed with caution. Alison

Wright Reid, advisor to the Association of British Orchestras, noted in 2008 that "Orchestras continue to have problems [with shields] and some have stopped using them."[38]

vii. *Elevate speakers.* If speakers are placed on the floor, low-frequency pitches will be lost to absorption, and musicians will respond by jacking up the volume. Putting speakers on stands halts the loss of bass. Then, both performers and listeners gain from cleaner, less overblown sound. But before you elevate a speaker, review the manufacturer's specifications to be sure that it's designed for hoisting. Also, locate house speakers such that they have an unobstructed sound line to an audience and the musicians won't be hit by the laserlike high-frequency pitches. If a house speaker is ever placed behind you, sit or stand to one side.

viii. *Improve monitoring.* When monitoring is upgraded, musicians hear themselves vividly and don't hike their volume. They curb both their sound exposure and their risk of overuse injury, plus they can better enjoy making music. Aside from relying on the in-ear monitors mentioned below, drummers and electric bass players can enhance their monitoring with bass shakers, hockey-puck-sized loudspeakers that amplify the lowest pitches. Other devices are available to aid nonamplified instrumentalists—for example, orchestral cellists and bassists—who might use personal monitoring systems that connect earpieces with either microphones or transducers attached to their instruments. In venues in which performers have persistent problems hearing themselves or each other, more expensive solutions are also conceivable. Some concert hall managers, for instance, enlist moveable acoustic shells or fasten sound-dispersing materials to ceilings and walls.

b. Reduce and manage exposure

Whatever the acoustic setting, you still have to regulate how much sound you and your groups produce. You also need to be cognizant of the sound levels that you encounter apart from making music. Here are some strategies to reduce and manage your sound exposure:

i. *Practice at lower volumes.* The most straightforward technique to trim your music-related sound dosage is to cut volume in practice and rehearsal. Some players might also employ mutes during portions of their solo practice. Amplified groups can turn down their amplifiers, and drummers might employ lightweight or soft-tipped sticks. Trumpeter and researcher Kris Chesky encourages conductors to emphasize softer playing, to mix in many dynamic contrasts, and to restrict peak levels to musically appropriate moments.[39]

ii. *Intersperse louder and softer pieces.* Organize rehearsals and practice sessions so that boisterous pieces are framed by more tranquil ones. And take breaks in quiet spaces to give your ears a rest.

iii. *Practice efficiently* (see part I). In solo practice, establish clear interpretive and technical maps in order to optimize your learning and minimize the need for you to repeat material.

iv. *Prepare for noisy situations.* If you're planning to attend the likes of a sporting event, dance club, rock concert, or fireworks exhibit or if you're going to operate power equipment, use earplugs (figure 13.41). In very loud situations, however, plugs alone might not provide enough protection. In the vicinity of gunshot-level sound or if you work with strident machinery, you should wear special earmuffs in tandem with plugs.

v. *Turn down the stereo.* A clarinetist I'll call Jeff studied music at a Midwestern university. During spring break of his sophomore year, he and some friends drove 24 hours nonstop to Florida with the car stereo blaring all the way. Upon arrival, his ears were ringing, sounds seemed dampened, and he couldn't make out speech when there was background noise. He returned to school with unrelenting symptoms, and tests revealed permanent damage.

   When you listen to recorded music—whether in the car, with a personal stereo, or elsewhere—moderate the volume. If you turn it up for one song, turn it down after the song ends. On road trips, switch off the stereo for long stretches, and periodically use earplugs when you aren't driving, both for relaxation and to protect your hearing when someone else cranks up the volume. Never overload your ears with hours and hours of intense sound.

vi. *Hum.* A bonus tactic to lessen the impact of earsplitting impulse sounds is, believe it or not, to hum. When you vocalize, a muscle attached to one of the tiny bones in the middle ear contracts into a position that hinders sound waves from penetrating to the inner ear.[40] By humming, you get at least a few decibels of attenuation for several seconds (the degree and duration of the effect varies among individuals). If you expect a cymbal crash, let's say, begin to hum just prior to the bang, and carry on humming throughout. For a few people, however, such vocalizing yields no effect, so you can't count on humming as an everyday technique, but use it as an emergency maneuver.

vii. *Ask for help.* If you're concerned about the sound levels in the settings where you practice and perform, consult with your teachers, colleagues, and music directors to identify and remedy problems. For example, if you feel stressed due to the volume produced by one of your ensembles, or if you experience tinnitus or muffled hearing during or after a re-hearsal, report it to the conductor. Also, ask your private teacher about protective strategies specific to your instrument or section. Sometimes, though, when musicians get together in certain combinations or for extended periods, their sound levels inevitably exceed safe limits. That's where earplugs come in.

c. Wear earplugs

Just as people don protective eyewear when handling materials that could injure their eyes, earplugs are primary safety tools for anyone who deals with harmful levels of sound. High-fidelity plugs actually help musicians hear bet-ter when the volume soars—the effect is akin to the way sunglasses enhance vision in bright light. Here I describe two classes of earplugs: those that only attenuate sound and those that both attenuate and also electronically feed sound to a musician's ears (generally known as in-ear monitors).

Attenuating earplugs

There are two types of high-fidelity, sound-reducing earplugs designed for musicians: premade and custom fitted. Unlike the foam earplugs avail-able at drugstores, musicians' plugs supply a precise amount of attenuation while preserving sound quality. Foam plugs have a less balanced sound and, for many musicians, attenuate too much to be useful when fully inserted. Nonetheless, as discussed a little later, foam plugs have a place in some musicians' toolkits; plus, they're suitable when you need protection from nonmusical sounds or simply want to wear plugs for relaxation. Incidentally, if you've ever considered stuffing your ears with cotton or tissue, then you should know that doing so affords little protection and isn't a strategy that audiologists advocate.

- *Premade earplugs:* Premade plugs provide an inexpensive way for mu-sicians to get started with personal hearing protection. The most com-mon variety designed for musicians attenuates sound by 20 dB and can be worn with a neck cord (figure 13.41). At the time of this writing, a pair costs less than $15 (*musiciansway.com* includes links to the web-sites of earplug manufacturers and retailers).

- *Custom-fitted earplugs:* Custom plugs are created by an audiologist using a mold of your ear canal; they deliver superior sound and are more effective than the premade types. Within the typical custom plug, a button is mounted that supplies 9, 15, or 25 dB of attenuation (figure 13.41). The 15 dB version has the most realistic frequency response and is the model suited to most performers. Percussionists, however, may opt for the 25 dB sort. If you're not sure what degree of attenuation you require, an audiologist or your teacher can advise you. It's best to go with the least possible attenuation so that you're adequately protected in loud ensembles but you can still hear clearly enough to pick up spoken directions and the subtleties of soft passages. Also, it takes a skilled professional to craft a comfortably fitting plug, so hire a practiced audiologist.

A pair of custom plugs costs roughly $150–$200, plus a couple of visits to an audiologist. If that strikes you as expensive, weigh the cost in comparison to that of prescription eyeglasses or the ultimate price of sustaining hearing loss. Such plugs are quite durable, too, and should last for many years.

Another comparably priced custom plug is the vented/tuned plug. It doesn't use a button but has a vent that filters high-frequency sounds and leaves lower frequencies mostly untouched. It can also be tuned somewhat to attenuate more or less of the high frequencies. It's used by cellists, bassists, and solo vocalists because it leaves their own sounds more intact. Clarinet and sax players may also favor the vented/tuned plug because the vent permits bone-conducted sound to escape from the ear. Your teacher or an audiologist who works with musicians can help you decide whether the vented/tuned plug is for you.

Figure 13.41 shows three kinds of attenuating earplugs. The top two pairs are foam plugs purchased at a national drugstore chain and have noise reduction ratings of 28 dB. On the lower left is a pair of premade musician's plugs with an attached neck cord—they supply 20 dB of attenuation. On the lower right are custom-fitted musicians' plugs with 15 dB buttons.

Even with the superior sound afforded by custom plugs, some brass and wind players choose foam or premade plugs because, when they play, their jaw movements alter the diameter of their ear canals. Rigid custom plugs can't adapt to those changes, but both foam plugs and the soft flanges on premade plugs can expand and contract, giving a more flexible fit throughout a player's range. If you're a brass or wind player, start with a premade plug. Then, if you're interested in a custom model, seek out an audiologist who works with musicians, and bring your instrument to your appointment so that the audiologist can evaluate how your playing affects the dimensions of your ear canal.

Musicians have diverse strategies for using plugs. In large ensembles, some instrumentalists will mark their scores with cues for when to insert and remove their plugs. Depending on the repertoire they're playing, they might rely on plugs only when the volume skyrockets. On other days, when their total sound exposure is greater, those same musicians might wear plugs

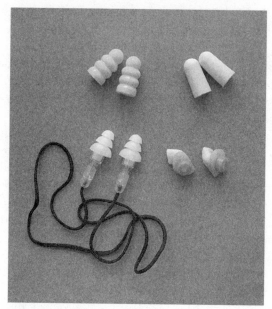

Figure 13.41. Various earplugs.

throughout much of a rehearsal. In another situation, a pianist won't need earplugs at all during solo practice but will wear them throughout rehearsals with a jazz big band. Performers in drum corps, marching bands, percussion ensembles, and pep bands might leave their plugs in for the majority of rehearsals—especially when rehearsing indoors—and also during lengthy or thunderous performances. The key is to pay attention to your daily sound exposure and then use plugs accordingly.

When you begin wearing earplugs, allow time to adjust. For one thing, it may feel odd to have something stuck in your ear. For another, plugs transform the way you hear yourself and others. Many musicians discover that the reduction in loudness relaxes them. Others find the change in sound to be jarring. For instance, if you're a vocalist or you play a brass or wind instrument, the perceptual shift caused by earplugs will be more dramatic for you than for musicians whose sound isn't so heavily conducted through the jaw and skull. Whatever your experience, be patient. You may want to try out plugs as a listener first: Don a pair at home, and then survey a mix of music on your stereo.

When wearing earplugs, be mindful to play or sing as usual and not boost your volume. Some musicians, upon the initial use of plugs, develop injuries because they play or sing with added force.

There isn't yet any inclusive research into how readily musicians acclimate to using earplugs, but surely every performer would rather not need them.

So do what you can to modify your acoustic environment, trim your volume, and manage your sound exposure. Then you won't constantly require earplugs. Still, at large-group rehearsals and when you perform piercing repertoire, the consistent use of plugs may be the only way that you can prevent hearing loss.

In-ear monitors

You've probably seen custom-fitted in-ear monitors used by performers in the rock and commercial music industries. These devices look like hearing aids; they strongly attenuate sound but also contain tiny speakers that connect to a group's sound system (see *musiciansway.com* for examples). Typically, a transmitter wired to a PA sends a signal to a cell-phone-sized appliance worn by a musician, perhaps as a belt pack. That appliance connects to two earpieces and equips the musician to control the volume. The latest versions of these plugs also contain miniature microphones on the exterior of the earpieces—these enable musicians to hear ambient sounds, as well as the feed from a PA.

Custom in-ear monitors are the superior choice for musicians who habitually work in amplified, high-volume conditions. Although top-level systems are pricey, the cost is justified by the musical and health benefits.

In-ear monitors also come in less-expensive, noncustom types that have removable foam or other compressible material surrounding the in-ear speakers. If the foam provides ample attenuation, these monitors can suffice. But if they don't block enough sound, then they won't furnish the protection that performers need. Your teacher and audiologist can help you assess the suitability of premade models.

❧

Whatever your musical style, stay open to new possibilities for hearing protection—more options will appear with future innovations. Also, when you assume the role of ensemble director or music educator, take the lead in informing other musicians about how to safeguard their hearing.

In sum, hearing conservation, like all forms of self-care, is an ongoing process. And given that musicians are at high risk for incurring sound-induced hearing loss, you need to take action now. So appreciate healthy hearing, schedule regular hearing exams, recognize dangers, heed warning signs, and protect your hearing.

14

Succeeding as a Student

In this chapter:

- Choosing and working with teachers
- Dealing with criticism
- Five career-building maneuvers
- Counteracting substance abuse
- Boosting creativity

Succeeding as a Student

The art of music is so deep and profound that to approach it very seriously only is not enough. One must approach music with a serious vigor and, at the same time, with a great, affectionate joy.

—Nadia Boulanger, pianist and composer

When you enroll in a college music program, your life changes dramatically. You're confronted with a new school environment, elevated artistic standards, and unfamiliar teachers and peers. The challenge, however, isn't merely to perform at a high level and become part of a campus community, although those can be formidable challenges. Amid the pressures to excel, you also have to fuel your joy in making music so that your imagination and productivity expand.

You won't achieve such comprehensive success if you just go with the flow. To prosper in the music-school setting and thereby assemble a foundation for lifelong creativity, you must make wise, proactive moves. This chapter examines many of those moves.

Student-Teacher Dynamics

Establish an honest dialogue with your teacher.
　　　　　—Wynton Marsalis, trumpeter and bandleader

Although music students rely on teachers for guidance, principled educators hope that their students will mature into self-directed artists who no longer need their guidance. During your apprenticeship, therefore, you're in the intriguing position of being subordinate to teachers while also having to learn how to succeed as an independent musician. The lessons you take with your major teacher can supply the ideal laboratory in which to attain self-sufficiency. But to shape a learning atmosphere that supports your future autonomy, you need to make informed choices about whom you study with; plus, you require skills in order to work in partnership with your teachers. Here are three concepts to keep in mind.

> **Optimizing Student-Teacher Relations**
>
> 1. Choose teachers carefully
> 2. Communicate
> 3. Be an active learner

1. Choose teachers carefully

There are plenty of fine educators in the world—and some not-so-fine ones, too. In addition, there are different styles of teaching. How do you recognize teachers who are both adept and suited to your personality and goals?

Your current instructors can be prime resources for identifying prospective teachers. However, as a free-thinking artist, you should also investigate on your own. Whether you're searching for a teacher before, during, or after college, your first task is to consider the attributes of effective teachers; your second is to screen teachers for those qualities.

Attributes of effective teachers

Effective teachers are leaders. Author Warren Bennis pinpoints four things that people should look for in leaders and, by inference, in teachers:[1]

i. *Purpose:* Expert teachers are purposeful; they convey clear educational objectives and build shared meaning with their students.

ii. *Trust:* They engender trust because they model high artistic standards, organized thinking, and articulate speech.

iii. *Optimism:* They have can-do attitudes that inspire students to work hard and surmount problems.

iv. *Results:* Above all, capable teachers get results. Their students grow into confident performers who possess easeful techniques and artistic interpretive skills.

Bennis further states that the best leaders also motivate others. They help people feel significant, excited about their work, and connected to a community. I'll add that top music educators also exhibit compassion—they care about students and are sensitive to the intricacies of striving in the arts.

Screening teachers

With these attributes in mind, here are five approaches to help you single out teachers who can meet your needs:

i. *Observe teachers in action.* Visit music schools, and sit in on lessons and classes. Are the teachers you observe compassionate, purposeful, articulate, and optimistic? If you hear the teachers perform, do they embody the artistic excellence you seek? Educators don't need to be working soloists, but if they continue to concertize, they should exemplify professionalism.

ii. *Attend student performances.* Do the students demonstrate self-assured performance skills coupled with interpretive and technical facility? Or are they crippled by anxiety, wooden in their expression, and ignorant of stage deportment?

iii. *Get together with students.* Are the students energized by their work, and do they show a sense of community? Or do you detect indifference, frustration, or venomous competition?

iv. *Take lessons.* Seize chances to study with teachers that you'd like to appraise—festivals and workshops make definitive testing grounds. Is a teacher interested in you and able to elicit improvements in your skills? Does the teaching style mesh with your learning style?

v. *Audition for teachers and ask questions.* If you audition for a teacher, perform thoroughly prepared material, and pose questions such as the following:

- "What would you say my current strengths and weaknesses are?"
- "If I were to study with you, what would be some of your goals for my first semester?"
- "How do you suggest that students go about learning new pieces?"
- "How do you help students get hold of performance skills?"
- "How do you teach technique and interpretation?"

Apt educators will give answers that indicate that their methods are detailed and in harmony with your ambitions.

Your teachers should have high expectations for you, and you for them. When you take the time to choose a teacher carefully, you start your collaboration with foreknowledge of how you'll work together and with a virtual guarantee of success.

2. Communicate

When you begin studying with a new teacher, neither of you is well versed in the other's communication style, and that lack of familiarity creates a breeding ground for misunderstanding. To avoid confusion about instructional aims, below are two questions to ask yourself and to discuss with your instructor at the outset of your student-teacher partnership. The first question is adapted from an article titled "Outcome-centered Learning" by music educator Paul Broomhead:[2]

- What are the primary ways in which you want to be different after taking lessons this term, and, correspondingly, how does your teacher want you to be different?
- What are your intermediate and long-term goals as a musician?

Throughout your student-teacher collaboration, questioning remains the most helpful communication habit that you can adopt. Do you know, for instance, whether your practice is producing the results that your teacher foresees? If you don't receive comments in that regard, the only way you'll know is to inquire. So before concluding a lesson, be sure that both you and your teacher spell out the objectives for the coming week. At your subsequent session, ask questions like these to assess how well you're achieving lesson aims:

- "Am I accomplishing what you expect?"
- "In what ways am I practicing most and least successfully?"
- "How might I alter my practice to overcome my weaknesses?"
- "Are my technique and musicianship improving as you think they should? Is there anything that I should be doing differently to upgrade my skills?"

To preserve your teacher's advice, audio- or video-record your lessons, and then review afterward and take notes. Also try to practice on the heels of each meeting to instill information while it's fresh. The most important practice session of the week isn't the one right before your lesson; it's the one right after.

3. Be an active learner

Artistic growth can continue throughout a musician's life. Even so, this growth hinges on a person's willingness to change. In effect, the artists who keep on creating are those who keep on changing.

Sometimes, though, change can be tough. When musicians resist change—when they want to remain in their customary boxes—they spurn new ideas. But those who embrace active learning search out the new—they accept that, to advance, they have to go outside of their comfort zones.

I get the impression that many more students could be active learners. Violin teacher Mimi Zweig agrees: "The biggest challenge with my new students," she explains, "is to convince them to be excited about solidifying their foundations."[3] Active learners present no such resistance. They're enthusiastic about every facet of their musical development, foundational aspects no less than interpretive ones. Still, they won't blindly consent to teachers' prescriptions. They need to know the *why* behind every *how*.

To become a more active learner, ask questions, and branch out to investigate a range of your musical interests. No matter how brilliant your teachers may be, you can't count on them to provide for all of your educational needs. Don't be content, therefore, to cruise along in a teacher's slipstream. Be a voracious consumer of information and experience. Beyond practicing efficiently, also attend concerts and workshops, collaborate with fellow musicians, listen to recordings, and read about music and creativity. You are the one who will shape yourself into the artist that you aspire to be.

Appreciating Criticism

A fear of criticism equals a fear of performing.
—Eric Maisel, author and psychologist

Whenever you perform, but especially in a lesson, a rehearsal, or an audition, you open yourself up to criticism. There's no way around it. Playing or singing entails self-exposure, and the road to improvement is paved with evaluations. Music students who are overly sensitive to critiques tend to shy away from educational and performance opportunities. They might not see the connection, but their aversion to criticism causes them to pass up going to auditions, asking questions in lessons, or participating in master classes.

Given that criticism is integral to your creative work, this section looks at ways to make it a positive force in your life.

Eric Maisel explains that there are two basic kinds of criticism: fair and unfair.[4] Fair criticism is accurate and appropriate. In music lessons, for example, a teacher's statements such as "Lighten your touch" or "The staccatos are too short" are fitting critiques intended to better your skills. Similarly, in an ensemble rehearsal, if you start on the wrong measure and the conductor points out, "You're a measure behind," that's legitimate. Fair criticism isn't sugarcoated, though, and you shouldn't expect it to be.

Unfair criticism, however, is inaccurate or inappropriate. Such critiques often stem from misunderstandings—for instance, when someone blames you for something that you didn't do—or they may arise from emotional explosions. Whichever sort of criticism you face, the following three-part approach will help you extract the most gain.

First, welcome fair criticism; it's crucial to your development. Wise artists, in fact, seek out critical evaluations because they know that input from other musicians will promote their growth. Second, listen objectively to a critique so that you can sift out the meaning without getting irritated by any prickly words. Third, respond constructively. Here are some examples.

> **Appreciating Criticism**
> - Welcome fair criticism
> - Listen objectively
> - Respond constructively

Dealing with Fair Criticism

Suppose that you perform a solo at a public master class. At the conclusion of your performance, the audience applauds heartily, but then the teacher says, "It was too fast." You hear no recognition of all of the good things you did, just those few words. With a discerning attitude toward criticism, you'll be unfazed. After all, you came for a critique, and even though the remark didn't come in a cushy container, it was fair criticism nonetheless.

A constructive response would either be a question concerning the teacher's preferred tempo or your performance of a phrase at a slower pace that feels right to you. Both comebacks help you get what you came for: advice. Rather than passing judgment on the suggested tempo, you try it out because you welcome novel ideas. You take pleasure in learning how the change of tempo impacts the music.

A student who is less proficient at handling criticism, however, might become defensive or feel sheepish upon hearing the critique. Then, not only would the session be less productive, but it's also conceivable that the student will dread future workshops, dodge them, and thereby miss out on valuable opportunities for learning.

Dealing with Less-Than-Fair Criticism

When you receive an inaccurate critique, offer an immediate clarifying response. For instance, if a conductor accuses you of being unprepared for a rehearsal, yet your part wasn't available until five minutes earlier, calmly report on the part's unavailability. In that way, you thwart mixups and pre-empt anyone from harboring resentment.

But when a critique is tinged with scorn, you might ignore the comment, or, as portrayed on page 118, you could use an "I" statement to convey how the jibe affects you. A classic circumstance would be when you deliver a top-notch performance, and afterward someone disdainfully says, "I've heard better." Such words say nothing about you but reveal volumes about the person who utters them. To deflect the negativity and shore up your inner peace, it's often best to disregard those types of scoffs. If the critic is a person close to you, you might follow up later with an "I" statement: "I was glad that you came to my show, but when you said, 'I've heard better,' I felt put down."

As it happens, though, many of the critiques you'll hear will be more subtly unfair than the preceding examples. Let's say that, at another master class, the teacher listens to your performance and then pronounces, "That version of the music is full of misprints; I can't work with that edition." Listening objectively, you're grateful to know that you're in possession of an inferior edition—fair enough. But is the instructor saying that he won't teach you? As with any critique that might be ambiguous or unfair, it's up to you to reply.

After asking which edition the teacher favors, move on to something like "Can you help me with interpretive things that would apply to any edition?" It's hard to imagine how a teacher could decline such a request. By being open to criticism, listening perceptively, and responding constructively, you foster a situation in which you can access the teacher's expertise. Instead of getting sidetracked by negative emotions, you focus on the music. Conversely, students who react to unfair critiques with anger or embarrassment let their emotions hijack their reasoning power. They may throw up their hands as opposed to asking for the guidance that will help them progress.

One of the chief skills needed to cope with criticism is the ability to establish boundaries between yourself and the assessments you receive. When someone critiques your work, treat it as information and not as a jab at your character. Even when you mess up badly and draw some heated but fair criticism, accept that it's normal to feel regret. Still, refuse to put yourself down. Learn from your mistakes and go forward.

Often, however, musicians don't erect emotional boundaries. When criticism cuts their way, instead of responding usefully, some performers rage within. But left to simmer, mishandled criticism corrodes creativity. Psychologist Andrew Evans writes that the most biting criticisms can "stay in the brain like curses."[5]

With adept management of criticism, you can neutralize most of the toxic effects and carry on with gusto. Nevertheless, if, in spite of your attempts to stay cool, your hackles rise whenever you hear critiques, consult a therapist. Becoming more self-aware will help make you a better artist.

❦

The above scenarios apply to the criticisms you hear, but you're also going to be in collaborative situations where you'll be the one dishing out the remarks. To communicate your opinions tactfully, apply the guidelines in chapter 6. As author Anne Lamott quips, "You don't always have to chop with the sword of truth. You can point with it too."[6]

Embracing Career Challenges

To be a musician in the service of music is not a job; it is a way of life.

—Isaac Stern, violinist

Some of your most gratifying musical experiences, both in and out of school, will be those that serve the greater good. Whether you contribute on a grand scale, like Isaac Stern, or you donate a single concert to those who wouldn't hear music otherwise, the satisfaction of serving humanity will probably be the richest reward that you will ever receive.

For music and service to become your way of life, however, you must confront economic realities. You have to find ways to unite your passion for music with an income-producing career. Financial independence may or may not be of concern to you today, but the earlier you begin contemplating career directions, the sooner you can make choices that will prepare you to thrive. Just as important, if you live with friction between your love of music and anxiety over career prospects, the emotional chafing will almost certainly hinder your creativity. Therefore, the goal here is to help liberate you from any such internal conflict while describing five career-building maneuvers.

Career-Building Maneuvers
1. Draft a career plan
2. Educate yourself
3. Network
4. Fill many niches
5. Polish your image

1. Draft a career plan

When college-bound music students report their educational plans to family and friends, they often hear this question: "So, what are you going to do for a living?" It's a fair question, and these pages will help you answer it intelligently.

Diverse careers are available to musicians because people worldwide consume huge amounts of music-related products and services every day. There's also a shortage of school music teachers, so full-time employment is virtually ensured for graduates with degrees in music education. The issue you must resolve as a student is not so much whether you'll find work upon completing college because, if you plan well, there's work to be had. You first need to discover whether you want the employment that realistically exists for you. Then, if you're dedicated to becoming a professional, you have to prepare to compete in the marketplace. And that will require learning about yourself and the music profession.

Begin by answering this question: What do you envision doing when you're a successful musician? Aim to define success broadly. Career counselor Angela Myles Beeching cautions that "with a narrow view of success, musicians unconsciously limit their career options."[7] For instance, if your concept of success is restricted to being an international soloist or performing with a major symphony or opera company—maybe the Los Angeles Philharmonic or the Metropolitan Opera—then you're probably headed for difficulties in life.

Difficulties are probable because few aspiring soloists rise to international stature, and there are few openings in major orchestras and opera companies each year. Because every top-level position attracts a horde of eager artists, it's doubtful that any one musician will make it through the audition process. Most performers who hold lofty positions have worked their way up and excelled for many years.

If your only goal is to win the audition lottery, and you haven't developed any other interests or skills—such as teaching, gigging, conducting, or contracting—then what will you do while you're "working your way up"? Can you be happy and financially solvent during that time? The prospects don't look promising. And if a solo career or top-tier orchestra post fails to materialize for you, will you be dejected? If you have no other desire in life, yes. Dreaming large is fine, but putting all of your eggs in one career basket isn't a smart bet for either your livelihood or your happiness.

Another problem with holding a restricted view of success is that it can undermine your creativity and well-being. When students have no ambitions other than to be full-time soloists or members of major orchestras, they can't avoid the fear that things might not work out. The fear may be a conscious or an unconscious one, but when students cling to exclusive career goals, and when attaining those goals calls for beating long odds, they're giving in to a notion of the world that's more fantasy than reality. To go on believing in the fantasy, students have to convince themselves day in and day out that the profession operates differently from the way their common sense tells them it does. The daily delusion then prevents them from exploring their capacity for creativity, service, and income in other areas. In addition, their unrealistic outlook buys them a ticket to emotional pain.

Forward-thinking students uncover multiple career avenues that they would enjoy. Some of their choices may involve long odds, but others will compensate by being more likely winners. Also, many students don't expect to make their living from music at all; they pursue undergraduate music degrees as a context in which to acquire an inclusive liberal arts education.

The following are descriptions of four freshmen music students and their initial career plans. Later I'll propose ways to ripen such basic sketches into full-blown artistic visions.

- Sylvia has sung roles in musicals since elementary school. As a high school senior, she also volunteered as an understudy to the director at the community theater in her hometown. Although she's a voice major and hopes to perform in operas and recitals, she's also furthering her knowledge of conducting and stage directing with an eye toward working as a director of choral or theatrical music.

- Chelsea took up the clarinet in fifth grade and became a standout in her high school concert band. She also plays jazz and klezmer music with her uncle's amateur group. Given her passion for improvising, as well as band and orchestral playing, her plan for entering college is twofold: 1. to major in music education and prepare to head up a band or jazz program at either the secondary or collegiate level; 2. to form a gigging jazz combo while refining her expertise as a classical player.

- Reggie started violin lessons before the age of four and began studying with the local concertmaster when he was 11. During high school, he won prizes in state and national competitions, and over the past two summers he played in the first-violin section at a prestigious festival. He's hoping to become a soloist or land a seat in a major orchestra, which he realizes are long shots, but he's also weighing a career as a university professor in the tradition of his mentor at the summer festival, who is both a violinist and a conductor.

- Dan is a jazz/rock bassist who began playing at age 13. During the summer after high school, he worked as an intern with a realty company in the town where his family takes beach vacations. He plans to obtain a dual degree in music and marketing and then reside near the beach,

where he can earn a living in the real estate business while also performing with his own jazz and rock groups. Eventually he wants to
sponsor after-school jazz courses at area high schools because he was
introduced to music through such a program.

Probe every aspect of what "being a successful musician" means to you,
and then draft a career plan that combines your abilities and desires. Next,
learn all you can about how to progress toward your goals.

2. Educate yourself

To discover more about the music profession and how you might fit in it,
I recommend two strategies: First, gain awareness of various career paths;
second, get experience in many areas.

Gain awareness of various career paths

For starters, hash over a range of professional options with your major
teacher. Then, if your school offers courses in career development, sign up.
But don't wait until you take a class to put your career ideas in motion. Visit
your institution's career office, and make an appointment with a counselor
who can help you analyze your interests, comb resources, and set down action plans.

Some of the most instructive activities that you can do with a career counselor or in a course are case studies and mock career projects. Through such
exercises, you grasp the inner workings of the music trade and can decide
how different sides match up with your personality. For example, a pianist
who wants to perform solo recitals might research how other pianists built
their careers. He'd then study methods of locating venues for future concerts
and formulate techniques to pitch programs to hypothetical presenters. In
the process, he'd reap professional skills and get a glimpse of the soloist's life.

Get experience

To add to the experience that you pick up in school, attend workshops and
festivals that provide professional-grade education. If you want to delve into
chamber music, opera, jazz, film music composition, and the like, summer
programs abound, and most of them give scholarships. If you're curious about
career tracks that you haven't yet been exposed to, do some observing. You
might check out a commercial recording session, or you could enroll in a
conducting class and then shadow a conductor through some rehearsals and
meetings. Another tactic is to volunteer a bit. Perhaps assist a school music
teacher or, like Sylvia, help out at a community theater.

Aside from observing and volunteering, the best way to get experience is to begin working. Tell your teacher about the occupations that appeal to you, and then, as soon as your qualifications warrant, try subbing in orchestras, teaching, gigging, accompanying, concertizing, or whatever.

Jump-start your self-education this week. To supplement what you learn here, read an online article, borrow a career guide from a library, or drop in at your campus career office and introduce yourself.

3. Network

None of the employment in music is generated by machines; it all comes from people. By getting to know numerous performers, teachers, and presenters, you integrate yourself into the music world and increase your career potential. In reality, every prominent musician is part of an extensive professional network.

The first network that you assemble comprises your classmates and teachers. Be a supportive colleague whom your fellow students hold in esteem— you may all be professionals before long, and your connections can yield frequent career leads. Also recognize that your teachers have massive networks that you can plug into. Take care to sustain positive relationships with your professors so that their backing and their networks will be there when you need them.

Your school is the foundation of your network, but you should extend your connections far beyond your immediate surroundings to build a vast address book of contacts. Here are five routes to doing so:

- *Attend conferences.* When you go to events such as the convention of the National Flute Association, you're able to interact with hundreds of performers and teachers in your specialty and also avail yourself of concerts, educational sessions, and product showcases.
- *Participate in summer music festivals.* Whether you study in your home country or abroad, the musicians you perform with at festivals usually hail from far-flung locales, and you can often supply each other with valuable ideas and contacts.
- *Perform in and attend local concerts.* Become acquainted with the musicians and presenters in your area.
- *Take part in online communities.* Cultivate an online presence through your personal pages and by supporting other musicians.

- *Join music organizations.* If you're focused on music education, sign up with or inaugurate a student chapter of an organization such as the American String Teachers Association.

4. Fill many niches

Peter Spellman's career primer, *5 Essentials of Music Career Success,* gives this advice: "Your goal, to use marketing lingo, is to 'position' yourself in your 'market' as the go-to person for that particular skill or talent."[8] In other words, when someone wants to hire a musician in your field, if you've secured a reputation as a go-to person, then much of the work comes to you. The more niches you occupy as a go-to musician in your community, the more prospects you'll have. Jennifer, a pianist, understood that principle intuitively. Here's a summary of how she put together a prosperous career starting in her freshman year of college and continuing through graduation.

Jennifer came to college with a draft career plan to perform solo recitals, accompany, and teach privately. She also had a background in church music, having worked for the music director for her hometown congregation. During her first semester, she answered an ad for a church accompanist and began working Wednesday evenings and Sunday mornings at a church near campus. She let her boss know that she was fond of teaching, and soon she had a few students.

Meanwhile, by her second semester on campus, Jennifer had become known as a go-to pianist for student voice recitals. Her years of church work had made her an ace sight-reader and collaborator. Most of the accompanying that she did at school required little practice on her part, so she was able to play for many concerts and rehearsals and was paid for her services, while on her own she primarily practiced solo repertoire.

Back at the church, the music director hired her to play a solo recital on a Sunday afternoon. The response was so enthusiastic that the director emailed colleagues at dozens of affiliated congregations. That summer, Jennifer traveled through three states and performed 15 well-paid concerts for sister churches; each congregation then invited her to return the next summer and perform again.

In her junior year, Jennifer took a choral conducting class. By February, she had twice substituted for the choir director at her church. She left her position as church accompanist that August to be a better-paid assistant music director at a larger congregation, and she still worked only twice a week. She also taught six students who came to the studio that she set up in her apartment.

As her senior year began, Jennifer had ample earnings from teaching, accompanying, solo performance, and working at the church. Her calendar was full, so instead of turning down offers, she began contracting other pianists whom she trained to teach at her home studio and to do some of the accompanying that she couldn't take on herself. Of course, she netted a portion of the fees from all of those engagements. Although she was a student, she was also a respected professional who was filling many niches as soloist, accompanist, teacher, assistant director, and contractor. In every one of those roles she had emerged as one of the go-to people in her city.

After graduation, Jennifer stayed in town, took on more concerts and students, and became music director at the church where she had worked as an accompanist. Now, five years later, she's a happy artist-teacher with a sizable income and a widespread following.

The transition from college to the professional world is one of the most momentous occasions in a person's life. Will your changeover be smooth or rocky? The ease of your entry into the music profession will largely depend on the doors you open while you're a student. You can't control what opportunities might arise, but if you fill many niches, you'll create multiple income-producing channels that will be there, ready for you to step forward.

5. Polish your image

To find your place in the music world, there are two images that will need your attention: your self-image and your professional image.

Polish your self-image

Newly arrived college students often feel insignificant. After all, when you show up on campus as a freshman, you're at the bottom of the academic totem pole; it's natural to be intimidated. But if you concur with Isaac Stern that you're a "musician in the service of music," then there is no totem pole—you're a contributor to a great cause. As a student, it's your role to learn and grow, making more and more contributions as your abilities allow. You have a place, so carry on with a strong sense of purpose. Conductor Benjamin Zander writes, "Throw yourself into life as someone who makes a difference, accepting that you may not understand how or why."[9]

Also avoid ranking yourself against other performers. Violinist Andrés Cárdenes recalls how his teacher at Indiana University, Josef Gingold, helped him transform his contentious mindset to one that led to his success: "I was a very confused eighteen-year-old with a highly competitive attitude," Cárdenes admits. "Mr. Gingold taught me that the beauty in playing the instrument is not to be better than the next person but to stay true to oneself, to set one's own standards and keep to them, not just in violin playing but in life itself."[10] I can't imagine better advice.

Last of all, although career success depends on sufficient practice, you won't have much of a self-image if you seldom exit the practice room to partake in life. Alongside the hours that you reserve for work, also socialize, enjoy recreation, and maintain a healthy lifestyle. Devoting yourself to music shouldn't preclude balanced living.

Polish your professional image

A performer's reputation is enhanced by or diminished with each musical interaction. Therefore, stand by the elements of professionalism catalogued in chapter 6: punctuality, preparation, courtesy, and integrity. Here are four additional habits to live by:

- *Be easy to reach.* If you hope to be contacted for bookings, then it's vital to be known as someone who answers the phone, checks email, and responds promptly to messages.

- *Dress for the occasion.* When Jennifer auditioned for those church vacancies, she didn't wear the jeans that she sported around the music school. She chose attire that communicated she was a reliable performer who was ready to shoulder responsibilities.

- *Clean up your online presence.* If you have any funky pages scattered around the Web, look at them from the viewpoint of a prospective employer. Be sure that you won't be raising any eyebrows.

- *Create promotional materials.* To share your contact information, keep business cards handy. Print cards with your name, specialty, email, mobile phone, mailing address, and any website. Also, if you don't yet have a résumé, it's time. When you're ready to line up regular professional engagements, you'll also need a first-rate photo, bio, website, and demo recording. Career guidebooks list ways to put such items together. The staff at a campus career office can assist as well.

When it comes to professional accomplishment in music, the biggest difference between prolific and stagnant musicians isn't necessarily talent; it's this: Successful musicians will do things that faltering musicians won't. Committed performers will abide by their practice schedules and their self-care routines. They'll hone career strategies, relate positively to colleagues, book self-produced concerts, ask mentors for help, and so on. Whatever it takes, they'll do it.

Those who waffle on their commitments will come up with endless reasons not to make phone calls, schedule coaching sessions, or learn new material. If you ever perceive yourself waffling, talk to your teacher or a therapist. Life's too short to live without celebrating your gift for making music.

Counteracting Substance Abuse

Any musician who says he is playing better either on the needle or when he is juiced is a plain straight liar. . . . You can miss the most important years of your life, the years of possible creation.

—Charlie Parker, saxophonist and composer

Substance abuse problems aren't exclusive to musicians, but according to the website of the Louis Armstrong Center for Music and Medicine in New York, "when compared to other professionals, there is a notably higher incidence of depression and chemical dependency among musicians and performing artists."[11] Your activities in music will likely bring you in contact with colleagues who have substance-abuse issues, and you could be at greater risk for problems yourself.

In this section, I point up some of the ruinous effects of substance abuse and suggest ways to dodge trouble and get help if you need it. I'll begin with the stories of Sierra and Kyle, two music students who learned the hard way about the consequences of using illegal drugs.

Sierra's legal nightmare

Sierra grew up in a Pacific Northwest town that tolerated marijuana use. After arriving on the East Coast for college, she thought nothing of it when she repeatedly bought marijuana on the street and shared it with friends in the dorm. Before long, the campus police caught two of those friends smoking, and both students named Sierra as the source of the drugs.

When police officers arrived at Sierra's dorm room, they quickly found her stash. She was handed over to the local city police, charged with possession and distribution of marijuana, and jailed. Her parents bailed her out of the city lockup, but she was expelled from the school, where she had been granted a full scholarship. With the help of a pricey lawyer, she struck a plea bargain that allowed her to avoid a prison sentence. The blot on her record, however, means that she's no longer eligible for federal financial aid, which she needs to pay for college. Today she works as a waitress in her home state and is trying to save enough money to return to school and start repaying her parents, who mortgaged their home to cover her legal bills.

Sierra isn't alone in being blind to the legal ramifications of drug use—many student-users don't grasp the severity of the drug laws. If you buy or sell illegal drugs, you involve yourself in criminal activity. In the eyes of the law, you're a criminal.

From ecstasy to agony

The legal and financial consequences of drug use are awful, but the health effects can be utterly devastating. I'm sure you know that a drug-induced high occurs because of changes in the brain. Are you aware, though, that inducing those changes can result in irreversible brain damage? Kyle wasn't. He had no idea that swallowing a pill would upend his life.

Kyle was a third-year voice student at a university music school. Besides being a fine classical artist, he also sang lead in a part-time rock band. One night, at a postgig party, he got caught up in the revelry and took a drug that someone claimed was ecstasy. The next day he was walking around the school cafeteria and greeting people by saying, "Hi, I'm God. Welcome to heaven."

He was admitted to the local hospital, where his parents were told that college-age students who take drugs sometimes develop permanent psychosis. Tragically, that's what happened to Kyle. Years later, he continues to have hallucinations and hear voices. He takes antipsychotic medications, which allow him some semblance of normal function, but he's unemployed and rarely makes music any more.

If you perform in nightclubs, you're going to be exposed to a culture that's awash in alcohol and drugs. On campuses, too, you'll be faced with offers to alter your mental state in all sorts of ways. Kyle assumed that the drug he took was a mild recreational tonic. He may have hesitated before he swallowed, but, in spite of any qualms, he went along and paid a horrible price. If you're ever in a parallel situation, you need to be better prepared than Kyle was. And you should know how to get help if a substance abuse problem starts brewing.

Prepare yourself

First, recognize that there is no such thing as a wholly safe recreational drug, legal or illegal. Alcohol, no less than other drugs, can wreak havoc by leading to car crashes, addiction, brain injury, and death from overdose. Binge drinking, for example, is especially deadly. The National Institute on Alcohol Abuse and Alcoholism grimly reports that, in the United States, approximately 1,500 college students die annually from injuries tied to alcohol consumption.[12] So think twice before you imbibe—there's nothing wrong with enjoying alcohol-free drinks where others swig the hard stuff. If you do drink, do so in moderation, and assign a designated driver. The U.S. Department of Health and Human Services defines moderate drinking as "the consumption of up to one drink per day for women and up to two drinks per day for men."[13]

Regarding illegal drugs, people who partake put their lives in jeopardy. For one thing, you never know what you're getting; for another, you can't predict how your body might react. Added to that, there are the legal hazards. The smartest move is to steer clear of all such substances. If you're at a party, as Kyle was, and drugs are brought out, take a simple action: Leave. You don't have to explain to anyone. Just remove yourself from the situation.

Getting help

Plenty of renowned musicians have survived their bouts with substance abuse and moved on to caution others. Singer-songwriter Paul Simon says, "It was very unsatisfying, the drug use, although I started out loving it. But at the end, it was bad. I couldn't write. It made me depressed. It made me anti-social."[14] Simon overcame his drug habit and returned to healthy living. Still, don't be lulled into thinking that substance abuse is something you can ignore for now and resolve later.

When you hear musicians like Simon describe how they rose above their troubles, remember that there are hosts of others who couldn't recover or didn't endure. "So many of my friends shouldn't have died," said pianist and composer Dave Brubeck. "They just believed they were indestructible and they lived too hard and those things finally catch up with you."[15]

The physicians and counselors at health centers are trained to assist people with substance-abuse issues. If you suspect that you have a problem or you want to help someone who does, put aside any doubts and make an appointment. Confidentiality laws protect you from legal entanglements.

Boosting Creativity

I'm always thinking about creating. My future starts when I wake up every morning. . . . Every day I find something creative to do with my life.

—Miles Davis, trumpeter and bandleader

Mature artists, like Miles Davis, generate creative energy day after day. Through the ups and downs of life, they work intently and imaginatively. The five creativity-boosting habits here will help you stockpile comparable stores of inspiration.

1. Forge an artistic vision

Your most fertile source of creative energy is a compelling artistic vision. It marries what you do today with what you want to be doing in the future. It melds your artistic desires with career options, thereby clarifying the draft career plan you created earlier (p. 300). When you practice with a vision in your heart, you work toward goals for the next hour, the next week, the com-

> **Boost Your Creativity**
>
> 1. Forge an artistic vision
> 2. Practice consistently
> 3. Make meaning
> 4. Be playful
> 5. Build community

ing year, and your entire lifetime. "Vision is the art of seeing things invisible," wrote author Jonathan Swift.[16] With a powerful vision, you'll see through any setbacks and stay connected to the big picture.

A vision packs the most punch when it's specific, realistic, and altruistic. Vague fantasies, in contrast, evaporate like fog. And if your vision is only about you, that single root will be too slim to sustain you during hard times. A draft career plan suffices when you arrive at school, but as your knowledge and experience grow, your preliminary ideas should coalesce into a far-reaching strategy. As an example, Celia's artistic vision merged her love of performance, education, and radio with her wish to make music lessons available to children from low-income families.

Celia's artistic vision

- Play viola in a string quartet that performs and records classics and contemporary music.
- Perform in the viola section of a regional orchestra. Eventually, audition successfully for a major orchestra.
- Volunteer to lead sectional rehearsals for local high school orchestras.
- Found a nonprofit teaching studio that provides lessons in stringed instrument playing and has a charitable endowment that awards scholarships to disadvantaged children.
- Host a radio program or webcast that features recordings of string quartet music.
- Continually elevate interpretive, technical, and professional skills.

Notice that Celia's vision doesn't include nebulous statements like "Contribute to the cultural life in my community." Instead, Celia specified how she'd make contributions. Furthermore, all of her aspirations were realistic given her artistic trajectory. As a 20-year-old, she had already played principal viola in her university orchestra, she had performed in quartets for two years, she was involved in radio in both high school and college, and she had been teaching intermittently. She didn't yet know how to run an independent teaching studio, but she would learn the basics in a career development course.

Today she's a busy professional. Upon earning her Master of Music degree, she won a full-time seat in the viola section of a second-tier U.S. orchestra. She also performs with a string quartet. Due to several relocations, she hasn't been able to launch that teaching studio or radio program, although they're still part of her long-range plan. Her volunteer efforts in schools, however, have made her a celebrity among area students and teachers.

Start formulating your artistic vision as soon as you have the expertise to flesh out your initial career sketch. List ideas on a computer file, have periodic discussions with your teacher, and stay open to revision—as you advance, insights will surface, and you'll want to steer your career in new directions.

2. Practice consistently

Creativity requires industry. Because imagination alone produces nothing, it's not enough to have an imaginative vision. Creative people work. And through their work, their artistry blooms.

So craft a stable practice schedule, draw on the self-motivating tactics in chapter 5, and be on the lookout for procrastinating behaviors. Seek help from your teacher or a therapist if you can't dependably practice or fulfill your obligations. Procrastination negates creativity. Every musician must learn to recognize and counteract it before it escalates into a disabling habit.

A consistent practice agenda, though, shouldn't straitjacket you into restrictive routines. On most days, when you begin to practice, your physical and mental faculties will line up promptly. At other times, you may feel a bit out of sorts.

Rather than practicing long hours on the good days and none on the tougher ones, seasoned artists adjust the contents of their practice so that they work reliably but not inflexibly. Cellist William Pleeth reasoned that pushing through your typical practice itinerary on an off day is "like getting your car stuck in the mud and sitting there with your foot still pressed against the accelerator, spinning your wheels, in the hope that the same techniques you used for normal road driving would somehow get you out." He goes on to say that "under different conditions we should be able to use ourselves completely differently."[17]

For instance, when you don't warm up quickly, amend your warm-up routine. If you ordinarily get under way with scales or arpeggios, opt for a favorite piece at a moderate tempo—choose something easy to execute but replete with emotion. As you play or sing, bring *habits of excellence* (p. 20) to every phrase. Then proceed with small practice tasks that you'll easily accomplish, and take frequent, short breaks. By being patient, your coordination will often be restored, and you can meet your practice goals. If things continue to feel off kilter (and assuming that you aren't ill), do more mental than physical practice, conclude early, and plan to practice again in a few hours, perhaps after getting some exercise. It's better to do 30 minutes of high-quality work than to spin your wheels for hours. But if off days occur repeatedly, get help.

3. Make meaning

Psychologist and author Eric Maisel discusses three types of meaning that people experience in life.[18] One is *received* meaning, the kind that's supplied via families and cultural surroundings. Another is *sought* meaning, which results from looking outside yourself. The third and most pertinent to your musical mission is *created* meaning, your own personal meaning.

Meaning, not originality, is what matters most in your day-to-day practice. Some people might argue that you're being creative only when you come up with something that hasn't been done before, but I think differently. You're creative when you produce music and ideas that hold meaning for you. You'll have lots of original notions, but meaning doesn't hinge on uniqueness. Meaning you make for yourself.

Whatever you value most in music, pursue it. If you're enthralled by a style of world music, explore it. Do both traditional and experimental compositions float your boat? Go after them. Create meaning in everything that you practice, even the most mundane of materials. Can a scale be meaningful? Yes, intensely so, as violinist Josef Gingold made clear in describing his teacher, Eugène Ysaÿe. "Ysaÿe could play a scale," Gingold reminisced, "and it was the most heavenly thing you had ever heard."[19]

Scales, your old friends, help you upgrade tone, rhythm, articulation, easefulness, and more. They can be nurseries of creativity or barren drills. The choice is yours. Nonetheless, whether you're working on a scale or a masterpiece, the more depth you bring to your sound, the more meaning you'll make and the more exhilarating your practice will be. And when your every phrase permeates with soul, your listeners will sense it—because by making meaning, you make art.

4. Be playful

Playfulness and creativity go together like music and dance—one sets the other in motion. Psychologist Mihaly Csikszentmihalyi warns that creativity will fizzle if "too many obstacles are put in the way of risk and exploration."[20] When you're being playful, you take whatever creative risks you please.

Cellist Pablo Casals, for example, began every day by playing the music of Bach on the piano because he felt that doing so served as "a sort of benediction on the house." He also asserted that, when he played Bach, "the music is never the same for me, never. Each day it is something new, fantastic and unbelievable."[21] His habit of savoring Bach's music was not only beautiful but also playful. Why not saturate your own warm-ups with playfulness and wonder and maybe toss in some laid-back improvisation?

Of course, playfulness doesn't belong just at the outset of practice but throughout as well. When working with new repertoire, if you adopt a playful approach to discovering interpretive possibilities, you'll be more open to novelty. For instance, if your first instinct is to crescendo to the climax of a phrase, also try contradicting that instinct: Test a sudden dip in volume at the top, and investigate how it sounds if you delay the peak's arrival with a pause. Similarly, when a new technique feels unbalanced, make up some exercises, and play around by moving through a series of physical motions until you achieve poise.

Playfulness in practice helps you follow your heart, tackle problems inventively, and not be too regimented. Take heed, though, that you don't turn recklessly playful. Your fun-loving stance should buoy your *habits of excellence* and not send artistic fidelity out the window.

5. Build community

One of the most inspiring features of music schools is their vibrant sense of community. By enrolling in an educational program, you plug into a network that can be a source of lasting support. But communities don't evolve automatically. It takes deliberate effort to nurture relationships.

Maintain an interest in your peers' activities: Attend their performances; encourage their dreams. Collaborate, too, by playing in ensembles, collectively improvising, or starting a performance-development group (p. 199). Later on, when people go their separate ways, stay in contact. Also form a network of mentors, including teachers and alumni of your school, who can aid your passage through the stages of your career. Let your community feed your creativity.

⁂

Ultimately, your musical progress will depend more on your skillfulness with the creative process than on any talent. Talent represents your innate potential; it's like a wind that blows throughout your lifetime. Creative skills—especially the practice, performance, and self-care skills covered in this book—

are the sails you deploy to catch that wind and carry your artistry forward. Masterful skills weave bigger sails, capture more air, and give rise to greater accomplishment. Whether your talent flows gently or surges with gale force, without sails, the wind streams past and you go nowhere.

Amassing the know-how of a professional musician takes time and diligence, but the personal investments you make will bring rewards beyond measure. As you move ahead, there will be triumphs and stumbles. Some things will come easily; others will call for persistent toil. Still, the path you take is your path and no one else's, so welcome it. Sometime in the future, when you look back, the complex route you took will make perfect sense.

Psychologist Rollo May wrote, "Creativity arises out of the tension between spontaneity and limitations, the latter (like the river banks) forcing the spontaneity into the various forms which are essential to the work of art."[22] Don't fight the limitations. Work within them to be productive today and tomorrow. Forge an artistic vision, practice consistently, make meaning, be playful, and build community. That's the musician's way.

Notes

Preface

1. Victor Hugo, *William Shakespeare* (Paris: Librairie internationale, 1867), 76 (digitized May 14, 2007, by Google).

Chapter 1: Getting Organized

Epigraph quotations are from the following sources: Stuart Nicholson, *Ella Fitzgerald: A Biography of the First Lady of Jazz* (New York: Da Capo, 1995), 243; Yehudi Menuhin, foreword to Madeline Bruser, *The Art of Practicing: A Guide to Making Music from the Heart* (New York: Bell Tower, 1997), xiii; Grace Glueck, "Art: How Studios Look to the Painters Who Work in Them," *New York Times* (June 29, 1984), http://query.nytimes.com/gst/fullpage.html?res=9D00E7DC1539F93AA15755C0A 962948260&sec=&spon= (Nov. 18, 2008); Annie Dillard, *The Writing Life* (New York: HarperCollins, 1989), 32; Lene M. Ellington, "Quotes," *The Official Website of Duke Ellington,* www.symphonicpops.com/ellington/de_website/about/quotes.htm (Dec. 28, 2008); Tobias Matthay, *Musical Interpretation* (1913; repr., Westport, Conn.: Greenwood, 1970), 5.

1. Doris Fielding Reid, *Edith Hamilton: An Intimate Portrait* (New York: Norton, 1967), 45.
2. Samuel Applebaum and Sada Applebaum, *The Way They Play,* bk. 4 (Neptune City, N.J.: Paganiniana, 1975), 29.
3. Ralph Manchester, *Wellness Practices for Musicians Videoconference* (Winston-Salem: University of North Carolina School of the Arts, Apr. 11, 2006).

Chapter 2: Practicing Deeply, I

Epigraph quotations are from the following sources: "Authentic Voice: An Interview with Meredith Monk," *Mountain Record: The Zen Practitioner's Journal* 22(4) (Summer 2004): 54–58, www.mro.org/mr/archive/22–4/articles/monk.html (Oct. 11, 2006);

Tryon Edwards, *A Dictionary of Thoughts* (Detroit: F. B. Dickerson, 1908), 212; Tobias Matthay, *Musical Interpretation* (1913; repr., Westport, Conn.: Greenwood, 1970),
159; Eric Maisel, *Writers and Artists on Devotion* (Novato, Calif.: New World Library,
2004), 151; William Pleeth, *Cello* (New York: Schirmer, 1982), 11.

1. David Blum, *The Art of Quartet Playing: The Guarneri Quartet in Conversation
   with David Blum* (Ithaca, N.Y.: Cornell University Press, 1986), 101.
2. Kato Havas, *Stage Fright: Its Causes and Cures with Special Reference to Violin
   Playing* (London: Bosworth, 1973), 136.
3. Wynton Marsalis, *Marsalis on Music* (New York: Norton, 1995), 130.
4. David Blum, *Casals and the Art of Interpretation* (New York: Holmes and Meier,
   1977), 161.
5. Samuel Applebaum, Mark Zilberquit, and Theo Saye, *The Way They Play*, bk. 13
   (Neptune, N.J.: Paganiniana, 1984), 278.
6. Diran Alexanian, *J. S. Bach: Six Suites pour violoncelle seul* (Paris: Éditions Sal-
   abert, 1929), vi–ix.
7. James M. Thurmond, *Note Grouping: A Method for Achieving Expression and
   Style in Musical Performance* (Galesville, Md.: Meredith Music, 1991), 52.
8. Friedrich Kerst, *Mozart: The Man and the Artist, as Revealed in His Own Words,*
   trans. Henry Edward Krehbiel (1905; repr., New York: Dover, 1965), 25.
9. Erich Leinsdorf, *The Composer's Advocate: A Radical Orthodoxy for Musicians*
   (New Haven, Conn.: Yale University Press, 1981), 49.
10. Blum, *Casals and the Art of Interpretation,* 49.
11. W. Timothy Gallwey, *The Inner Game of Tennis* (New York: Random House,
    1974), 59.
12. Julie Lyonn Lieberman, *You Are Your Instrument* (New York: Huiksi Music,
    1995), 84.

Chapter 3: Practicing Deeply, II

Epigraph quotations are from the following sources: Ian Crofton and Donald Fraser,
Dictionary of Musical Quotations (New York: Schirmer, 1985), 79; Frederick H.
Martens, *Violin Mastery* (1919; repr., Mineola, N.Y.: Dover, 2006), 49; Abby White-
side, *Abby Whiteside on Piano Playing* (Portland, Ore.: Amadeus, 1997), 110; David
Blum, *Quintet: Five Journeys toward Musical Fulfillment* (Ithaca, N.Y.: Cornell Univer-
sity Press, 1999), 8.

1. Eloise Ristad, *A Soprano on Her Head: Right-side-up Reflections on Life and Other
   Performances* (Moab, Utah: Real People, 1982), 116–117.
2. Elyse Mach, *Great Contemporary Pianists Speak for Themselves,* vol. 2 (1988;
   repr., Mineola, N.Y.: Dover, 1991), 104.
3. W. Stephen Smith, *The Naked Voice: A Wholistic Approach to Singing* (New York:
   Oxford University Press, 2007), 140–141.
4. Abby Whiteside, *Abby Whiteside on Piano Playing* (Portland, Ore.: Amadeus,
   1997), 54.
5. Ivan Galamian, *Principles of Violin Playing and Teaching* (Englewood Cliffs, N.J.:
   Prentice-Hall, 1962), 95.

6. Lene M. Ellington, "Quotes," *The Official Website of Duke Ellington*, www.symphonicpops.com/ellington/de_website/about/quotes.htm (Dec. 28, 2008).

7. Sue Graham Mingus, *Tonight at Noon: A Love Story* (Cambridge, Mass.: Da Capo, 2003), 112.

8. John Gottman, *Raising an Emotionally Intelligent Child* (New York: Simon and Schuster, 1998), 20.

9. Ken Robinson, *Out of Our Minds: Learning to Be Creative* (West Sussex, UK: Capstone, 2001), 114.

10. Smith, *Naked Voice*, 119–121. Used by permission of Oxford University Press, Inc.

Chapter 4: Practicing Deeply, III

Epigraph quotations are from the following sources: William Pleeth, *Cello* (New York: Schirmer, 1982), 9; Elyse Mach, *Great Contemporary Pianists Speak for Themselves,* vol. 2 (1980; repr., Mineola, N.Y.: Dover, 1991), 29; Linda J. Noyle, ed., *Pianists on Playing: Interviews with Twelve Concert Pianists* (Metuchen, N.J.: Scarecrow, 1987), 147; Ellen Langer, *The Power of Mindful Learning* (Cambridge, Mass.: Perseus, 1997), 41.

1. Elyse Mach, *Great Contemporary Pianists Speak for Themselves,* vol. 1 (1980; repr., Mineola, N.Y.: Dover, 1991), 119.

2. Rita Aiello and Aaron Williamon, "Memory," in *The Science and Psychology of Music Performance: Creative Strategies for Teaching and Learning,* ed. Richard Parncutt and Gary E. McPherson, 171 (New York: Oxford University Press, 2002).

3. Susan Hallam, "Approaches to Instrumental Music Practice of Experts and Novices: Implications for Education," in *Does Practice Make Perfect?* ed. Harald Jørgensen and Andreas Lehmann, 89–107 (Oslo: Norwegian State Academy of Music, 1997).

4. Linda J. Noyle, ed., *Pianists on Playing: Interviews with Twelve Concert Pianists* (Metuchen, N.J.: Scarecrow, 1987), 97.

5. Janet Cromley, "To Really Remember, Sleep on It," *Los Angeles Times* (Apr. 30, 2007), www.articlebrain.com/Article/To-really-remember—sleep-on-it/88 (Jan. 11, 2008).

6. Jane Ginsborg, "Strategies for Memorizing Music," in *Musical Excellence: Strategies and Techniques to Enhance Performance,* ed. Aaron Williamon, 136 (New York: Oxford University Press, 2004).

7. Marion Pratnicki, pers. comm. (Winston-Salem, N.C., Aug. 9, 2008).

8. David Dalton, *Playing the Viola: Conversations with William Primrose* (New York: Oxford University Press, 1998), 166.

Chapter 5: Practicing Deeply, IV

Epigraph quotations are from the following sources: David Mamet, *On Directing Film* (New York: Penguin, 1991), 6; Bill Cole, *John Coltrane* (New York: Da Capo, 2001), 43; Shinichi Suzuki, *Nurtured by Love: A New Approach to Education, trans. Waltraud Suzuki* (Hicksville, N.Y.: Exposition, 1969), 94.

1. Len Lyons, *The Great Jazz Pianists: Speaking of Their Lives and Music* (New York: William Morrow, 1983), 221.

2. Kathryn Lucktenberg, "Review of 'Playing the Violin: An Illustrated Guide,' by Mark Rush," *American Music Teacher* 56(5) (Apr./May 2007): 82.

3. Lawrence Dillon and Bonnie Davidoff, eds., *In Tune: The Newsletter of the School of Music at the University of North Carolina School of the Arts* (May 2007), www.uncsa.edu/music/whatsnew/May07.pdf (Nov. 22, 2008).

4. Sam Thompson and Andreas C. Lehmann, "Strategies for Sight-reading and Improvising Music," in *Musical Excellence: Strategies and Techniques to Enhance Performance*, ed. Aaron Williamon, 146 (New York: Oxford University Press, 2004).

5. Whitney Balliett, *American Musicians II: Seventy-two Portraits in Jazz* (New York: Oxford University Press, 1996), 426.

6. Robby Barnett, "Designing Our Experience" (lecture, University of North Carolina School of the Arts Digital Arts Symposium, Winston-Salem, N.C., Apr. 7, 2006).

7. Julia Cameron, *The Vein of Gold* (New York: Putnam, 1996), 164.

8. Ashton Applewhite, William R. Evans III, and Andrew Frothingham, *And I Quote: The Definitive Collection of Quotes, Sayings, and Jokes* (New York: St. Martin's, 2003), 126.

9. Lene M. Ellington, "Quotes," *The Official Website of Duke Ellington*, www.symphonicpops.com/ellington/de_website/about/quotes.htm (Dec. 28, 2008).

10. Eric Maisel, *Writers and Artists on Devotion* (Novato, Calif.: New World Library, 2004), 1.

11. Paul Salmon and Robert Meyer, *Notes from the Green Room* (New York: Lexington Books, 1992), 68.

12. Anne Lamott (lecture, San Francisco Jewish Community Center, San Francisco, Calif., Dec. 11, 2007).

13. David W. Barber, *The Music Lover's Quotation bk.* (Toronto: Sound and Vision, 2003), 65.

14. Charlene W. Billings, *Grace Hopper: Navy Admiral and Computer Pioneer* (Berkeley Heights, N.J.: Enslow, 1989), 114.

Chapter 6: Musical Collaboration

Epigraph quotations are from the following sources: Wayne Enstice and Paul Rubin, *Jazz Spoken Here: Conversations with Twenty-two Musicians* (Baton Rouge: Louisiana State University Press, 1992), 28; David Blum, *The Art of Quartet Playing: The Guarneri Quartet in Conversation with David Blum* (Ithaca, N.Y.: Cornell University Press, 1987), 24; Annie Dillard, *The Writing Life* (New York: HarperCollins, 1989), 69; Wynton Marsalis, *Marsalis on Music* (New York: Norton, 1995), 134; Miles Davis, *Miles: The Autobiography* (New York: Simon and Schuster, 1990), 399.

1. Stephen Pologe, pers. comm. (Winston-Salem, N.C., Mar. 26, 2007).

2. David Blum, *The Art of Quartet Playing: The Guarneri Quartet in Conversation with David Blum* (Ithaca, N.Y.: Cornell University Press, 1987), 7.

3. Whitney Balliett, *American Musicians: Fifty-six Portraits in Jazz* (New York: Oxford University Press, 1986), 254.

4. Samuel Applebaum, Mark Zilberquit, and Theo Saye, *The Way They Play*, bk. 13 (Neptune, N.J.: Paganiniana, 1984), 278.

5. Taimur Sullivan, pers. comm. (Winston-Salem, N.C., Aug. 15, 2008).

Chapter 7: Unmasking Performance Anxiety

Epigraph quotations are from the following sources: Bart Barnes, "Charismatic Conductor Brought Glory to the National Symphony," *Washington Post* (Apr. 28, 2007), www.washingtonpost.com/wp-dyn/content/article/2007/04/27/AR2007042702496 .html (Apr. 28, 2007); Linda J. Noyle, ed., *Pianists on Playing: Interviews with Twelve Concert Pianists* (Metuchen, N.J.: Scarecrow, 1987), 35; Gary Mortenson, "A Tribute to the Life and Career of Vincent Cichowicz," *International Trumpet Guild Journal* (June 2007): 10; Kato Havas, *Stage Fright: Its Causes and Cures with Special Reference to Violin Playing* (London: Bosworth, 1973), 5; Shannon Sexton, "A Breath-taking Performance: Yoga for Stage Fright," *Yoga International* (Aug./Sept. 2004): 80; Paul Zollo, *Song Talk* interview (1990), www.artgarfunkel.com/articles/songtalk.html (Nov. 18, 2008); Eric Maisel, *Performance Anxiety* (New York: Back Stage Books, 2005), 175.

1. Martin Fishbein, Susan E. Middlestadt, Victor Ottati, Susan Straus, and Alan Ellis, "Medical Problems among ICSOM Musicians: Overview of a National Survey," *Medical Problems of Performing Artists* 3(1) (March 1988): 1–8.

2. Mark Ross Clark, *Singing, Acting, and Movement in Opera* (Bloomington: Indiana University Press, 2002), 105.

3. Paul Salmon and Robert Meyer, *Notes from the Green Room* (New York: Lexington Books, 1992), 131.

4. Glenn D. Wilson, *Psychology for Performing Artists*, 2d ed. (London: Whurr, 2002), 211.

5. David Blum, *Casals and the Art of Interpretation* (New York: Holmes and Meier, 1977), 209.

6. Hugh Stephenson and Nicholas F. Quarrier, "Anxiety Sensitivity and Performance Anxiety in College Music Students," *Medical Problems of Performing Artists* 20(3) (Sept. 2005): 119–125.

7. Frank R. Wilson, foreword to Barbara Schneiderman, *Confident Music Performance* (St. Louis, Mo.: MMB Music, 1991), iii.

8. Mitchell W. Robin and Rochelle Balter, *Performance Anxiety: Overcoming Your Fear in the Workplace, Social Situations, Interpersonal Communications, and the Performing Arts* (Holbrook, Mass.: Adams Media, 1995), 52.

9. Philip Farkas, *The Art of Musicianship* (Bloomington, Ind.: Musical Publications, 1976), 48.

10. Alice Brandfonbrener, "Beta-blockers in the Treatment of Performance Anxiety," *Medical Problems of Performing Artists* 5(1) (March 1990): 23–26.

11. Lee Birk, "Pharmacotherapy for Performance Anxiety Disorders: Occasionally Useful but Typically Contraindicated," *Journal of Clinical Psychology* 60(8) (Aug. 2004): 867–879.

12. David Dubal, *Reflections from the Keyboard: The World of the Concert Pianist* (New York: Summit, 1984), 19–20.

Chapter 8: Becoming a Performing Artist, I

Epigraph quotations are from the following sources: Sir Michael Tippett, interview by F. David Peat (June 1996), www.fdavidpeat.com/interviews/tippett.htm (Nov. 18, 2008); Shirlee Emmons and Alma Thomas, *Power Performance for Singers: Transcending the Barriers* (New York: Oxford University Press, 1998), 3; Whitney Balliett, *American Musicians: Fifty-six Portraits in Jazz* (New York: Oxford University Press, 1986), 214; David Dubal, *Reflections from the Keyboard: The World of the Concert Pianist* (New York: Summit, 1984), 21.

1. Barry Green, *The Mastery of Music: Ten Pathways to True Artistry* (New York: Broadway, 2003), 177.

2. Linda J. Noyle, ed., *Pianists on Playing: Interviews with Twelve Concert Pianists* (Metuchen, N.J.: Scarecrow, 1987), 23.

3. Green, *Mastery of Music,* 179.

4. Thich Nhat Hanh, *Peace Is Every Step: The Path of Mindfulness in Everyday Life* (New York: Bantam, 1991), 8.

5. Eric Maisel, *Performance Anxiety* (New York: Back Stage Books, 2005), 197.

Chapter 9: Becoming a Performing Artist, II

Epigraph quotations are from the following sources: Karen Hagberg, *Stage Presence from Head to Toe* (Lanham, Md.: Scarecrow, 2003), 7; Barry Green, *The Mastery of Music: Ten Pathways to True Artistry* (New York: Broadway Books, 2003), 174; Whitney Balliett, *American Musicians: Fifty-six Portraits in Jazz* (New York: Oxford University Press, 1986), 214; Claire Chase, "Winter-term Project Fights Performance Anxiety with Don Greene's Optimal-performance Workshop," *Oberlin Online: Backstage Pass,* www.oberlin.edu/con/bkstage/200001/greene_don.html (Aug. 2, 2007); Ian Whitcomb, *After the Ball: Pop Music from Rag to Rock* (New York: Simon and Schuster, 1973), 203.

1. Jacqueline Trescott, "Kennedy Center to Honor Five High-wattage Cultural Lights," *Washington Post* (Sept. 7, 2005), C-1, www.washingtonpost.com/wp-dyn/content/article/2005/09/06/AR2005090600861.html (Nov. 25, 2008).

2. Dale Reubart, *Anxiety and Musical Performance: On Playing the Piano from Memory* (New York: Da Capo, 1985), 43.

3. Emanuel Ax, "When to Applaud," *Emanuel Ax's Official Blog,* http://emanuelax.wordpress.com/2008/11/14/when-to-applaud (Dec. 28, 2008).

Chapter 10: Becoming a Performing Artist, III

Epigraph quotations are from the following sources: David W. Barber, *The Music Lover's Quotation Book* (Toronto: Sound and Vision, 2003), 87; Barry Green, *The Inner Game of Music*, with W. Timothy Gallwey (New York: Doubleday, 1986), 127; Whitney Balliett, *American Musicians II: Seventy-two Portraits in Jazz* (New York: Oxford University Press, 1996), 164; David Saito-Chung, *Yahoo! News*, http://news.yahoo .com/s/ibd/20060707/bs_ibd_ibd/200677lands (July 19, 2006).

1. Ken Robinson, *Do Schools Kill Creativity?* Recorded lecture, Feb. 2006, www.ted .com/index.php/talks/view/id/66 (June 7, 2007).
2. Ross Harbaugh, "What? You're Not Getting Along? 26 Ensemble Savers," *American String Teacher* 41(4) (Autumn 1991): 97–99.
3. Paul Salmon and Robert Meyer, *Notes from the Green Room* (New York: Lexington Books, 1992), 137.
4. Ibid., 38.
5. William Westney, *The Perfect Wrong Note: Learning to Trust Your Musical Self* (Pompton Plains, N.J.: Amadeus, 2003), 142.
6. William Pleeth, *Cello* (New York: Schirmer, 1982), x.

Chapter 11: Performing like a Pro

Epigraph quotations are from the following sources: Joseph Kahn and Daniel J. Wakin, "Classical Music Looks toward China with Hope," *New York Times* (Apr. 3, 2007), www.nytimes.com/2007/04/03/arts/music/03class1.html (Nov. 18, 2008); Nat Shapiro, *An Encyclopedia of Quotations about Music* (Garden City, N.Y.: Doubleday, 1978), 204; Linda J. Noyle, ed., *Pianists on Playing: Interviews with Twelve Concert Pianists* (Metuchen, N.J.: Scarecrow, 1987), 111; Eckart Preu, *What Do We Have in Our Bag for You?* www.orchestraconductor.org/pages/blog.php?f=6 (Aug. 16, 2007); William Ganson Rose, *Success in Business* (New York: Duffield, 1913), 317; Rachel Barton Pine, "Getting the Most from Your Competition Experience," *American String Teacher* 57(2) (May 2007): 31; Russ Musto, "Branford Marsalis: It's All about the Band," *All About Jazz* (Jan. 12, 2005), www.allaboutjazz.com/php/article.php?id =15917 (Dec. 28, 2008).

1. Joseph Goldstein and Jack Kornfield, *Seeking the Heart of Wisdom: The Path of Insight Meditation* (Boston: Shambala, 1987), 172.
2. Online: www.brooklynphilharmonic.org/images/MOTW3American.pdf (Aug. 20, 2007).
3. Barry Green, *The Mastery of Music: Ten Pathways to True Artistry* (New York: Broadway Books, 2003), 184.

Chapter 12: Injury Prevention, I

Epigraph quotations are from the following sources: Thich Nhat Hanh, *Peace Is Every Step: The Path of Mindfulness in Everyday Life* (New York: Bantam, 1991), 12; Carol

Anne Jones, Richard Norris, Judy Palac, Robert T. Sataloff, Victor Sazer, Darin Workman, and Alice Brandfonbrener, "Music and Medicine: Preventing Performance Injuries," *Teaching Music* 9 (Oct. 2001): 24; Janet Horvath, *Playing (Less) Hurt: An Injury Prevention Guide for Musicians* (Kearny, Neb.: Morris, 2002), 15; Angela Myles Beeching, *Beyond Talent: Creating a Successful Career in Music* (New York: Oxford University Press, 2005), 229; Karen Hagberg, *Stage Presence from Head to Toe* (Lanham, Md.: Scarecrow, 2003), 71; Richard Norris, *The Musician's Survival Manual: A Guide to Preventing and Treating Injuries in Instrumentalists* (St. Louis, Mo.: MMB Music, 1993), 6.

1. Christopher Wynn Parry, "Managing the Physical Demands of Musical Performance," in *Musical Excellence: Strategies and Techniques to Enhance Performance,* ed. Aaron Williamon, 41–60 (New York: Oxford University Press, 2004). Also, Kris Chesky, George Kondraske, Miriam Henoch, John Hipple, and Bernard Rubin, "Musicians' Health," in *The New Handbook of Research on Music Teaching and Learning,* ed. Richard Colwell and Carol Richardson, 1023–1039 (New York: Oxford University Press, 2002).
2. Alice Brandfonbrener, "History of Playing-related Pain in 330 Freshman Music Students," *Medical Problems of Performing Artists* 24 (1) (March 2009): 30–36.
3. Emil Pascarelli and Deborah Quilter, *Repetitive Strain Injury: A Computer User's Guide* (New York: John Wiley and Sons, 1994), 3–4.
4. Danelle Cayea and Ralph Manchester, "Instrument-specific Rates of Upper-extremity Injuries in Music Students," *Medical Problems of Performing Artists* 13(1) (March 1998): 19–25.
5. William J. Dawson, *Fit as a Fiddle: The Musician's Guide to Playing Healthy* (Lanham, Md.: Rowman and Littlefield, 2008), 137.
6. Ibid., 37.
7. Alice Brandfonbrener, "Joint Laxity and Arm Pain in Musicians," *Medical Problems of Performing Artists* 15(2) (June 2000): 72–74.
8. Richard Norris, *The Musician's Survival Manual: A Guide to Preventing and Treating Injuries in Instrumentalists* (St. Louis, Mo.: MMB Music, 1993), 87–90. Also, Alan H. D. Watson, *What Studying Musicians Tells Us about Motor Control of the Hand,* www.musicandhealth.co.uk/articles/WatsonReview06.pdf (May 28, 2008).
9. Hans-Christian Jabusch and Eckart Altenmüller, "Epidemiology, Phenomenology, and Therapy of Musician's Cramp," in *Music, Motor Control, and the Brain,* ed. Eckart Altenmüller, Mario Wiesendanger, and Jürg Kesselring, 265 (New York: Oxford University Press, 2006).
10. Angela Myles Beeching, *Beyond Talent: Creating a Successful Career in Music* (New York: Oxford University Press, 2005), 230.
11. Barbara Paull and Christine Harrison, *The Athletic Musician: A Guide to Playing without Pain* (Lanham, Md.: Scarecrow, 1997), 12.
12. Alan H. Lockwood, "Medical Problems in Secondary School-aged Musicians," *Medical Problems of Performing Artists* 3(4) (Dec. 1988): 129–132.

13. Alice Brandfonbrener and James Kjelland, "Music Medicine," in *The Science and Psychology of Music Performance,* ed. Richard Parncutt and Gary McPherson, 86 (New York: Oxford University Press, 2002).

14. Anthony E. Kemp, *The Musical Temperament: Psychology and Personality of Musicians* (New York: Oxford University Press, 1996).

15. Norris, *Musician's Survival Manual.*

16. Alice Feinstein, ed., *Training the Body to Cure Itself: How to Use Exercise to Heal* (Emmaus, Penn.: Rodale, 1992), 306.

17. Kris Chesky, telephone conversation with author, May 22, 2008.

18. Emil Pascarelli and Deborah Quilter, *Repetitive Strain Injury: A Computer User's Guide* (New York: John Wiley and Sons, 1994), 96–97.

Chapter 13: Injury Prevention, II

Epigraph quotations are from the following sources: Whitney Balliett, *Collected Works: A Journal of Jazz, 1954–2000* (New York: St. Martin's, 2002), 209; Pedro de Alcantara, *Indirect Procedures: A Musician's Guide to the Alexander Technique* (New York: Oxford University Press, 1997), 266; Elliott Murphy, "Townshend, Tinnitus, and Rock 'n' Roll," *Rolling Stone* 556/557 (July 13–27, 1989), 101.

1. Gyorgy Sandor, *On Piano Playing: Motion, Sound and Expression* (New York: Schirmer, 1995), 31.

2. Richard Norris, *The Musician's Survival Manual: A Guide to Preventing and Treating Injuries in Instrumentalists* (St. Louis, Mo.: MMB Music, 1993), 39.

3. Jaume Rosset i Llobet and George Odam, *The Musician's Body: A Maintenance Manual for Peak Performance* (London: Ashgate, 2007), 57.

4. *Advice for Care of the Voice,* The Texas Voice Center, www.texasvoicecenter.com/advice.html (Apr. 21, 2007).

5. *Fit to Sing,* British Association for Performing Arts Medicine, Factsheet 3, www.bapam.org.uk/docs/3_Fit_to_sing.pdf (Oct. 11, 2007).

6. Richard Miller, *Solutions for Singers: Tools for Performers and Teachers* (New York: Oxford University Press, 2004), 18.

7. Robert Thayer Sataloff, "Care of the Professional Voice," in *Performing Arts Medicine,* 2d ed., ed. Robert Thayer Sataloff, Alice Brandfonbrener, and Richard Lederman, 149 (San Diego: Singular, 1998).

8. Ibid.

9. *Advice for Care of the Voice.*

10. David Blum, *Quintet: Five Journeys toward Musical Fulfillment* (Ithaca, N.Y.: Cornell University Press, 1999), 174.

11. *How Can Professional Voice Users Avoid Voice Disorders?* Lions Voice Clinic of the University of Minnesota, www.lionsvoiceclinic.umn.edu/page4.htm#treat (Oct. 11, 2007).

12. *Advice for Care of the Voice.*

13. Friedrich S. Brodnitz, *Keep Your Voice Healthy,* 2d ed. (Boston: College-Hill Press, 1988), 77.

14. Ibid.
15. Clark A. Rosen and Thomas Murry, *Guidelines for Singers: The Do's and Don'ts.* University of Pittsburgh Voice Center, www.pitt.edu/~crosen/voice/guidelines .html (Nov. 18, 2008).
16. *Preventing Voice Disorders: Invest in Your Voice.* University of Pittsburgh Voice Center, http://voicecenter.upmc.com/InvestVoice.htm (Oct. 8, 2007).
17. Jason Victor Serinus, "Interview: A Conversation with Cecilia Bartoli in Salzburg," *Secrets of Home Theater and High Fidelity* (June, 2004), www.hometheaterhifi .com/volume_11_2/feature-interview-cecilia-bartoli-6-2004.html (December 28, 2008).
18. Kris Chesky, "Hearing Conservation in Schools of Music: The UNT Model," *Hearing Review* 13(3) (March 2006): 48.
19. Marshall Chasin, *Hear the Music: Hearing Loss Prevention for Musicians* (Colorado Springs, Colo.: Westone Laboratories, 2001), 80.
20. *NIOSH Exposure Guidelines: Criteria for a Recommended Standard: Occupational Noise Exposure,* NIOSH Publication 98–126 (June 1998), www.cdc.gov/niosh/ docs/98-126 (Oct. 8, 2007).
21. Glen Gower, *What's That Ringing in Your Ears?* www.carleton.ca/catalyst/2002/ s7.shtml (Oct. 8, 2007).
22. *Decibel Trivia: Decibel Comparison Chart,* www.hearnet.com/at_risk/risk_trivia .shtml (Oct. 8, 2007).
23. *Hearing Damage: What Is It?* www.hearnet.com/at_risk/risk_at_risk2.shtml (Oct. 8, 2007).
24. Karl Strom, ed., "News: ASHA Study Assesses Portable Music Players," *Hearing Review* 13(3) (March 2006): 18.
25. Susan L. Phillips, Julie Shoemaker, Sandra T. Mace, and Donald Hodges, "Environmental Factors in Susceptibility to Noise-induced Hearing Loss in Student Musicians," *Medical Problems of Performing Artists* 23(1) (March 2008): 20–28.
26. Vanessa L. Miller, Michael Stewart, and Mark Lehman, "Noise Exposure Levels for Student Musicians," *Medical Problems of Performing Artists* 22(4) (Dec. 2007): 160–165.
27. Susan L. Phillips and Sandra Mace, "Sound Level Measurements in Music Practice Rooms," *Music Performance Research* 2(1) (2008): 36–47, www.mpr-online .net/vol2_no1.html (Dec. 28, 2008).
28. Kevin Sallows, *Listen while You Work: Hearing Conservation for the Arts* (Vancouver: Safety and Health in Arts Production and Entertainment, 2001), 24, www.shape.bc.ca/resources/pdf/listen.pdf (Oct. 8, 2007).
29. Susan L. Phillips, *Hearing Conservation for Musicians Videoconference* (Winston-Salem: University of North Carolina School of the Arts, Apr. 10, 2008).
30. *NIOSH Safety and Health Topic: Safety and Hearing Loss Prevention: Frequently Asked Questions,* www.cdc.gov/niosh/topics/noise/faq/faq.html#tooloud (Oct. 8, 2007).
31. Chasin, *Hear the Music,* 72–73.
32. *Hearing Damage: What Is It?* Also, Sallows, *Listen while You Work,* 16.

33. Chasin, *Hear the Music,* 50.

34. Marshall Chasin and John Chong, "Four Environmental Techniques to Reduce the Effect of Music Exposure on Hearing," *Medical Problems of Performing Artists* 10(2) (June 1995): 66–69.

35. Ibid.

36. Janice E. Camp and Sanford W. Horstman, "Musician Sound Exposure during Performance of Wagner's Ring Cycle," *Medical Problems of Performing Artists* 7(2) (June 1992): 37–39.

37. Chasin, *Hear the Music,* 74, 85.

38. Alison Wright Reid, *A Sound Ear II* (London: Association of British Orchestras, 2008), 27, www.abo.org.uk/pdfs/information/A_Sound_Ear_II.pdf (May 27, 2008).

39. Kris Chesky, "Preventing Music-induced Hearing Loss," *Music Educators Journal* 94(3) (Jan. 2008): 36–41.

40. Chasin, *Hear the Music,* 87.

Chapter 14: Succeeding as a Student

Epigraph quotations are from the following sources: Ian Crofton and Donald Fraser, *A Dictionary of Musical Quotations* (New York: Schirmer, 1985), 80; Wynton Marsalis, *Marsalis on Music* (New York: Norton, 1995), 136; Eric Maisel, *Performance Anxiety* (New York: Back Stage Books, 2005), 130; Isaac Stern, *My First 79 Years* (New York: Da Capo, 2001), 3; Nat Shapiro and Nat Hentoff, *Hear Me Talkin' to Ya: The Story of Jazz as Told by the Men Who Made It* (Mineola, N.Y.: Dover, 1966), 379; Miles Davis, *Miles: The Autobiography* (New York: Simon and Schuster, 1990), 408.

1. Warren Bennis and Joan Goldsmith, *Learning to Lead: A Workbook on Becoming a Leader,* 3d ed. (New York: Basic Books, 2003), xvi–xvii.

2. Paul Broomhead, "Outcome-centered Learning," *Teaching Music* 13(4) (Feb. 2006): 53–55.

3. Tiffany Martini, "A Talent for Teaching," *Strings* 146 (Feb. 2007): 49.

4. Eric Maisel, *Performance Anxiety* (New York: Back Stage Books, 2005), 132.

5. Andrew Evans, "Performance Anxiety and the Musician's Hand," in *The Musician's Hand,* ed. Ian Winspur and Christopher Wynn Parry, 182 (London: Martin Dunitz, 1998).

6. Anne Lamott, *Bird by Bird: Some Instructions on Writing and Life* (New York: Doubleday, 1994), 156.

7. Angela Myles Beeching, *Beyond Talent: Creating a Successful Career in Music* (New York: Oxford University Press, 2005), 9.

8. Peter Spellman, *5 Essentials of Music Career Success,* www.musiccareers.net/articles/careers_in_music/music_career_success (May 6, 2007).

9. Rosamund Stone Zander and Benjamin Zander, *The Art of Possibility* (Boston: Harvard Business School Press, 2000), 59.

10. David Blum, *Quintet: Five Journeys toward Musical Fulfillment* (Ithaca, N.Y.: Cornell University Press, 1999), 78.

11. Louis Armstrong Center for Music and Medicine, www.wehealny.org/services/ BI_LAC/index.html (Jan. 12, 2007).
12. National Institute on Alcohol Abuse and Alcoholism, *College Alcohol Problems Exceed Previous Estimates* (Mar. 17, 2005), www.niaaa.nih.gov/NewsEvents/ NewsReleases/College.htm (Oct. 9, 2007).
13. U.S. Department of Health and Human Services, *Dietary Guidelines for Americans, Chapter 9: Alcoholic Beverages* (2005), www.health.gov/dietaryguidelines/ dga2005/document/html/chapter9.htm (May 17, 2008).
14. Eric Maisel, *Staying Sane in the Arts: A Guide for Creative and Performing Artists* (New York: Putnam, 1992), 58.
15. Hedrick Smith, "Talking with Dave Brubeck: Dave on Paul Desmond and the Quartet," *Rediscovering Dave Brubeck,* www.pbs.org/brubeck/talking/daveOnPaul .htm (Dec. 28, 2008).
16. Jonathan Swift, "Thoughts on Various Subjects," in *The Works of Jonathan Swift,* vol. 10, ed. John Nichols (London: 1801), 246 (digitized Apr. 7, 2006, by Google).
17. William Pleeth, *Cello* (New York: Schirmer, 1982), 12.
18. Online: www.ericmaisel.com/mmeaning.html (Dec. 30, 2007).
19. Blum, *Quintet,* 77.
20. Mihaly Csikszentmihalyi, *Creativity: Flow and the Psychology of Discovery and Invention* (New York: HarperCollins, 1996), 11.
21. Pablo Casals, *Joys and Sorrows: Reflections* (New York: Simon and Schuster, 1970), 17.
22. Rollo May, *The Courage to Create* (New York: Norton, 1975), 115.

Selected Bibliography

Alcantara, Pedro de. *Indirect Procedures: A Musician's Guide to the Alexander Technique.* New York: Oxford University Press, 1997.

Altenmüller, Eckart, Mario Wiesendanger, and Jürg Kesselring, eds. *Music, Motor Control, and the Brain.* New York: Oxford University Press, 2006.

Balliett, Whitney. *American Musicians: Fifty-six Portraits in Jazz.* New York: Oxford University Press, 1986.

———. *American Musicians II: Seventy-two Portraits in Jazz.* New York: Oxford University Press, 1996.

Beeching, Angela Myles. *Beyond Talent: Creating a Successful Career in Music.* New York: Oxford University Press, 2005.

Bensen, Herbert, and Eileen M. Stuart. *The Wellness Book: The Comprehensive Guide to Maintaining Health and Treating Stress-related Illness.* New York: Birch Lane, 1992.

Blum, David. *The Art of Quartet Playing: The Guarneri Quartet in Conversation with David Blum.* Ithaca, N.Y.: Cornell University Press, 1986.

———. *Quintet: Five Journeys toward Musical Fulfillment.* Ithaca, N.Y.: Cornell University Press, 1999.

Brandfonbrener, Alice. "Beta-blockers in the Treatment of Performance Anxiety." *Medical Problems of Performing Artists* 5(1) (March 1990): 23–26.

———. "Joint Laxity and Arm Pain in Musicians." *Medical Problems of Performing Artists* 15(2) (June 2000): 72–74.

Brodnitz, Friedrich S. *Keep Your Voice Healthy,* 2d ed. Boston: College-Hill Press, 1988.

Burt-Perkins, Rosie, and Janet Mills. "The Role of Chamber Music in Learning to Perform: A Case Study." *Music Performance Research* 2(1) (2008): 26–35. Online: www.mpr-online.net/vol2_no1.html.

Chaffin, Roger, Gabriela Imreh, and Mary Crawford. *Practicing Perfection: Memory and Piano Performance.* Mahwah, N.J.: Erlbaum, 2002.

Chasin, Marshall. *Hear the Music: Hearing Loss Prevention for Musicians.* Colorado Springs: Westone Laboratories, 2001.

———, guest ed. "Special Edition: Music and Hearing Loss." *Hearing Review* 13(3) (March 2006): 22–80.

Colwell, Richard, and Carol Richardson, eds. *The New Handbook of Research on Music Teaching and Learning.* New York: Oxford University Press, 2002.

Csikszentmihalyi, Mihaly. *Creativity: Flow and the Psychology of Discovery and Invention.* New York: HarperCollins, 1996.

Davidson, Jane W., ed. *The Music Practitioner: Research for the Music Performer, Teacher, and Listener.* London: Ashgate, 2004.

Dawson, William J. "Experience with Hand and Upper Extremity Problems in 1,000 Instrumentalists." *Medical Problems of Performing Artists* 10(4) (December 1995): 128–133.

———. *Fit as a Fiddle: The Musician's Guide to Playing Healthy.* Lanham, Md.: Rowman and Littlefield, 2008.

———. "Upper Extremity Overuse in Instrumentalists." *Medical Problems of Performing Artists* 16(2) (June 2001): 66–71.

Duke, Robert A. *Intelligent Music Teaching: Essays on the Core Principles of Effective Instruction.* Austin, Tex.: Learning and Behavior Resources, 2005.

Ericsson, K. Anders, Ralph Th. Krampe, and Clemens Tesch-Römer. "The Role of Deliberate Practice in the Acquisition of Expert Performance." *Psychological Review* 100(3) (1993): 363–406.

Fishbein, Martin, Susan E. Middlestadt, Victor Ottati, Susan Straus, and Alan Ellis. "Medical Problems among ICSOM Musicians: Overview of a National Survey." *Medical Problems of Performing Artists* 3(1) (March 1988): 1–8.

Gallwey, W. Timothy. *The Inner Game of Tennis.* New York: Random House, 1974.

Green, Barry. *The Mastery of Music: Ten Pathways to True Artistry.* New York: Broadway Books, 2003.

Greene, Don. *Performance Success: Performing Your Best under Pressure.* New York: Routledge, 2002.

Hagberg, Karen A. *Stage Presence from Head to Toe.* Lanham, Md.: Scarecrow, 2003.

Horvath, Janet. *Playing (Less) Hurt: An Injury Prevention Guide for Musicians.* Minneapolis, Minn.: Janet Horvath, 2009.

Jørgensen, Harald, and Andreas C. Lehmann, eds. *Does Practice Make Perfect? Current Theory and Research on Instrumental Music Practice.* Oslo: Norwegian State Academy of Music, 1997.

Kemp, Anthony E. *The Musical Temperament: Psychology and Personality of Musicians.* New York: Oxford University Press, 1996.

Langer, Ellen J. *The Power of Mindful Learning.* Cambridge, Mass.: Perseus, 1990.

Lehmann, Andreas C., John A. Sloboda, and Robert H. Woody. *Psychology for Musicians: Understanding and Acquiring the Skills.* New York: Oxford University Press, 2007.

Leinsdorf, Erich. *The Composer's Advocate: A Radical Orthodoxy for Musicians.* New Haven, Conn.: Yale University Press, 1981.

Loehr, Jim, and Tony Schwartz. *The Power of Full Engagement.* New York: Simon and Schuster, 2003.

MacDonald, Glynn. *Illustrated Elements of Alexander Technique*. London: Element, 2002.

Maisel, Eric. *Coaching the Artist Within*. Novato, Calif.: New World Library, 2005.

————. *Performance Anxiety: A Workbook for Actors, Singers, Dancers, and Anyone Else Who Performs in Public*. New York: Back Stage Books, 2005.

Matthay, Tobias. *Musical Interpretation*. 1913. Reprint, Westport, Conn.: Greenwood, 1970.

McCormick, John, and Gary E. McPherson. "Self-efficacy and Music Performance." *Psychology of Music* 34(3) (July 2006): 322–336.

Middlestadt, Susan E., and Martin Fishbein. "The Prevalence of Severe Musculo-skeletal Problems among Male and Female Symphony Orchestra String Players." *Medical Problems of Performing Artists* 4(1) (March 1989): 41–48.

Miller, Richard. *Solutions for Singers*. New York: Oxford University Press, 2004.

Miller, Vanessa L., Michael Stewart, and Mark Lehman. "Noise Exposure Levels for Student Musicians." *Medical Problems of Performing Artists* 22(4) (December 2007): 160–165.

Nachmanovitch, Stephen. *Free Play: Improvisation in Life and Art*. New York: Penguin Putnam, 1990.

Nagel, Julie Jaffee. "In Pursuit of Perfection: Career Choice and Performance Anxiety in Musicians." *Medical Problems of Performing Artists* 3(4) (December 1988): 140–145.

Nhat Hanh, Thich. *Peace Is Every Step: The Path of Mindfulness in Everyday Life*. New York: Bantam, 1991.

Norris, Richard. *The Musician's Survival Manual: A Guide to Preventing and Treating Injuries in Instrumentalists*. St. Louis, Mo.: MMB Music, 1993.

Parncutt, Richard, and Gary E. McPherson, eds. *The Science and Psychology of Music Performance: Creative Strategies for Teaching and Learning*. New York: Oxford University Press, 2002.

Pascarelli, Emil, and Deborah Quilter. *Repetitive Strain Injury: A Computer User's Guide*. New York: John Wiley and Sons, 1994.

Paull, Barbara, and Christine Harrison. *The Athletic Musician: A Guide to Playing without Pain*. Lanham, Md.: Scarecrow, 1997.

Peters, Cheryl, Jadine Thom, Elaina McIntyre, Meghan Winters, Kay Teschke, and Hugh Davies. *Noise and Hearing Loss in Musicians*. Vancouver: SHAPE (Safety and Health in Arts Production and Entertainment), 2005. Online: www.shape.bc.ca/resources/pdf/noisehearinglossmusicians.pdf.

Phillips, Susan L., and Sandra Mace. "Sound Level Measurements in Music Practice Rooms." *Music Performance Research* 2(1) (2008): 36–47. Online: www.mpr-online.net/vol2_no1.html.

Pleeth, William. *Cello*. New York: Schirmer Books, 1982.

Reid, Alison Wright, and Malcolm Warne Holland. *A Sound Ear II*. London: Association of British Orchestras, 2008. Online: www.abo.org.uk/pdfs/information/A_Sound_Ear_II.pdf.

Rink, John, ed. *Musical Performance: A Guide to Understanding*. New York: Cambridge University Press, 2002.

Ristad, Eloise. *A Soprano on Her Head: Right-side-up Reflections on Life and Other Performances.* Moab, Utah: Real People, 1982.

Robin, Mitchell W., and Rochelle Balter. *Performance Anxiety: Overcoming Your Fear in the Workplace, Social Situations, Interpersonal Communications, and the Performing Arts.* Holbrook, Mass.: Adams Media, 1995.

Robinson, Dan, and Joanna Zander. *Preventing Musculoskeletal Injury for Musicians and Dancers.* Vancouver: SHAPE (Safety and Health in Arts Production and Entertainment), 2002. Online: www.shape.bc.ca/resources/pdf/msi.pdf.

Rosset i Llobet, Jaume, and George Odam. *The Musician's Body: A Maintenance Manual for Peak Performance.* London: Ashgate, 2007.

Sallows, Kevin. *Listen while You Work: Hearing Conservation for the Arts.* Vancouver: SHAPE (Safety and Health in Arts Production and Entertainment), 2001. Online: http://shape.bc.ca/resources/pdf/listen.pdf.

Salmon, Paul G., and Robert G. Meyer. *Notes from the Green Room: Coping with Stress and Anxiety in Musical Performance.* New York: Lexington, 1992.

Sataloff, Robert Thayer, Alice G. Brandfonbrener, and Richard J. Lederman, eds. *Performing Arts Medicine,* 2d ed. San Diego: Singular, 1998.

Shearer, Aaron. *Learning the Classic Guitar.* 3 vols. Pacific, Mo.: Mel Bay, 1990–1991.

Sloboda, John. *Exploring the Musical Mind: Cognition, Emotion, Ability, Function.* New York: Oxford University Press, 2005.

Smith, W. Stephen. *The Naked Voice: A Wholistic Approach to Singing,* with Michael Chipman. New York: Oxford University Press, 2007.

Spahn, Claudia, Bernhard Richter, and Ina Zschocke. "Health Attitudes, Preventive Behavior, and Playing-related Health Problems among Music Students." *Medical Problems of Performing Artists* 17(1) (March 2002): 22–28.

Steptoe, Andrew. "Negative Emotions in Music Making: The Problem of Performance Anxiety." In *Music and Emotion,* ed. Patrik N. Juslin and John A. Sloboda, 291–307. New York: Oxford University Press, 2001.

Thurmond, James Morgan. *Note Grouping: A Method for Achieving Expression and Style in Musical Performance.* Galesville, Md.: Meredith Music, 1991.

Tubiana, Raoul, and Peter C. Amadio, eds. *Medical Problems of the Instrumentalist Musician.* London: Martin Dunitz, 2000.

Watson, Alan H. D. *What Studying Musicians Tells Us about Motor Control of the Hand.* United Kingdom: Music and Health, 2006. Online: www.musicandhealth.co.uk/articles/WatsonReview06.pdf.

Williamon, Aaron, ed. *Musical Excellence: Strategies and Techniques to Enhance Performance.* New York: Oxford University Press, 2004.

Williamon, Aaron, and Sam Thompson. "Awareness and Incidence of Health Problems among Conservatoire Students." *Psychology of Music* 34(4) (2006): 411–430.

Williamon, Aaron, and Elizabeth Valentine. "The Role of Retrieval Structures in Memorizing Music." *Cognitive Psychology* 44 (2002): 1–32.

Wilson, Glenn D. *Psychology for Performing Artists,* 2d ed. London: Whurr, 2002.

Winspur, Ian, and Christopher Wynn Parry, eds. *The Musician's Hand: A Clinical Guide.* London: Martin Dunitz, 1998.

Zaza, Christine. "Prevention of Musicians' Playing-related Health Problems: Rationale and Recommendations for Action." *Medical Problems of Performing Artists* 8(4) (December 1993): 117–121.

———. "Research-based Prevention for Musicians." *Medical Problems of Performing Artists* 9(1) (March 1994): 3–6.

Zetterberg, Carl, Helena Backlund, Jenny Karlsson, Helen Werner, and Lars Olsson. "Musculoskeletal Problems among Male and Female Music Students." *Medical Problems of Performing Artists* 13(4) (December 1998): 161–166.

Index